The Paradox of Professionalism

THE PARADOX OF PROFESSIONALISM

REFORM AND PUBLIC SERVICE IN URBAN AMERICA, 1900–1940

Don S. Kirschner

CONTRIBUTIONS IN AMERICAN HISTORY, NUMBER 119

Greenwood Press
NEW YORK·WESTPORT, CONNECTICUT·LONDON

Library of Congress Cataloging-in-Publication Data

Kirschner, Don S.
  The paradox of professionalism.

  (Contributions in American history, ISSN 0084-9219 ;
no. 119)
  Bibliography: p.
  Includes index.
  1. Social reformers—United States—History—20th
century.   2. Social workers—United States—History—
20th century.   3. City planners—United States—
History—20th century.   4. Public health personnel—
United States—History—20th century.   5. City and town
life—History—20th century.   I. Title.   II. Series.
HN64.K625   1986   361.2'5'0973   86-399
ISBN 0-313-25345-5 (lib. bdg. : alk. paper)

Library of Congress Catalog Card Number: 86-399
ISBN: 0-313-25345-5
ISSN: 0084-9219

First published in 1986

Greenwood Press, Inc.
88 Post Road West, Westport, Connecticut 06881

Printed in the United States of America

The paper used in this book complies with the
Permanent Paper Standard issued by the National
Information Standards Organization (Z39.48-1984).

10 9 8 7 6 5 4 3 2 1

For Teresa

Contents

Introduction

Different societies respond in different ways to the dislocations of the modern world. In one nation the pressures polarize social classes and lead to a state of civil strife in which the forces of revolution and reaction play out their grim drama on a bloody stage. In another, these pressures are released short of revolution and lead instead to a succession of lesser adjustments with correspondingly less violence. The United States went through both of these stages. The earlier phase culminated in the sectional strife of the mid-nineteenth century; after that, accommodations were made without explosive intensity, if not without considerable pain and some violence.

By the turn of the century a wide variety of reform groups had come onto the scene, each of which was trying to gain control over some aspect of this process of accommodation in the cities. Some of them aimed to regulate the practices of corporations, others to rationalize the structure of urban governments; some sought to eliminate alcohol from the life of the immigrant, others to eliminate immigrants from the life of the nation.

As the clamor for change mounted and the variety of reforms multiplied in those yeasty years, several groups appeared that were concerned primarily with the health and welfare of urban people, and more generally with the dynamics of urban life. Coming largely from the middle and upper reaches of American society, they shared a common assumption that the origins of human misery and social upheaval were environmental, and therefore that a more benign environment would minimize social disorder and increase the potential for personal happiness and human fulfillment. They were the reformers whose efforts to humanize the industrial order were eventually institutionalized in the services that made the United States a welfare state. This book is about how these well-fixed social reformers and their successors perceived the urban milieu in the early decades of the twentieth century, what they proposed to do about it, and what that did to the way they thought about themselves.

In recent years various studies have shown that these individuals fell into categories that were more sharply defined than the term "reformers" might suggest. Their reform activities led them to create entirely new occupations and then to elaborate those occupations into professions through the years. It is this process of professionalization that I want to follow, especially as it developed in the minds of social workers and public health personnel, along with city planners and the architects who gravitated toward the planning movement. All of these groups worked close to the heart of reform in the cities earlier in the century.

Some cautionary notes are in order at this point. First of all, this is not a book about how the reformers acted on their perceptions. It is essentially an intellectual history of the professionalization of reform. The link between what these professionals thought about social policy and what they did about it is the subject for another book. By the same token, it is necessary to emphasize that this is not a book about urban people and problems, but about how the reformers perceived urban people and problems. Thus, to take one example, the pages on the "New Negro" in Chapter 5 are not intended as a discussion of Harlem in the 1920s, but as an illustration of how black Americans increasingly entered the consciousness of reformers in that decade.

Second, I have found it necessary to go over some matters that are already familiar lore to historians. In recent years, for instance, a significant body of writing has described some rather hostile feelings that the reformers harbored toward the new immigrants in the cities and has argued that there was a repressive side to their efforts in the Progressive era—indeed that their goal was social control in the face of urban disorder more than it was humanitarian reform in the face of social injustice. Curiously, this argument then virtually disappears from the historical writings about professionals in the 1920s and 1930s. In Chapter 2, therefore, I focus on this theme in the Progressive era (hopefully with some fresh material), in part to engage myself in the discussion of social control and in part to provide a perspective for the recurrence among the professionals of such subjects as ethnicity, localism, and social control in the years that followed.

One of the themes of this book is that the common concerns of the reformers drew them together into a vaguely defined demi-class in American society. This leads to a final caveat, for there is a conceptual assumption here that demands explanation. The reformers were drawn from quite distinct occupations, with different levels of training, different skills, and often different perspectives on urban problems. The reader may well question a scheme that obscures these differences in order to portray the professionals as a demi-class in American society. Actually, this should not be a problem as long as it is clear that I am using the word "professional" as a tool of discourse and not as an axiom. We do the same thing, for instance, when we speak of "skilled workers," "small businessmen," and "new immigrants." Each of these is an abstraction, a tool of discourse that permits us to emphasize common characteristics by obscuring differences. When we want to emphasize the differences—when we change the *terms* of the discourse—we lay aside these tools for others.

It might avoid some confusion if I mention also that my use of the word "professional" throughout the book refers specifically to these reformers in social welfare, public health, and city planning, and not, for instance, to such other professionals as corporation lawyers or physicians in private practice, many of whom supported other reform movements early in the century. In fact, I use such terms as "professionals," "new professionals," "public-service professionals," "policy" or "social-policy" workers, "experts," and simply "reformers" interchangeably to designate the practitioners of these three occupations.

Since the 1930s, of course, experts have become a fixture in our world because we are not equipped to handle the volume and complexity of knowledge necessary to manage a technological society without them. As the handmaidens of modernization they advise us on everything from how to spray our crops to how to fight our wars—and, by the way, how to preserve our sanity as we contemplate the likelihood of surviving either of these activities. Now, after several decades of having experts supervise our public affairs, we find ourselves closer to extinction than to utopia, and we begin to wonder if we weren't tricked somewhere along the line.

We weren't, of course, but still our discomfort lingers and finds an easy target in the public-service professionals. After all, they are experts in the disorders of urban life, and in spite of their expertise, urban life does not seem to be notably more orderly today than it was a half-century ago. Actually the new professionals have had a mixed press over the years. The early reviews were generally quite favorable, no doubt because most of the critics shared the assumptions of the reformers. In recent years, however, the critics have grown increasingly hostile as they have watched the costs mount and the reforms get caught up in the very machinery that was set up to administer them.

There is another reason why the evaluations of these individuals have changed. It involves the conflicting strains in their own thinking. Like the people they set out to help, the reformers were affected by the transition from village to urban society. In a classic example of cultural lag, they responded at different rates to the material and nonmaterial changes that took place around them. As a consequence their ideas were characterized by certain tensions and ambiguities that influenced the way they viewed social change as well as the way they related to their clients. Early historians perceived only one aspect of their thought and praised them for it. Many later historians concentrated on a different aspect and condemned them for it. The fact is that both strains were present throughout most of the era, permitting historians to single out whatever seemed most relevant to them at a given time. These tensions and ambiguities constitute another theme in the book.

In some degree these ambiguities probably contributed to the erratic course of reform sentiment in these years. During the Progressive era, for instance, when the reformers were establishing their credentials as professionals, they were fervent and more or less united in their quest for broad social change. After the war their ardor cooled and they fragmented, following narrow, often trivial paths of change to no common purpose at all. Then in the 1930s they rediscovered social passion under the stimulus of New Deal welfare and housing programs. This rhythm of reform is yet another theme of the book.

This is scarcely a novel thesis. In fact it is essentially the restatement of a very old one. Yet I believe it merits some emphasis here for two reasons. First of all, it explains the old theme in a different way. Historians used to discuss this rhythmic pattern as a long-term struggle between "conservative" businessmen and "liberal" reformers. I am suggesting instead that it is in some degree the result of the internal dynamics of reform thought itself, and in a somewhat different way from the one suggested by Robert Wiebe some years ago. Second, this explanation stands apart from the "organizational thesis" that defines so much of the best recent work on these decades. In one perspective the course of change is as intermittent as a pulse; the professionals ebbed and flowed between commitment and detachment. In the other the emphasis is on continuity; change is more or less linear.

Since I find the organizational thesis on the whole persuasive, I have no intention of using this book to flog it. I do suggest, however, that we approach it with an eye to the peaks and valleys of social process that resist the bulldozer of modernization theory. Indeed, perhaps the next great synthesis of recent American history will find a way to make these two analytical frameworks more compatible than they have been so far.

Today's smoothly professional public-service workers are a world removed from their generally ill-trained forerunners at the turn of the century. They are also under heavier fire than at any time since then. In retrospect it is easy enough to see past their honorable intentions to the flaws that have contributed to this negative assessment. That is one of the advantages of explaining the past. It is also one of the disadvantages, because nothing comes more easily than judgments against our ancestors for underestimating their task and leaving the mess for us to clean up. These reformers were not saints, but they were not rascals either. To put them in perspective, perhaps we should try to imagine America's cities in this century without them and the reforms they sponsored. That is a sobering thought.

I am grateful to the Canada Council for funding the early stages of this study so generously with a Research Grant and a Leave Fellowship, and to Simon Fraser University for a President's Research Grant. Library personnel, the unsung heroes of our labors, were unfailingly helpful to me. I want to thank those at Simon Fraser University, the University of British Columbia, the University of Washington, the Seattle Public Library, the University of Chicago, and the Center for Research Libraries in Chicago for their assistance.

I also want to express my appreciation to the editors of *Historical Reflections* for permission to use material that they published in their Summer 1975 issue; and to the editors of *American Studies* for permission to reprint, with few changes, articles that they published in Spring 1978 and Fall 1980.

I am particularly fortunate for the encouragement I received from two friends whose very different sensibilities intersected in this work and complemented each other perfectly. I am delighted to acknowledge my debt to Samuel Mc-Seveney, who stole time from his own heavy schedule at Vanderbilt University to comment at length and incisively on the manuscript, and to my colleague, Michael Fellman, whose readings have helped guide this study to maturity over the past several years. Together they helped to clarify my thinking and to rescue me from more than a few literary excesses.

I have dedicated this book to my wife, Teresa, who unselfishly set aside her own scholarly projects at crucial moments in order to contribute her insights and her spirit to this work.

The Paradox of
Professionalism

1

The New Professions
Take Shape

At the end of the nineteenth century the problems of industrialization converged in the first nationwide urban crisis in American history. Shifting patterns of immigration, political and economic inefficiency, industrial strife, crippling poverty, and the chilling specter of epidemic disease stalking massive concentrations of people had been disrupting cities for years, of course, but in the 1890s these problems were focused and magnified by an economic depression of awesome proportions. Although two-thirds of the population were still rural, in a very real sense the United States entered the urban era at that time.

A handful of generally wellborn Americans responded to the crisis in a novel manner. Refusing to accept refuge in the established argument that personal hardship was necessarily a consequence of personal inadequacies, they insisted instead that the crisis was a matter of environmental pathology that was susceptible to social diagnosis and treatment. Sustained by an unwavering commitment to this theory, these individuals confidently set out to solve the problems of urban disorder. By the late 1890s they were already identifiable as a salty band of social reformers. As they worked out the logic of their environmental assumptions, they contributed to the genesis of various new public-service professions after the turn of the century, and eventually to the formation of a subclass in American society.

The process by which concern for the poor was transformed from charity work into settlement work and finally into social welfare reformism lay at the heart of this development.[1] The charity movement of the nineteenth century had rested upon the doctrine of personal responsibility, according to which poverty was the result of a morally defective character. Therefore, the best treatment for this condition was a little bit of charity and a lot of moral instruction.

The charity outlook was challenged in the 1890s by a group of young social justice reformers who were just then gathering in the new settlement houses of the cities. Unlike the charity leaders, these settlement workers rejected the doctrine of personal responsibility and embraced instead an environmental theory of poverty and social disorder that seemed to them more consistent with the realities of industrial society. Low wages, erratic employment, desperately long hours for women and children, hazardous factory conditions with no compensation for injury or death, dangerously overcrowded tenements—these, they felt, were the real sources of human misery. It was not individuals who were flawed, but society itself. Proceeding from these assumptions, settlement workers concluded that the solution to the problems of poverty lay not in exhorting the individual to higher levels of morality, but in reforming society. On the whole these reformers were somewhat more ambivalent toward the poor than the charity workers had been. Like the charity workers, they were distraught at the potential for cultural disruption and social disorder that lurked in such a large class of downtrodden foreigners, yet their environmental assumptions disposed them to be less hostile toward the poor and in time to feel genuinely sympathetic toward them.

Settlement workers gained a hearing at the National Conference of Charities and Corrections (NCCC) in the 1890s and found it to be an ideal institutional setting to propagate their ideas on a wide variety of problems relating to poverty: slums, disease, crime and delinquency, child and female labor, wages, hours and factory conditions, and the breakdown of family life. They began as a small enclave in this stronghold of the charity movement and proceeded to suffuse it with their own spirit and ideas. By 1909 their influence had grown to the point where Jane Addams, the most renowned of the settlement leaders, was elected president of the NCCC, and in the years that followed, the social justice outlook almost completely dominated the organization. By 1917, when it changed its name to the National Conference of Social Work (NCSW), it had emerged as the organizational embodiment of the new social welfare professionalism. Because of the broad interests of these innovators, they acted throughout the Progressive era to unify the disparate reform movements that grew in the cities.

The environmental theory that informed these developments was coolly received at first and placed a heavy burden of proof upon the social justice reformers. In the face of an entrenched ethic of personal responsibility they were compelled to demonstrate that individual degradation had social causes. In the spirit of the age they adapted the methods of science to their needs. Some of the early reformers, for instance, employed primitive methods of data collection to reveal the impact of factory and sweatshop conditions on the health and safety of workers. Florence Kelley helped to blaze this trail with her investigations into the work environment of children in Chicago. Kelley led a Hull House group which gathered the evidence used to secure the Illinois Factory Act of 1893.

Thereafter social investigators refined this technique of amassing data to support their demands for social reform. Diligently they applied it to industrial conditions, housing, social insurance, and other problem areas, watching with satisfaction as the evidence to support their environmental assumptions mounted. As the sheer volume of information from social research piled up, the generalists of reform gave way to a growing number of specialists in such fields as child labor, social insurance, and housing. Then, shortly before American entry into World War I, social casework, with its emphasis on individual adjustment, emerged as still another area of specialization. By the end of the Progressive era, social welfare reformism encompassed a complex network of subspecializations.

In broad outline these same developments characterized the modernization of public health.[2] Before the 1880s the public health movement had been guided by the dirt theory, which held that communicable diseases originated in decayed organic matter and were conveyed by the unhygienic conditions that prevailed in the cities, especially in slum neighborhoods. The movement was often led by sanitation engineers who stressed control of the physical environment through modern techniques of plumbing and sewerage as the primary deterrents to disease. These methods contributed to the fight against infectious diseases in the nineteenth century and no doubt had a benign effect upon the aromatic qualities of industrial cities, but ultimately they were limited by the very theory that sustained them.

Meanwhile the groundwork for a new approach to communicable diseases was being laid by Robert Koch and Louis Pasteur in Europe. In the 1880s word of their dramatic discoveries crossed the Atlantic and was then confirmed by a succession of experiments on both sides of the ocean that identified bacteria as the cause of contagious diseases. Even more exciting was the development of vaccines that promised mass immunization from these scourges.

In the 1890s public-health activities in the United States began to move in new directions as the germ theory of disease caught on nationwide. Experiments and knowledge in bacteriology and immunology piled up so rapidly that awareness, even among specialists, began to lag. This prompted the American Public Health Association (APHA) to set up a Laboratory Section in 1899 as a clearing house for the rapidly growing inventory of information in these fields. As researchers worked out the logic of the germ theory, they opened up other areas of specialization. By early 1900s the growing interest in the demography of births, disease, and deaths raised questions about the social distribution of morbidity and mortality, and led to the creation of a Section of Vital Statistics by the Association in 1906. Two years later, as the social implications of public health were coming into focus, the APHA established a Sociological Section to encourage studies of the relationship between the social environment and communicable diseases. After 1910 many health specialists, captivated by the success of scientific techniques in isolating the bacterial causes of infectious diseases, and in producing antitoxins for some of them, began to argue for a more narrowly medicobiological approach to public health that would concentrate primarily on the individual, implicitly relegating considerations of the social environment to the background.[3] By then the field of public health was carving itself into areas so specialized that the practitioners were beginning to experience some difficulty communicating with one another.

In the past, control over public-health organizations had often been an issue over which politicians and public-spirited amateurs had struggled fiercely. With the triumph of the scientific outlook and the growth of areas of specialization, these controversies now seemed irrelevant to the new prophets of public health, since neither the politician nor the dilettante was qualified to oversee the activities of bacteriologists, entomologists, chemists, physicians, sanitary engineers, statisticians, and even legal experts. The point at which all these lines of expertise intersected must itself become a new profession.[4]

Of course, the conception of public health as a separate profession that unified several other fields of special knowledge implied training of a type that scarcely existed at the time. There was some work in public health offered at a few eastern universities, but it was usually given only casually as an optional series of lectures along the way to a degree in medicine or engineering. Now, as the fever of professionalism rose in the Progressive era, public-health devotees prepared for the future with suggestions for entire courses of study leading to degrees in public hygiene. In 1909 Robert Weston, a prominent health official, laid out one such program in the *American Journal of Public Hygiene (AJPH)*. Weston prefaced his remarks by affirming that "specialization is in accordance with the spirit of the age and in that spirit must the future be faced." He demonstrated that his vision was not rivited to the microscope by asserting that the very nature of *public* health required that it be firmly tied to social moorings. Thus the curriculum that he outlined provided for a solid grounding in history, economics, and sociology, as well as for immersion in laboratory methods and statistical analysis, whether the student pursued a degree in public health through medicine or sanitary engineering. Beyond that he proposed graduate work leading to a Ph.D. based upon "a thesis which should embody the results of some original investigation which should reveal an ability to attack public health problems in a scientific way."[5] So much for amateurism!

The modern city-planning movement had its origins paradoxically in the World's Columbian Exposition of Chicago in 1893—paradoxically because this "plaster fantasy," as Mel Scott calls it, did not address urban problems at all. Instead it hid them behind a dazzling facade of classical columns and placid lagoons that reflected nothing so much as the aspirations of a new cultural and industrial elite.[6] Nevertheless, the fair did demonstrate the enormous possibilities inherent in large-scale planning by a group of experts who shared a particular esthetic ideal.

Over the next fifteen years esthetic considerations prevailed among planners. This was the era of the "city-beautiful" movement, with its vision of manicured parks, imposing monuments, and dramatic civic centers finding expression in the neoclassical schemes of such men as George Kessler, Frederick Law Olmsted, Jr., and above all Daniel Burnham, who had coordinated the planning for the Exposition of 1893. The capstone of Burnham's career, and of the entire city-beautiful era, was the publication in 1909 of the *Plan of Chicago*, a breath-taking enterprise that extended the esthetic commitment from its customary locale near the city center outward to the city limits and beyond. It was the first realistic effort at a plan for an entire city and the first great city plan to be adopted in the United States.

But Burnham and his associates had more on their minds than parks and statues. Indeed the Chicago plan was a pivotal development in the city-planning movement, for in its bold proposals to improve transit, transportation, and freight-handling facilities it sought to fuse esthetic ideals with commercial needs, and thus pointed the way toward a more functional approach to urban design. At the same time, many social workers, sanitarians and housing experts began to see how city planning could be broadened even further to include their own interests. Esthetic, commercial, and social perspectives on planning were rap-idly converging in a view of the city as an organic system of interdependent parts, each of which was serviced by a crew of specialists who were already at work searching out the facts that were relevant to their own areas of expertise. In the eyes of many urban planners, how a city functioned was clearly becoming more important than how it looked.

This functional approach to city planning opened the movement up for the first time to the eclectic reformers who roamed freely through America's prob-lem areas in the Progressive era. Such people as Benjamin Marsh began to see planning as a cure for many of the social ills of the nation. In 1908 Marsh organized a group of New York social workers and housing experts into the Committee on Congestion of Population. The purpose of the committee was to publicize the wretched living conditions of the urban poor in order to generate support for properly planned housing reforms. In March the committee spon-sored an exhibition that dramatically portrayed the consequences of slum con-ditions. This "Congestion Show" attracted thousands of spectators who were introduced to the notion that the worst social and economic problems of the city could be solved by planning and zoning. The leading journal of social work reported effusively on the show and thereafter supported planning whole-heartedly as a means of improving urban housing conditions.

By 1910 functionalism in city planning was already superceding the city-beautiful idea. But functionalism toward what end? Not all planners were as enthusiastic as Marsh and his followers about planning as a social panacea. As early as 1912 those who were more concerned with the physical than with the social aspects of urban life began to assert themselves, especially as it became apparent how much resistance social planning would encounter. Fearful of the legal impediments to comprehensive planning, men like Edward Bassett of New York lowered their gaze from the far horizons of the reformers to the immedi-acy of street plans and "use districts" (that is, planning a district according to its use) as the best means of bringing some sort of order, no matter how piece-meal and temporary, to the turbulent cities.

As was the case with social work, city planning evolved before there were fixed qualifications or formal training in the field. In the early years it was dominated by landscape architects, but it included engineers, sanitarians, architects, health officials, housing specialists, lawyers, and businessmen as well. In fact city planning in those days was an activity that was open to almost anyone who wanted to help plan a city. These pioneer planners took a major step toward professionalization in 1909 when they responded to the urging of Marsh and other reformers by founding the National Conference on City Planning (NCCP), which met annually thereafter to sort out their widening interests and give some shape to the movement. Harvard University conferred a different sort of legitimacy to the field that year by offering the first course in city planning ever given at an American university. Finally in 1917 planners formed their own professional organization, the American City Planning Institute.

Each of these occupations followed similar lines of development, characterized by new theories, new methods, and new areas of specialization. In each case a group of experts emerged who claimed special competence in urban problems by virtue of their access to an expanding volume of more or less esoteric knowledge. In time, expertise donned the armor of professionalism in the form of special journals, organizations, and educational requirements. Soon the initiates shared an exclusive community of knowledge and activity that worked to limit the casual participation of part timers and outsiders.

All these reformers shared a common assumption that the urban environment was in some measure responsible for the conditions that absorbed their energies. Thus while the new public-service professions took root separately in the 1890s, they began to draw together after the turn of the century, as welfare experts, health workers, and city planners discovered one another prowling about the same slum neighborhoods in a common quest for social reform. Within a few years, however, countertendencies appeared in each of these professions. Casework in social welfare, a biological emphasis in health work, and zoning among city planners all implied a withdrawal from broad social reform in favor of more narrowly conceived goals. Nevertheless, throughout the Progressive era centripetal forces were dominant as the new professionals searched out a basis for cooperation across the lines of specialization.

The impetus for cooperation was provided by leading health, welfare, and planning reformers, who spoke at one another's annual conventions and wrote in the appropriate professional journals to encourage the exchange of ideas among different specialists. Physicians and health administrators, for instance, made regular appearances at the NCCC to read papers to the welfare workers on a broad range of topics involving the relationship between health and social conditions. In 1905, physicians read half a dozen papers at separate sections on "Children," "Care of the Sick," and "Warfare Against Tuberculosis." In 1911 housing, health, and recreation, which had been treated separately at the NCCC in the past, were brought together for the first time in one session. By

1917 the session on "Health" included two papers on nutrition, three on the coordination of health activities, and four on health and social welfare.[7]

Information flowed in the opposite direction also. Eugene Lies, a well-known charity worker, implored health officials not to deal with tuberculosis as if it struck in a social vacuum. Tuberculosis and poverty, he said, were so completely tangled together that they could not be understood separately. Each was a cause of the other and both, he concluded, were social diseases that required social treatment.[8] Some months later a Minnesota health official offered to his colleagues a more specific proposal for approaching epidemiology as a social phenomenon. He insisted that any proper investigation of a typhoid epidemic must include a detailed analysis of the sociology of the afflicted community. He singled out the ethnic, occupational, and class structures of the community, along with the social relations of its people, for particular attention in such an inquiry.[9]

It was at this time that city planners were beginning to shift their attention from the City Beautiful to the broader possibilities for change inherent in functional planning—from how the city looked to how it worked. Social justice leaders were quick to perceive how this new approach related to their own needs and set out to help steer planning toward the growing network of urban reformism. For a start, they turned over an entire issue of *Charities and The Commons* to the planners early in 1908. In the introductory essay Charles Mulford Robinson outlined for his social-welfare audience the most recent thinking about city planning and set the tone for the entire issue. Robinson, a founding father of the planning movement, cautioned his readers not to dismiss a city plan because it appeared to deal only with the "skeleton" of the city—with streets and buildings, parks and neighborhood centers. Beneath these changes in form, he said, the deeper purpose of the plan was to integrate urban life rationally "on lines of business convenience, of good sense, of social service, and of art." [10] Robinson and the other planners who contributed to this issue clearly saw the way in which functional planning reached beyond esthetic principles to the commitments of urban welfare professionals. Thus when the NCCP was organized a year later, it came as no surprise that *Charities and The Commons* gave its benediction by heralding the opening meeting and asserting flatly that there was not an urban center in the United States that did not need a city plan.[11]

The bond that was growing among these new urban service professions was strengthened by strategists who recognized almost immediately that common purpose called for common action. In 1909 a health official, speaking at the NCCC, urged social workers to involve themselves in health programs, which were, he pointed out, a kind of social service that was closely related to poverty and unemployment.[12] Meanwhile an editorial in the *AJPH* warned health workers that relations with social reformers had to be reciprocal, for if physicians and sanitarians did not work actively to support welfare professionals, they would be squeezed into the background of reform as mere technical advisers.[13] Two years later Charles Probst took up this theme in his presidential address to the APHA. Probst spoke at length about the national movements that were springing up to deal with housing, work, and recreation, and of their correlation with health problems. "The time is ripe," he said, "for cooperation! Cooperation of the widest sort."[14]

The APHA moved to encourage such cooperation that year by inviting representatives from a wide assortment of national agencies for social betterment to present papers to the health officers assembled at its annual meetings. Frederic Almy, a leading figure in the new social work, best summarized the theme of those meetings when he described the struggle against poverty, disease, and ignorance as a "holy war" of national dimensions. To fight it, he said, the new professionals must coordinate the activities of national organizations, which so far had been dissipating too much energy in separate struggles against such foes as tuberculosis, slum housing, impure milk, inadequate recreational facilities, and child labor, all of which were now vulnerable to concerted action.[15] The cooperative ideal, which had grown willy-nilly from the perceptions and needs of diverse professionals, came of age at that convention. Thereafter it was held as an axiom of reform.

From its inception the NCCP was a model of cooperative endeavor among experts from different fields, simply because there were as yet no experts actually trained in city planning. Meeting for the first time in Washington, D.C., the conference included representatives from the Committee on Congestion of Population, the American Institute of Architects, the American Society of Landscape Architects, the League of American Municipalities, the American Civic Association, and the NCCC. The relationship between planning and social reform became a tender issue in the next few years, but the mandate for cooperative action held firm. George B. Ford, a dominant voice at the conference in these formative years, and a spokesman for the broader view of planning, insisted that the team for formulating any effective city plan must include an engineer for its physical aspects, an architect for esthetic considerations, and a specialist as well for the social factors. Beyond that, he continued, the planner must not hesitate to consult experts in any other field as the occasion arose.[16] Planning, still the most amorphous of the service professions in the Progressive era, was the one most actively committed to integrating the expertise of many fields.

Still, before about 1909 the impulse for cooperation spread only slowly among the new professionals. In part, no doubt, this was due to the very newness of these fields, and the consequent uncertainty of direction in them. In part, however, it was because the flow of ideas across barriers of specialization was retarded by poor lines of communication. Annual meetings were too cramped in time and place to serve more than a few at a time, and by and large they served the same few year after year. Professional journals reached larger audiences, but most of them were too absorbed in the pleasures of self-discovery to yield space very generously to specialists from other fields. These meetings and journals played an important role in nursing the cooperative ideal through its formative years, but by themselves they were ill equipped to carry it much beyond that.

Instead, the communications gap was bridged by the appearance of several new periodicals that were conceived specifically to popularize expertise among the different specialists in urban problems, and even more broadly among the growing corps of concerned laymen who were gathering around the new professionals. Among the most significant of these periodicals were *The Survey*, *American City*, and *National Municipal Review*.

Successor to *Charities and The Commons* as the leading journal of social and settlement work, *The Survey* actually went beyond its predecessor in its commitment to the new welfare reformism. Paul Kellogg, who had served his apprenticeship in welfare journalism with *Charities and The Commons*, founded the new journal, and was to be its editor and guiding spirit for more than forty years. Under Kellogg's leadership, *The Survey* aimed consciously to mold disparate new professionals into a common class of public servants working to rationalize and humanize urban life. Experts in several fields who had already been moving individually in that direction "would need to learn from each other the essential information and design of each other's separate professions. It was to the process of mutual education that *The Survey* was chiefly dedicated."[17] To stimulate these processes *The Survey* included regular columns on health and city planning from the very beginning, along with a barrage of information on problems and progress in social work.

American City made its debut that same year. Arthur Grant, its editor, stated that the journal was founded expressly to overcome the limits to communication imposed by sporadic conventions, and that it must lead the way to cooperative action among civic organizations in various cities.[18] From its first issue it printed articles of general interest as well as highly technical studies on such matters as water purification and air pollution. Like *The Survey* it was a medium in which experts from different professions could exchange ideas. Unlike *The Survey* it beamed these ideas increasingly, as time passed, to elected officials and to the rising class of professional administrators who were beginning to manage the affairs of cities.

A somewhat different angle on reform was drawn in *National Municipal Review*, which first appeared in 1912. An offspring of the National Municipal League, it was the nearest thing among these journals to what James Weinstein and others have called "corporate liberalism," especially in the way it adapted moderate welfare reformism to the interests of corporate business enterprise. Whereas *The Survey* generally emphasized the moral necessity of reform, the *Review* often discussed the economic feasibility of reform. The difference was significant. In the first issue, John Ihlder wrote almost crudely in this vein. Ihlder, a housing expert who was gravitating toward the city planning movement, stated bluntly that bad housing caused high rates of mortality and was thus an expensive proposition. In those terms he justified his argument for slum clearance. "A life is coming to be regarded as a commercial asset," he said. "It must be made to yield as much as possible on the investment." [19] By opening its pages not only to reform-minded businessmen concerned with municipal finances and political corruption, but also to the often fractious service professionals concerned with social problems in the cities, *National Municipal Review* served as an important bridge between the professionals and the business community.

There was a great deal of overlap among these journals; yet each retained a distinctive character that justified its existence. *The Survey*, for all its avowed intent to transcend the limits of specialization, imparted the flavor and fervor of social work to most of the material it published. *American City*, which not only published many of the same experts who wrote for the other two journals but often reprinted articles and excerpts from them verbatim, still never lost sight of the politicians and administrators whom it made a special effort to reach. Less heated than *The Survey* and less technical than *American City*, *National Municipal Review* was more disposed than either to temper its reformism with specifically business principles. Yet differences in style and direction did not impede the larger mission of these journals to coordinate the ideas of specialists and project them outward to the growing body of experts and activists in all fields of urban affairs.

In fact the first giant stride toward making the cooperative ideal a reality had already been taken by the new professionals when they conducted the Pittsburgh Survey in 1907–1908. The Pittsburgh Survey was a surpassingly ambitious project, which Clarke Chambers describes as "the first major attempt to survey in depth the entire life of a single community by team research." [20] Guided by Paul Kellogg, the investigation brought together city planners, doctors, engineers, and labor experts, among others, and integrated their efforts within a social-welfare outlook. It had a tremendous impact upon service professionals and resonated widely in American society, in part because of its implications and in part simply because its mountains of data were dramatically summarized in human terms with shocking personal stories that informed the general public what the reformers had long known about the social consequences of long hours and low wages.

The survey idea struck a responsive chord and spread rapidly through the new professions in the next few years. Between 1910 and 1913 it was a common topic for discussion at both the NCCC and the NCCP. In 1913 Frederick Law Olmstead, Jr., the illustrious son of an illustrious father in matters of urban design, insisted that a planner should not even sit down to his drawing board until he had the facts of a comprehensive survey before him. [21] With a consensus growing over the need for such a survey, city planning was indeed moving into the era of the "City Scientific."

At the same time the idea spread to the public health movement. In a 1913 editorial, the *AJPH* traced the recent demand for surveys to the dislocation of social relationships that accompanied rapid urbanization. The editorial explained that the use of social surveys in nearly a score of cities already, with many more under way, reflected the development of new analytical methods for diagnosing urban problems, and gave hope to social, civic, business, and health leaders of new remedies through "the application of scientific methods for social betterment."[22] From time to time thereafter, health officers reported on health surveys that analyzed the broad social data of a community.

Here then were the factors that molded the new professionals in the United States: the laboratories and settlement houses where dedicated individuals first fought against disease, poverty, and social disorder on modern terms; the new areas of specialized knowledge that grew from the application of scientific methods to urban problems; the annual meetings and occupational journals where specialization moved in the direction of professionalism; the emerging professional leaders who preached a gospel of cooperation across the boundaries of expertise; the appearance of periodicals which spread the precepts of coordinated expertise nationwide among professionals, politicians, administrators, and businessmen; and the social surveys where experts from different disciplines united for the first time on a large scale in a common effort.

Still, there was more to these new professionals than the processes that gave them a form. Within that form there was a spirit at work that defined them more clearly in terms of how they perceived and evaluated various forces in the modern world: among other things, with images they held of the city itself; with the changing nature of American identity and values; with the methods necessary to influence public attitudes and behavior toward the reforms they sought; and with the role of politics and government in effecting and cementing social change.

II

To their dismay the public-service professionals found that the society they wanted to change with their special skills and knowledge was not always receptive to their efforts. Vested interests opposed them systematically, which did not surprise them, but as often as not the very people they wanted to help also resisted them, and that upset them terribly. When they analyzed this opposition, they discovered that the arguments against them were usually rooted in—or at least rationalized by—American individualism in one or another of its guises.

The individualistic ethos held that each person was responsible for his own well-being and could act much as he wished as long as he did not tread too heavily upon the lives, property, or sensibilities of others. It had originated in the natural-rights philosophy of the eighteenth century and had flourished in the highly atomized and highly mobile conditions of a rural society for several generations. By the end of the nineteenth century it had burrowed deep into American values and attitudes and was commonly reflected in the images that

Americans held of themselves. More than a nuisance, it stood as an obstacle to the new professionals, who thought not in terms of individuals in the countryside, but of densely packed blocs of people in the slums. And so the reformers set about to reassess the relationship of the individual to the community and to rearrange the priorities between them. The result was a growing commitment to the notion of collective or community rights.

By the early twentieth century the professionals were using this new collectivist creed to justify all of their programs. Clinton Rogers Woodruff was one of many who treated it in that manner. Secretary of the National Municipal League, and a widely respected participant in various urban causes of the era, Woodruff attacked individual rights as an impediment to housing regulation, and in general to the development of social responsibility. Expanding upon this theme, he said that the cities were finally beginning to realize "that the rights of the community are more important than the rights of the individual." Indeed, he continued, "the highest interests of the latter are best subserved through a cultivation, protection and enforcement of the rights and interests of the former." [23] The distinction that Woodruff made here between rights and interests is illuminating. He endowed the community with both, but preferred to limit the individual to interests alone. By serving the community the individual served himself, according to this view.

For public health workers the doctrine of community rights became a matter of dogma, in large part because bacteria paid no respect at all to individual rights. H. W. Hill discussed the problem in an editorial he wrote for the *AJPH*. In one's own home, Hill admitted, hygiene and morality were personal matters subject only to regulation by the family, not to coercion by outside forces. But the moment one left for his office, or any of his family left for school, or church, or theater, they entered a new environment where they lost control to countless outside forces. Contact with food, water, utensils, and with other people in public places exposed them to disease constantly. "By a thousand insidious pathways," Hill observed, "[people] touch, inhale and swallow discharges of many persons." To be sure, the likelihood of infection for any one person from any one contact was slight. But public health workers dealt with aggregate statistics, and they knew that hundreds of thousands of those single contacts had devastating social consequences, especially in the absence of sound health practices. Given those conditions, Hill concluded, the health officer had every right to impose controls on behalf of the public. [24]

At that, Hill was more generous than other health officials, many of whom insisted upon extending those controls to the individual even in his own home. More than anything it was the "white death," tuberculosis, which led them to believe they must show no mercy in the struggle against communicable diseases. Edward Otis, a Boston public-health doctor, urged health boards everywhere to comb through tenements, apartment by apartment and person by person, in order to give a tuberculosis examination to every single resident of the slums. He assumed that members of "the intelligent and better classes" could safely be left to the care of their own physicians, but he insisted that "if we would control tuberculosis in the tenements, we must control the tenements and the conditons of life in them." His plan included the compulsory institutionalization of anyone who refused to comply with tuberculosis regulations.[25] That was a specific application of what the assistant surgeon general meant some years later when he proclaimed in more general terms that "we are now emerging from the stage of individualism into the stage of collectivism and [thus] we as health wardens must reach out and touch every activity in the community."[26]

Lawrence Veiller also contributed to this growing attack on unfettered individual rights. Veiller had been the prime mover in New York's seminal housing reform act at the turn of the century, and for a generation was perhaps the premier housing reformer in the nation. He had an invincible confidence in the capacity of housing reform to solve every problem he found in American cities. Was poverty oppressive in the slums? Better housing would relieve it. Were morals low in the slums? Better housing would elevate them. Was delinquency high in the slums? Better housing would lower it. Was disease rampant in the slums? Better housing would cure it.

At the National Housing Conference in 1912 Veiller fixed his attention on the overcrowding that often resulted from the immigrant practice of taking in lodgers. He condemned this practice because it contributed to the appalling rates of disease and death produced by congestion in the urban slums. Convinced that the immigrants were motivated far more by greed than need, he found absolutely no redeeming qualities in this "lodger evil" and asserted that the community had every right to protect itself by stamping it out. He scoffed at any "sentimental plea" for individual rights, and he flogged one of America's sacred cows when he warned his audience "not to be led astray by the argument that the workingman's home is his castle, that its privacy cannot be invaded by officials for inspectional purposes any more than the rich man's."[27]

This was no mere metaphor for Veiller. When he spoke of invading the workingman's home, he meant just that. In great detail he described how an attempt to control the lodger problem in New York had failed some years earlier. At that time the health officers and police had made it a policy to carry out their inspections in the middle of the night when they were most likely to find the lodgers in and the residents off guard, or so they thought. They would knock on the door and then be forced to wait interminably before they were admitted by a "very sleepy Italian family" whose members were all wide-eyed innocence about the presence of any lodgers. Then, accompanied by the grumbling family, the inspectors would conduct a room-by-room search of the apartment. Ordinarily they found no one because the lodgers, alerted by the knocking, had taken flight to the fire escapes, where they hid while the inspection team completed its rounds. And on those rare occasions when the inspectors actually bagged a lodger the results were not better than when they didn't. The violators—that is, the tenants who had taken in lodgers—would appear in court the next morning, always with sad stories of an unemployed cousin staying for just a night or two until he found a job. Somehow, Veiller observed sarcastically, these violators always turned out to be sobbing widows ("Why they always should have been 'widows' I have never been able to find out.") with countless children in tow. Invariably the magistrate, a political hack controlled by the machine, would dismiss the case and end the hearing with a lecture to the policeman about finding something better to do with his time than harassing poor, unfortunate widows. Small wonder that the policy had been abandoned. Veiller supported its revival in 1912 because he was convinced that a new wrinkle in the law would produce very different results. Under the old law the penalties were aimed at the tenants of the apartments. This time they would fall on the landlords of the buildings. Thus instead of the tenants appearing before sympathetic judges, they would have to confront angry landlords. Faced with the prospect of eviction, Veiller suggested, they would begin to see the lodger situation in an entirely different light.[28]

There is no reason to question Veiller's colorful details. No doubt lodgers did disappear at the first rap on the door. No doubt "widows" did lay on a heavy coat of pathos in court. No doubt collusion between immigrants, judges, and political machines was commonplace. Granting all that, what stands out is how Veiller put those details together, what he made of them. After all, in other hands they can be arranged in a variety of ways to convey different meanings and justify different conclusions. Using the same dramatic framework as Veiller, for instance, one can turn them around to illustrate the tragic fate of immigrants in a world they never made; or present them as melodrama in which heartless villains persecute helpless victims; or arrange them as satire, with victims vanquishing oppressors by guile and deception, a variation of what Lawrence Levine, in a different context, calls "Laughing at the Man," where roles are reversed to reveal the smart as stupid and the stupid as smart.[29] They can even be projected as slapstick, with cops running around frantically inside the building while lodgers fly up and down the fire escape outside. The point is that Veiller perceived greed where others perceived need, deception where others perceived defense. Immigrants were angry at the authorities and wanted them to ease up. Veiller was angry at the immigrants and wanted to pursue a policy of uncertain constitutional status in order to conquer communicable diseases. Given the strength of his commitments, he did not give a second thought to sacrificing the rights of the individual in the name of the community.

William Dudley Foulke pushed the logic of community rights even further. Late in 1915, nearing the end of his term as president of the National Municipal League, Foulke stood at the juncture of reform and war, and pondered the prospects for urban reconstruction. Deeply impressed by Germany's performance in the war against superior numbers and resources, he argued that Americans must somehow absorb the German ideal of collectivism without falling prey to the Prussian ideal of authoritarianism. For a start he suggested that serious consideration be given to the possibility of peacetime conscription for public service after the war. "But we must go further," he said:

The public welfare may require of some that they shall marry and rear children for the sake of the community. They must be ready to do it whether they so desire or not. It may require of some, that they shall give up the use of intoxicating liquor or discontinue some other habit that involves extravagance or demoralization . . . whether there is a prohibitory law or not. It may require periods of training either for military service or in organizing the industries of state or city for purposes of defence or social betterment, and those on whom the call is made must be willing to sacrifice their private interests and respond to the appeal.[30]

Fifty years earlier the individual, in theory at least, had been supreme and the community had counted for little. In order to establish a better balance between individual and community, reformers in the Progressive era had been at work fashioning their doctrine of collective rights. Foulke carried the idea much further than his contemporaries. Although his position was a perfectly logical extension of the doctrine, his emphasis on collectivism was so ponderous that the balance broke down completely. The individual counted for little; the community was supreme. No doubt Foulke's diction was characteristically American. "Community" came as easily to him as "state" or "fatherland" to many Europeans. Otherwise, however, his ideas had overtones that anticipated developments in Italy, Germany, and Spain between the wars.

Of course none of this was yet apparent in 1915. For the new professionals the problem was at hand and the doctrine of community rights was a practical necessity. At the Toronto meetings of the NCCP in 1914 the Canadian planners made that clear to their American colleagues. How, they asked mockingly, could Americans boast of their vaunted democracy when it was so severely compromised by a Constitution that exalted individual privilege at the expense of the community?[31] More specifically, how did they propose to remake American cities without running afoul of some individual's property rights with every move they made?

That question of private property and the Constitution was really the nub of the problem. The various levels of government had always been warmly responsive to propertied interests in the United States, but their generosity became positively prodigal late in the nineteenth century. This development encountered fierce resistance, especially in the controversy that arose over some novel readings of the recent Fourteenth Amendment to the Constitution. When the amendment was ratified in 1868, its intent had been to protect the freed men in the South from losing their newly won rights, no more, no less. Beginning in the mid-1880s, it was turned to completely different ends in a startling series of court decisions. At issue was the famous "due process" clause of the amendment which specified that no state could "deprive any person of life, liberty, or property, without due process of law." By the 1880s the Supreme

Court had begun to interpret this clause in ways that pinched in on the traditional right of states to promote the general welfare. The whole issue centered on a few vitally important questions of definition: What was a person? What was liberty? What was property? What constituted due process of law?

When the Fourteenth Amendment was written into the Constitution, these words had had meanings in law that were reasonably well understood.[32] As things worked out, however, the obvious answers to these questions were not necessarily the correct answers. Thus in 1868 "liberty" was generally understood to mean freedom from physical restraint, such as imprisonment; "property" alluded to some material thing, such as a house or a piece of land; "due process of law" referred only to procedures; and a "person" was—well, a person. By the time the Supreme Court finished redefining these terms some of them had been bent into wondrous new shapes. "Liberty" no longer meant only freedom from personal restraint but now also included the right to follow any lawful occupation and to live and work wherever one wished. "Property" included not only the ownership but also the free use of one's property and might even refer to one's expected future earning power. A "person" was not only a living organism with a certain more or less predictable number and location of thumbs, ankles, and kidneys, but might also be something as absolutely incorporeal as a corporation. "Due process of law" now referred to the substance of a law, as well as to its procedure; in the name of *process* a court might strike down a law whose *content* it held to be arbitrary or unjust. "Liberty of contract" tied the new meanings of liberty and property together; related to due process, for example, it could be invoked to protect a "person" (who might be the Standard Oil Corporation) from the "abritrary" loss of either "liberty" or "property."

Thus the problem was not simply that individualism was built into the structure of American values, but that it was also built into the structure of American property relations. It was defined by due-process clauses in federal and state constitutions, gilded by the tenet of liberty of contract, modernized by the covenient legal definition of a corporation as a person, and zealously protected by federal and state courts everywhere. Demands for housing, zoning, and labor laws, to mention just a few, were bound to threaten someone's property rights under these definitions and thus to be cast into the courts where they would be at the mercy of judges who were not often given to generous judgments on those matters.

For the new professionals, whose very *raison d'être* was to reform society by imposing restraints on property rights and individual liberty, the implications of all this were staggering. Many social workers, for example, wished to push through laws limiting the number of hours that a person might work in one day. Would such a law violate liberty of contract and due process as manufacturers claimed? Health workers had shown that phosphorous was the cause of "phossy jaw," a disease that was disfiguring and even fatal to workers engaged in the manufacture of matches. Could a state ban the use of phosphorous in the manufacture of matches on grounds of health? Such a law would force the manufacturers to use a more expensive process to make matches, and that could very well put them in a poorer competitive position against foreign manufacturers. Would that constitute deprivation of property in the form of expected future earnings? And what about those midnight raids on lodgers or the forced institutionalization of reluctant consumptives? These were not hypothetical questions. They referred to specific situations, and they struck to the very marrow of reform. If the answers in all cases favored individual or propertied interests, then the professionals might just as well pack it in.

For city planners the situation was especially difficult. At least in public health there were precedents for community controls that reached back over decades. The struggles of health boards were thus not over the basic principle of controls, which was already firmly established in law, but over the nature and extent of controls. Modern city planners had not yet been able to confirm even the fundamental principle. They were breaking new ground, and they quickly discovered that whether they wanted to let light into a district by limiting building heights, or facilitate traffic flow by cutting diagonal boulevards through rectangular street patterns, or replan an entire city according to the most modern thinking, their plans always threatened some individual's property rights.

Hobbled in this way by America's tradition of individualism, the early planners usually looked to Europe for inspiration on collective rights. Arnold Brunner cited Paris, Vienna, and Berlin in this context as models of beauty and efficiency because they held the municipality above the individual, in contrast to American cities which he felt to be choking on their own excessive individualism. He ridiculed the city-beautiful mentality then in vogue for its narrow "desire to tie pink bows on the lampposts, or . . . to place statues along the car tracks." The real challenge was to harness the efforts of many individuals and give them a single direction. "The crowd left to its own devices is only a mob," he said, "but the same crowd, organized, drilled and properly led, becomes an army. Physically considered, our cities are now in the mob state."[33]

When social workers began to demand welfare legislation, they too discovered the pitfalls of American individualism as it related to liberty of contract and due process of law. Although they never really had an easy time of it, their early efforts were at least rewarded with state laws to regulate factory conditions and abolish child labor. But the further they pressed, the more resistance they met until about 1910, when they wrote social insurance onto their agenda and ran into a stone wall of individual rights. Like their counterparts in health and planning, they found it necessary at this point to make an issue of the obsolescence of individual values. They generally traced American individualism back to the eighteenth century or earlier and then followed its development across an empty continent heavy with untapped resources, where it had been an affordable luxury. Unfortunately the tendency of the courts to make a "fetish" of individual freedom had produced the human tragedy of contemporary society, where the individual had lost control of his destiny to the forces of an industrial economy. Social workers pointed to studies on accidents, unemployment, and old age, which proved that "the simple creed of individualism" was inadequate to deal with the perpetual state of crisis in which most workers lived. Nothing less than "collective remedies" carried out through "an aggressive program of governmental control" would cure these social ills.[34]

They also found it useful to make comparisons with European nations. All social welfare reformers were impressed with the social insurance schemes in Europe, and especially with those in Germany. Isaac Rubinow drove the point home when he contrasted a hypothetical working-class family in "democratic America" with its counterpart in "monarchical Leipzig" and concluded sadly that the German family was better off in many ways because it was covered by health insurance. Rubinow found it hard to swallow that almost every country in Europe provided at least a minimum of health coverage for its wage workers while the United States provided none. Like others at the time, he identified American particularism as the cause. Because health insurance had to be compulsory, it was not permitted in the United States on the grounds that it would interfere with the property rights of the employers who would have to help finance it. Rubinow argued that the nation could no longer afford such logic. The interests of the worker, the employer, and the "community at large," he said, could only be served in the modern era by a thorough system of health insurance.[35]

Fortunately there was a way out of this bind in the police power of the state. Now, for the new professionals, unschooled as most of them were in the language and labyrinths of constitutional law, the phrase "police power" no doubt evoked frightening images of men in blue with guns and billy clubs at the ready to enforce the law, instead of suggesting, as it should have, that property rights were not absolute but were subject to modification by the states. Specifically the police power could be invoked to promote the general welfare through legislation designed to protect public health, public safety, and public morals. Thus property rights and the police power were almost directly antithetical to one another, held in a delicate and shifting balance by fragile court majorities and changing public attitudes toward such things as morality or the ways in which sunlight and fresh air related to health. Could a legislature ban the manufacture of cigars in unsanitary tenement apartments? The concept of police powers suggested that it could in the name of public health. The concept of due process suggested that it could not, because such a law would constitute an infringement upon an individual's freedom to pursue a lawful occupation in a place of his own choosing. Could a city pass an ordinance authorizing midnight searches for lodgers? In 1912 the need to control health and morals suggested that it could. The right to freedom in one's own quarters suggested that it might violate due process.

In order to provide a basis for sorting things out and making decisions in such cases, the courts set up certain guidelines on these matters late in the nineteenth century. First of all, they insisted that it was not enough for a legislature simply to assert that a law would promote health, safety, or morals. It had to demonstrate that the law really was likely to promote these areas of the general welfare. Secondly, they determined that the courts themselves would be the final arbiters of this question. A legislature could pass a law to promote public health, but only the courts could judge whether the facts justified the law. That made the qualities and quirks of individual judges more important than ever.

To educate the professionals on these questions legal experts appeared at professional meetings and wrote in reform journals on the meaning of the police power, and in many cases its relevance to specific legislation. The labor legislation of the Progressive era was one example. In 1910 Louis Greeley, a Northwestern University law professor, spoke at the NCCC about the meaning of a recent decision by the Illinois Supreme Court to uphold the state's new ten-hour law for women. Greeley reminded his audience that the same court had overturned a similar law only fifteen years earlier. At that time the court had objected that the law justified maximum hours not in terms of the work that was done, but in terms of the sex of those who did it. Fixing the maximum number of hours was supposed to promote the public health, according to the law. Not so, said the court. First of all, it pointed out, there was no proof that there was any specific maximum number of hours beyond which a woman could not work without endangering her health. Secondly, even if it could be demonstrated that work beyond the eight hours specified in this law was somehow injurious to a woman, that would be a matter of *individual* health, not *public* health, and would not fall under the police power of the state. Thus the court struck down the law because it was arbitrary and because it did not relate to the end which it purported to serve. The decision concluded with a ringing affirmation of liberty and equality, after the fashion of that court. The "mere fact of sex," it proclaimed, must not be allowed to stand in the way of a woman's "fundamental and inalienable rights of liberty and property which include the right to make her own contract."

Whatever one thinks of the logic of the court in this decision, it did identify a sticky point in the logic of the legislature. The law did not say that work beyond eight hours was injurious to the health. It said that work beyond eight hours was injurious to the health of women. By singling out women, it seemed to imply that long hours of work did not particularly affect the health of men. Coupled with the court's argument about individual health and public health, this meant that any effort to pass such a law in the future, and to sustain it in court, would have to prove that the health of women was more fragile than the health of men, and that this fragility threatened the entire public for some reason that was unique to women. And that is precisely what the Illinois Supreme Court did with the ten-hour law of 1910, when it explained that "woman's physical structure and the performance of maternal functions place her at a great disadvantage in the battle of life." Physically impaired by excessive hours of work, women could not effectively rear "vigorous children." Thus it was of vital importance "to the public that the State take such measures as may be necessary to protect its women from the consequences induced by long, continuous manual labour." In this way then, because of the very womanness of women, Illinois's sexually biased ten-hour law "would directly conduce to the health, morals, and general welfare of the public." In 1895 the fact of sex had been "mere." In 1910 it was basic. Today it seems ironic that the "conservative" decision of 1895 was stated in terms of the social equality of women, while the "progressive" decision of 1910 was based upon their physical inferiority.

Greeley explained that this dramatic reversal was part of a nationwide trend for the courts, led by the federal Supreme Court, to pull back from their extreme position on liberty of contract in deference to the public welfare. To Greeley and other new professionals this meant that the Supreme Court would now yield to the reasonable judgment of legislators, thus giving a virtual carte blanche to the states for social reform. Greeley was euphoric. As he put it, "Individual freedom of contract, but a freedom controlled as the interest of the general welfare may require. What is there in this, *properly understood and applied*, to prevent any of the great measures for social amelioration now in sight." (My emphasis.) Indeed, he added, the legislatures might very well extend the concept of general welfare from its traditional emphasis on health and safety—what Greeley called "physical welfare"—to include "moral welfare" as well, by which he meant the recreation, reflection, and culture that were necessary for a "truly human existence."[36] Of course, the fatal flaw in his argument was the assumption that judges would always understand and apply the law "properly."

As things turned out, the courts were not quite ready yet to declare open season on substantive due process and liberty of contract. A year later the reformers were stunned when the New York Supreme Court struck down the state's workmen's compensation act, falling back on the due-process clause of the state's constitution and specifically denying that the law had any impact on public welfare. Perhaps reform was inevitable, but the professionals were learning that the path to it was not linear. They were also learning not to take the courts for granted.

For city planners the problem was less subtle, if no less difficult. At least they did not have to deal with the worst of the legal casuistry, the sort that endowed steelworkers with the inalienable right to work seven twelve-hour days a week at a blast furnace. They had only to cope with the property rights of various landowners, builders, and merchants. The trouble was that those rights seemed so manifest that the courts had upheld property in almost every confrontation with planners in the early years of the Progressive era. After 1910 more and more planners accepted zoning as the key to planning, which at least narrowed and clarified the problem for the reformers. All they had to do was persuade the courts that separating residential and commercial functions into different districts, or regulating the height and spacing of buildings, would promote public health or safety.

By 1914 the idea of districting filled the imaginations of planners, and the concept of police powers filled their discussions at the Toronto meetings of the NCCP. In particular it was Alfred Bettman, himself a lawyer, who undertook to enlighten the puzzled planners about a Constitution whose words were immutable but whose meaning apparently was not. What really changed, Bettman explained, were social conditions and the attitudes toward them. In a society of handicrafts and small businesses there was no need to remove industry and commerce from residential districts. In industrial society the need was urgent. The courts might use the same Constitution to defend property in the first instance and restrict it in the second, to strike down zoning under due process and later to uphold it under the police power, without contradicting themselves. At that point Bettman turned to the police power, patiently leading the planners through a primer on the subject, explaining that the word derived from the Greek *polis*, that it was related in the modern sense to ''policy'' rather than ''police,'' and that while it acted through restraint, the restraint was directed toward the public welfare. Where it involved such obvious cases as banning foundries from residential districts on grounds of health, he said, or restricting heavy traffic in them for reasons of safety, there was little doubt that police powers applied. But modern zoning had more subtle aims than those. When it came to regulating the precise location of specific structures in a commercial district, for instance, planners would need meticulous research and an imaginative legal strategy to justify application of the police power. For their part, he said, the courts would eventually come around to what the public was already willing to accept as necessary to promote the public welfare. In Bettman's view then, the police power, carefully nurtured and intelligently applied, would expand to meet public needs and public opinion, in spite of the barrier of individualism in property rights.[37]

In 1916 the Supreme Court confirmed Bettman's promises in a landmark decision that electrified planners. The case arose over an attempt by Los Angeles to close down a brickyard in an area that the city had recently annexed and designated as a residential district. The owner of the business challenged the ordinance and appeared to have a strong case for a variety of reasons. First of all, the brickyard had already been in business at that location before the area was annexed to Los Angeles, and after annexation it continued to operate unhindered until the ordinance was passed. Secondly, the city flatly refused to compensate the owner for his $50,000 investment. And finally, the brickyard could not in any way be characterized as a menace to public health or safety. In other words, the ordinance seemed to be retroactive, confiscatory, and arbitrary. According to Lawrence Veiller, its prospects for survival did not appear very bright, even after it was upheld by the California Supreme Court.

And yet, to the amazement of all observers the federal Supreme Court upheld the California decision, and in the process broke new constitutional ground by nimbly sidestepping the dubious area of public health and validating the ordinance in terms of the *general* welfare. Veiller called it "the most sweeping opinion [he had] ever had the pleasure of reading," and urged planners to read the entire decision. At the very least, he said, it removed all legal barriers from their efforts to separate residential and industrial districts. Beyond that, Veiller even believed that zoning regulations could now be devised that would shut apartment buildings—even "the best type of high-grade apartment house"—out of single-family residential districts, thus preventing congestion and promoting the general welfare. And, by the way, preserving the exclusive character of such suburbs as Shaker Heights outside of Cleveland, to which he alluded specifically at these Cleveland meetings of the NCCP.[38]

The incipient professionalism of these reformers forced them to sort through the primal values in American life and to clarify their position toward them. They discovered early in the Progressive era that their methods and goals had put them on a collision course with individualism and that the reforms they sponsored frequently perished in the legislatures or the courts at the hands of due process, which had become the legal instrument of individual rights. Frustrated in this way by a system that was not as responsive (to them) as they wished, they declared war on individual rights in the name of the community.

The new professionals were aware, however, that their struggle for community rights posed a threat to democracy, which, unlike individualism, was not a part of the national heritage that they chose to abandon. Germany typified the problem for them. When it came to recreation, housing, social insurance, land use, and city planning, Germany, more than any other nation, stood as a model for the reformers. Yet they knew that what they called "paternalism," "regimentation," "authoritarianism," and "autocracy" provided the framework for social planning and welfare there. As they saw it, Germany bought welfare at the expense of individualism and democracy. The reformers were willing to pay the price in individualism but were unwilling to sacrifice democracy in the transaction.

That presented them with a particularly delicate problem, for individualism and democracy were so intimately related in the nation's cultural mythology that it was difficult to discredit one without tarnishing the other. To their own satisfaction at least, they succeeded in separating the two by applying a kind of double standard according to which they perceived individualism as a product of culture, but refused to see democracy in the same context. They conceded that individualism had been relevant to nineteenth-century social and economic realities, or at least that it had been tolerable in those circumstances. But in the harsh conditions of industrial society they asserted in the strongest possible terms that it was no longer affordable because it was destructive of the general welfare. In other words, individualism was exclusively a product of time and circumstance, a passing phenomenon. To put it more forcefully, there was nothing in individualism that was essential to America, and therefore nothing fundamental would be lost in its demise.

They did not extend the flexible standards of cultural relativism to democracy, however. On the contrary, they implied that democracy was one of the eternal verities of American life and therefore something to be preserved at any cost. Thereafter they commonly justified their reforms in the name of democracy. Of course this meant that they had to redefine democracy, for in the past the term had referred essentially to a political *form*. In a way it was the institutionalized consequence of revolution. In the nation's consciousness revolution had brought liberty; democracy protected it. Liberty was valuable for what it was; democracy was valuable for what it did. In this light democracy was substantively neutral; it had no real content of its own. Thus to justify reform in the name of democracy, the professionals had to infuse the political form with social content. That is really what lay behind their efforts to elevate the principle of general welfare to a more lofty status. They were beginning to do with democracy what the courts had done with due process a generation earlier. They were beginning to "modernize" it by making it relevant to current needs. They were beginning to transform a procedural term into a substantive concept.

The goal of the new professionals was social welfare and their guide was science. Social and legal constraints led them to reject individualism and to modify the concept of democracy. In all these matters they were thoroughly modern and faced the future. Perhaps it is a tribute to their complexity that they faced the past at the same time, for they held fast to their recollection of the stable social order and close personal relations of a fading village America. In the years before America entered the Great War they cast about for some way to make that, too, relevant to the needs of an urban nation.

NOTES

1. The volume of literature on social welfare reform is intimidating. It can be sampled in Robert H. Bremner, *From the Depths: The Discovery of Poverty in the United States* (New York: New York University Press, 1956); Roy Lubove, *The Professional Altruist* (Cambridge: Harvard University Press, 1965), on the professionalization of social work; Allen F. Davis, *Spearheads for Reform* (New York: Oxford University Press, 1967), on the role of settlement houses in the Progressive era; Walter I. Trattner, *From Poor Law to Welfare State* (New York: The Free Press, 1974) and James Leiby, *A History of Social Welfare and Social Work in the United States* (New York: Columbia University Press, 1978), both of which are broad surveys of the movement. In addition, of course, there are biographies of most of the more important pioneers in social work.

2. The modernization of public health is traced in James H. Cassedy, *Charles V. Chapin and the Public Health Movement* (Cambridge: Harvard University Press, 1962), and Barbara Gutmann Rosenkrantz, *Public Health and the State* (Cambridge: Harvard University Press, 1972). John Duffy, *A History of Public Health in New York City, 1866–1966* (New York: Russell Sage Foundation, 1974), Stuart Galishoff, *Safeguarding the Public Health: Newark, 1895–1918* (Westport, Conn.: Greenwood Press, 1975), and Judith Walzer Leavitt, *The Healthiest City: Milwaukee and the Politics of Health Reform* (Princeton, N.J.: Princeton University Press, 1982) are informative for the cities

involved. For a broad survey by one of the pioneers in modern public health see C.-
E. A. Winslow, "A Half-Century of the Massachusetts Public Health Association,"
American Journal of Public Health (April 1940):325–335.

3. Barbara Gutmann Rosenkrantz, "Cart Before Horse: Theory, Practice and
Professional Image in American Public Health, 1870–1920," *Journal of the History of
Medicine* (January 1974):55–73.

4. "The American Public Health Association," *American Journal of Public Hygiene and the Journal of the Massachusetts Boards of Health* (November 1905):443–
445; "The Relations of Executive to Technical Men," Ibid. (August 1906):500–502;
H. M. Bracken, "Executive Sanitarians as Specialists," Ibid., 497–500.

5. R. S. Weston, "Public Health—A New Profession," *American Journal of Public Hygiene* (May 1909):212–217. See also Herbert D. Pease, "Training for Public
Health Service," Ibid., pp. 218–223. In 1911 the name of this journal was changed to
the *American Journal of Public Health*. Henceforth it will be abbreviated as *AJPH*.

6. Mel Scott, *American City Planning Since 1890* (Berkeley and Los Angeles: University of California Press, 1969), discusses the impact of the exposition on the move-
ment for city planning. The cultural implications of the fair are shrewdly analyzed by
John Cawelti in "America on Display: The World's Fairs of 1876, 1893 and 1933," in
Frederic Cople Jaher, ed., *The Age of Industrialism in America* (New York: The Free
Press, 1968), pp. 317–363; and Alan Trachtenberg, *The Incorporation of America: Cul-
ture and Society in the Gilded Age* (New York: Hill and Wang, 1982), pp. 208–234.
The early stages of planning in Chicago, which had the first great city plan, are dis-
cussed in Thomas Hines, *Burnham of Chicago: Architect and Planner* (New York:
Oxford University Press, 1974) and Carl W. Condit, *Chicago, 1910–1929: Building,
Planning and Urban Technology* (Chicago: University of Chicago Press, 1973).

7. See NCCC, *Proceedings*, for the dozen years or so before the United States
entered World War I.

8. Eugene T. Lies, "Tuberculosis and Poverty," *AJPH* (February 1909):71–75.

9. H. W. Hill, "The Epidemiological Diagnosis and Treatment of Typhoid Out-
breaks," Ibid. (May 1909):283–295.

10. Charles Mulford Robinson, "The Replanning of Cities," *Charities and The
Commons* (February 1, 1908):1489–1490.

11. "Every City Needs a City Plan Now," Ibid. (January 2, 1909):499.

12. Roy Smith Wallace, "Opportunities of Public Health Officials," NCCC, *Proceedings* (1909):182–192.

13. E. L. Tuohy, "Harmony in Public Health Work," *AJPH* (May 1909):224–226.

14. Dr. Charles O. Probst, "President's Address," Ibid. (January 1911):10–20.

15. Frederic Almy, "The Inter-relation of National Organizations Working in the
Interest of Health," Ibid., pp. 21–27. Almy became president of the NCSW in 1917.
See also Dr. Livingston Farrand, "Report for the Committee: The Public Health Situa-
tion," NCCC, *Proceedings* (1913):159–165.

16. George B. Ford, "The City Scientific," NCCP, *Proceedings* (1913):31–41.

17. Clarke A. Chambers, *Paul U. Kellogg and The Survey* (Minneapolis: University
of Minnesota Press, 1971), p. 45.

18. Arthur Grant, "The Conning Tower," *American City* (September 1909):20.

19. John Ihlder, "Private Houses and Public Health," *National Municipal Review*
(January 1912):54–60.

20. Chambers, *Paul U. Kellogg and The Survey*, p. 36.

21. Frederick Law Olmstead, Jr., "A City Planning Program," NCCP, *Proceedings* (1913):10–14. See also George B. Ford, "The Relation of the 'Social' to the 'Architectural' in Housing and Town Planning," Ibid. (1910):80–82; Jens Jensen, "Regulating City Building," *The Survey* (November 18, 1911):1203–1205; Clinton Rogers Woodruff, "Municipal Advance," *National Municipal Review* (January 1914): esp. 10–12.

22. "The Social Surveys," *AJPH* (July 1913):678–679.

23. Clinton Rogers Woodruff, "Forces Moulding the City of the Future," *Charities and The Commons* (November 5, 1906):235–237. Charles Mulford Robinson quoted this passage approvingly in "The City of the Future," Ibid., pp. 189–190. For a general discussion of collectivist ideas early in the twentieth century see James Gilbert, *Designing the Industrial State: The Intellectual Pursuit of Collectivism in America, 1890–1940* (Chicago: Quadrangle Books, 1972).

24. H. W. Hill, "Personal vs. Public Hygiene," *AJPH* (November 1908):382–384.

25. Edward O. Otis, "The Function of Health Boards in the Control of Tuberculosis," Ibid. (May 1908):205–213.

26. W. C. Rucker, "A Program of Public Health for Cities," Ibid. (March 1917):225–228.

27. Lawrence Veiller, "Room Overcrowding and the Lodger Evil," Ibid. (January 1913):11–23.

28. Ibid. See also Charles B. Ball, "Health Departments and Housing," Ibid., pp. 1–10. Ball quotes Veiller admiringly.

29. Lawrence W. Levine, *Black Culture and Black Consciousness* (New York: Oxford University Press, 1977), pp. 302–320.

30. William Dudley Foulke, "Coming of Age: Municipal Progress in Twenty-One Years," *National Municipal Review* (January 1916):12–22.

31. Flavel Shurtleff, "With the City Planners at Toronto," *The Survey* (July 11, 1914):390.

32. I am basing this brief summary of constitutional issues on the discussion in Sidney B. Fine, *Laissez Faire and the General Welfare State* (Ann Arbor: University of Michigan Press, 1956), pp. 140–151.

33. Arnold W. Brunner, "Readjusting a City for Greater Efficiency," *American City* (July 1912):4–8.

34. Henry R. Seager, "A Program of Social Reform," *The Survey* (April 2, 1910):25–31.

35. I. M. Rubinow, "Health Insurance," NCCC, *Proceedings* (1916):434–443.

36. Louis M. Greeley, "The Changing Attitude of the Courts Towards Social Legislation," Ibid. (1910):391–405. For a discussion of sexual bias in the courts on labor legislation see Judith Baer, *The Chains of Protection: The Judicial Response to Women's Labor Legislation* (Westport, Conn.: Greenwood Press, 1978). The police power was discussed in conjunction with most of the social reforms of the era. On factory legislation see John B. Andrews, "Industrial Diseases and Occupational Standards," NCCC, *Proceedings* (1910):440–449; on workmen's compensation see Miles M. Dawson, "Workmen's Compensation," *The Survey* (August 5, 1911):671–676; on tuberculosis control see Chester Bryant, "The Incorrigible Consumptive—The Isolation of Persons Ill with Communicable Diseases," *AJPH* (October 1915):1066–1074.

37. Bettman discussed these issues in comments he made at the 1914 and 1917 meet-

ings of the NCCP. See his comments in NCCP, *Proceedings* (1914):111–114, and Ibid. (1917):214–222.

38. Lawrence Veiller, "Districting By Municipal Regulation," Ibid. (1916):147–158.

2

Making Better Americans

Although more and more social reformers in the Progressive era were becoming enamored of their cities, most of them remained deeply troubled by the problems they perceived in them. There was too much poverty and congestion, too much disease and crime, too much family disintegration and immorality. When they set out to put things right, they as yet had no sense of themselves as professionals. What they had was a sense of the profound disjuncture between the city as it was and the city as it ought to be, between the reality and the ideal. Their professionalism emerged as they acted to close this gap.

The response of these reformers to the living and working conditions of the urban poor is a well-known and well-told tale. Dangerous factories, excessive hours of work, child labor, the insecurities of periodic unemployment, industrial accidents and old age, unsanitary and unsafe housing conditions—all of these were deservedly the objects of their indignation. Aroused, they pressed for legislation at the local and state levels, and finally through the federal government, to soften the oppressively harsh conditions of industry and society. Historians have located in their efforts one of the sources of the New Deal and the modern welfare state.

There is another part of the story that is only recently becoming familiar, and it bears exploration because it illuminates quite a different aspect of these reformers, and thus reveals the complexity of their perspectives on urban America. It is a story about their concern for the social unrest and moral decay of America, about the anxiety this caused them, and about what they hoped to do about it.

In the two decades before America entered World War I the reformers were persistently apprehensive at the prospect of social upheaval. They saw the symptoms all around them in the cities, and it gnawed away at the foundation of their optimism. When Clinton Rogers Woodruff pleaded for more parks to beautify the nation, he justified them not only in the esthetic terms of the city-beautiful movement, but also as a means of minimizing social strife. If you "neglect your industrial cities," he warned, " . . . there will be troublous times, the mutterings of which can even now be heard."[1] By relieving the tedium of working-class lives, he added, parks would make a valuable contribution to calming the troubles. These "mutterings" were audible to most of the reformers and put them very much on edge.

Nobody was more aware of urban tensions than the settlement workers. That was what had called them to reform in the first place. Robert Woods, of Boston's South End House, justified the profession of social work in terms of the need to overcome social conflict and defend a society that was "seriously threatened by internal foes."[2] Jane Addams, the revered founder of Hull House, was no less concerned with growing social divisions. She described how Chicago authorities had overreacted to a recent political assassination by arbitrarily and ruthlessly suppressing Jewish anarchists, thereby infuriating the entire Russian-Jewish community in the city. Radical organizations were feeding on this anger, and she warned that they would continue to thrive as long as city officials engaged in such inflammatory actions. The settlements stood ready, she said, to help calm this social unrest by explaining immigrant cultures to the rest of the city, and thus to build a bridge of understanding between these divided communities.[3] Graham Taylor, another of Chicago's famous settlement founders, lent an almost apocalyptic tone to the discussion when he reminded his readers of Alexis de Tocqueville's fear that America's cities might some day call forth a popular militia that would be "independent of the town population and able to repress its excess." The measure of his despair was the implication that matters were already reaching a point where such a repressive militia might become a necessary condition of city life.[4]

Other judgments were equally disturbing. Lawrence Veiller supported the new playground movement as a means of "reducing class antagonisms." Everyone, he said, was aware of "the treatment received by automobilists in passing through the poorer quarters of our larger cities." This was a class expression of "resentment at persons who are able to devote themselves so much to pleasure and recreation." If the poor were provided with the means of their own recreation in nearby playgrounds, their resentment might be neutralized. Moreover, he added, "organized play" did an excellent job of teaching one how to be a good loser, a quality that presumably would serve the poor well in the future.[5]

More bluntly still, Raymond Robins expressed the worst fear of the reformers. Acutely aware of the violence in modern industrial life, Robins blamed the rise of the militant Western Federation of Miners and, more broadly, the open warfare between labor and capital in the West, on the corruption of the mine owners. Then he added a provocative warning:

Either honest private business must wipe out dishonest private business, or the people will rise and wipe out both. You can take your choice, but you have got to choose. To sit idle is to rest on a volcano while underneath the fire burns. Those four hundred thousand votes cast for Debs meant something.[6]

The alarm was sounded constantly by the rhetoric of the reformers. America's cities were "swarming" and "seething." The social order was disintegrating. Such phrases as "great social upheavals," "industrial unrest," "class conflicts," "class antagonisms," and "social rumblings" were used regularly to alert concerned new professionals to the emergency and to the need for immediate and wide-ranging action to rid the nation of social strife.

This nervousness at the prospect of class conflict was magnified by the discomfort the reformers felt with the immigrants who were pouring into the industrial centers in those years. The variety was bewildering; the sheer number, staggering. How could one preach social reconciliation in the Tower of Babel? In the decade before the outbreak of World War I an average of 1 million immigrants per year entered the nation, the majority coming from peasant backgrounds in southern and eastern Europe. Without industrial skills to offer, often without even literacy in their own language, these newcomers were ill suited to the conditions of urban life in the New World and generally filled the lowest ranks of the labor force. They were the garment workers of New York, the steel workers of Pittsburgh, the packing-house workers of Chicago. For the most part desperately poor, often malnourished, and usually miserably housed, they were the people who crowded the problems that occupied the new professionals, and were thus central to the ways in which the reformers perceived the city in the Progressive era.

Because most of the reformers of those years came from Yankee Protestant backgrounds, it is not surprising that some of them were openly hostile toward the recent immigrants. These nativist social reformers were often informed by the thinking of the Immigration Restriction League and occasionally by the people who led the league.

Among these the most prominent was Joseph Lee, an upper-class Bostonian who was active in various reform affairs in the era and a guiding spirit of the Immigration Restriction League. In 1906 he was also the chairman of the Committee on Immigration of the NCCC. His report to the conference that year warned against further unrestricted immigration in strongly racist terms. "Nobody expects that as a result of contact with American institutions," he said, "the Negro will in any number of generations become white. And the inborn moral and mental characteristics appear to be as constant as the color of the skin." To Lee this observation carried the weight of scientific truth and applied as much to Yankee natives and immigrants as to Negroes. He rejected the argument that immigrants might simply be the products of bad governments, suggesting instead that bad governments were the products of people with inborn deficiencies. His message was straightforward: "Institutions . . . will in the end accurately reflect the abiding character of the people." Continued unrestricted immigration would force American institutions to conform to "the native character and genius of the races and classes of people whom we admit.''[7]

Still, the expressions of racial nativism and restrictionism represented only a minority of the new professionals. A more common response was simply exasperation, especially when some aspect of immigrant culture seemed to contribute to urban problems or to stand in the way of reform. That was evident, for example, in the way that custom and even practical necessity retarded the sanitation and nutritional reforms that public-health workers wanted to bring to the slums. Russians preserved their Old World custom of nailing windows shut against the winter cold; Italians built shelves in already cramped flats to serve as beds for their lodgers; and various immigrants fed their infants beer, wine, or garlic water to ward off disease. In obvious ways these practices frustrated the visiting nurses who were trying to spread their ideas about ventilation and sound nutrition to the immigrant poor, and they complained about it constantly.[8]

In contrast to this negativism there were many reformers who chose to emphasize the positive features of immigrant life. When *Charities* ran its series on different ethnic groups, the tone was decidedly friendly to the newcomers. Some of the essays were written by members of the specific ethnic groups under review, others by native Americans, but in all cases the purpose was to create a more sympathetic attitude toward the new immigrants.

The series followed two broad paths to this goal. As a rule the immigrant authors put special emphasis on the easy assimilability of their countrymen. Antonio Mangano praised New York's Italians, who had brought with them from the old country a love of freedom and independence that made them eminently suitable for American life. In just a few years they had founded their own chamber of commerce, mutal aid society, savings bank, school, and hospital. This highly developed organizational life assisted them in adapting to conditions in the New World without burdening native Americans.[9] When Alice Masaryk wrote of Chicago's rapidly growing Bohemian coummunity, she commented proudly on the remarkably high rates of literacy and industrial skills among the recent arrivals and the ease with which they took to mainstream American politics.[10] Basically Mangano and Masaryk were projecting the same message: the immigrants brought with them from the old country just the qualities they needed to help them adjust rapidly to American norms. Genes played no part in their discussion. Culture was all.

While the immigrants chose to stress their similarities to native Americans, the native Americans who contributed to this series often chose to laud the differences. With great compassion Lillian Brandt described the difficulties of Italian children who were caught between two worlds, but she cautioned social workers against trying to relieve the pressure on these children by forcing them into some preconceived idea of Americanism. She told them that they would do better to acquaint themselves with such typical Italian traits as naturalness, esthetic sensibility, kindliness, and social grace, and to encourage the children to develop these native qualities as they matured into young Americans.[11] Obviously not all stereotyping was negative. In this case the very "Italianness" of the children was desirable. Jane Addams was a major promoter of this new cosmopolitanism. In the report that she presented to the NCCC in 1909 for its Committee on Immigrants (just three years after Joseph Lee's racist plea to the conference for immigration restriction) she argued forcefully that immigrant parades and festivals, their clothes, their theater, and even their politics were a vital and inexhaustible source for the renewal of municipal society, art, and recreation.[12] Over the years, Hull House reflected Miss Addams's views on this matter by encouraging local ethnic groups to preserve their native customs and to display them with pride before other neighborhood residents at appropriate festivities sponsored by the settlement.

There was no real agreement among the reformers about the precise relationship of these immigrants to the urban crisis. A few of them traced urban decay in part to the inherent mental, physical, and moral defects of inferior types of Europeans. A far larger number reversed the order, blaming the environment, Old World and New, for various unattractive traits among the foreigners. A handful welcomed the newcomers for the cultural contributions they made to American Life. Some were plainly confused, uncertain of the balance between heredity and environment, and insecure in their judgments of immigrant customs and behavior. On the whole, the professionals were less hostile toward immigrants at the end of the era than at the beginning. No matter where they stood on this question, however, nearly all the reformers felt at least a nagging uneasiness in the knowledge that these new minorities, so different in manners, customs, and beliefs from old-stock Americans, were intimately linked to all the unsavory problems of industrial America. Committed as they were to improving the environment, the new professionals in the Progressive era generally agreed that immigrants were an integral part of the environment they wished to improve.

A different and more fundamental problem that the reformers perceived in the rapidly changing urban environment was the spread of moral rot. They likened this to a contagion and feared that it might spill out of the slums and infect the entire city. There had been a time, they believed, when conditions were different, when life had been of one piece, when work, recreation, meals, and prayer were daily communal affairs. The family in that culture had been strong and unified with "common interests and common understandings, because of common associations."[13] That unity was lost in the modern city, where tenement conditions changed families into masses with neither common occupation, nor common recreation, nor even common meeting ground to define and integrate them as coherent social units. Girls found it impossible to entertain their friends at home; boys found it impossible to release their energy in tenement cubicles; men found it impossible to relax from factory labor in the midst of family clatter. And so they all fled out onto the streets, leaving behind harried mothers with bawling babies as they escaped into their separate worlds.[14] Alienated finally from one another, they no longer existed as families in the eyes of the reformers, but only as relatives.

The activities that awaited them on the streets were almost universally demoralizing. Prostitution was an obvious target for reformers, who feared that the promise of easy money for easy virtue would prove irresistible in the bleak lives of poverty-ridden girls. Unchecked, they said, prostitution would impair health and industrial efficiency through the spread of venereal disease; would destroy the morals of anyone involved; would corrupt even the most innocent onlookers; and would contaminate nearby residential and business areas. Some of them wanted to segregate prostitution in red-light districts, but most of them agreed that nothing less than "absolute annihilation" would do. In either case, they shared the unspoken assumption that human behavior, left to its own devices, would gravitate toward evil and consequently that people had to be protected from even the most casual exposure to prostitution.[15]

Just as prostitution stood ready to entrap young girls, the gang life that swirled around the "street trades" stood as a threat to young boys. What the reformers saw here were youngsters—bootblacks, newsboys, messengers—roaming the streets at all hours of the day and night like animals in the jungle, without restraint, without roots, without shame. Many of them ran errands for prostitutes, and gambling was endemic among them. Without structure or discipline the streets prepared boys more for tramphood than manhood. The message was nearly always the same: freedom slipped easily into irresponsibility, and irresponsibility inevitably led to license. Without proper correctives, street behavior would follow a rising curve of antisocial activities from truancy through vagrancy to crime.[16]

Prostitution and the street trades were unpleasant and unacceptable, but they occupied only a small part of the population. A far more serious threat to the moral order was posed by commercialized recreation, which, in one form or another, was apparently irresistible to people of both sexes and all ages. Commercial recreation held a perverse fascination for such welfare reformers as Jane Addams in those years. When recreation was left casually in the hands of business interests, Addams noted, girls were denied a legitimate outlet for their natural love of pleasure, and were forced to gratify more "malignant and vicious appetites" in saloons and dance halls, where the "coarse and illicit merrymakings remind one of the unrestrained jollities of Restoration London . . . confusing joy with lust, and gaiety with debauchery." As examples of healthy alternatives she singled out Boston's municipal gymnasiums and cricket fields and Chicago's public parks. She would encourage social dancing as long as it was properly supervised and limited to those forms "which at once express and restrain, urge forward and set limits," and which generally expunge "dangerous expressions" without stifling joy.[17]

Unfortunately, more and more social dancing was being done in the new commercial dance halls, whose owners were quite uninterested in promoting the sedate steps described by Jane Addams. In fact, when the reformers looked into the matter, they were scandalized at what they discovered in the dance halls. Louise Bowen, a Chicagoan who specialized in juvenile problems, was one of many who addressed this problem. Like Addams, she knew that young girls needed some sort of recreational release after long days at monotonous jobs, and she bitterly resented the fact that they had no wholesome alternatives to the "lurid and dangerous pleasures" of the new dance palaces. Committed to the "scientific" investigation of social questions that characterized the era, Bowen's Juvenile Protective Association sent two married couples out for an entire winter to investigate the situation in dance halls all over Chicago. Their report was submitted months later, a jumble of statistics on everything from the quality of lighting in the hallways to the quantity of spittle on the floors. But one thing stood out starkly in the report: the owners and managers of these establishments condoned and often encouraged sexual promiscuity on the premises. Most of the dance halls served liquor, and the owners made no effort to prevent boys from deliberately getting adolescent girls drunk. Small wonder that in over half the places observed "immoral dancing and open embracing were indulged in." Even those dance halls that did not serve alcohol were usually adjacent to saloons, and many were conveniently close to disreputable lodging houses where young couples could play out the final tragic act in this drama of moral destruction.[18]

The new ragtime music, and the dances tailored to it, added to the sleazy atmosphere of the dance halls and to the problems of the girls who frequented them. Belle Israels spoke despairingly at the NCCC about girls who fell victim night after night to the new "dancing mania" in places where liquor, throbbing music, and lewd dancing conspired to break through even their stoutest defenses.[19] The next speaker addressed the problem of sexuality in young women directly. While women were as capable of reason and objectivity as men, she said, there was still a sense in which they were the more emotional sex, because "by their very physiological structure they have a more massive sex organization which finds direct expression through feeling and sentiment." Until recently, she added, girls had been completely sheltered and had had no outlet for these seething feelings, "except in harmless forms of poetry or music or the explosive form of hysteria." Nowadays, however, with increasing freedom from parental control, more and more girls were exposing those feelings prematurely in the shoddy surroundings of commercial dance halls. "The intensity of emotion in girls is justified by its great biological purposes" of reproducing the race, she asserted. The challenge was to contain it for the appropriate time and circumstances.[20]

Modern social dancing was the most frequently cited example of dangerous recreation among the young, but there were others scarcely less threatening. The reformers soon discovered the new amusement parks, such as Chicago's Riverview, where open gambling, drinking, embracing, and other forms of objectionable behavior were tolerated and often led to sexual adventures in nearby prairies. And then there were the summer excursion boats which rented staterooms, no questions asked, for as little as one dollar for the day-long cruise in the waters around New York City. The heavy demand on these staterooms had even created a new class of imaginative young entrepreneurs who used the rooms for their own pleasure at the beginning of the voyage, and then sublet them by the hour to a succession of eager couples for the remainder of the day.[21]

Another form of commercial recreation was the "cheap theater," which in various guises was spreading like a plague through the working-class and entertainment districts of the cities. Unlike most other forms of commercial recreation, the cheap theater made no distinctions of age or sex; it threatened the morals of everyone equally. Moreover, it became apparent in time that any particularly militant attempt to regulate it could put the reformers on a collision course with the First Amendment to the Constitution, a confrontation that most of them preferred to avoid.

Early in the era discussions of the cheap theater commonly dealt with such varieties of showmanship as vaudeville, melodrama, and burlesque, which the reformers judged as sensational, lewd, and generally demeaning.[22] Before long this concern with cheap theater began to concentrate on motion pictures, and with good reason. By 1909 when reformers first began to sound the alarm, 4 million Americans were going to the movies every day. Three years later daily attendance reached the astounding number of 7 million, even though films had scarcely yet ventured beyond the unsophisticated two-reel comedy or melodrama. Here obviously was a force for good or evil that reformers would have to reckon with.[23]

In 1909 *The Survey* consecrated movies as a reform issue by publishing its first serious essay on the subject. The author, Lewis Palmer, was impressed by the universal appeal of this "world in motion," but he was particularly intrigued by the special appeal it had in America for the poor. He noted that

certain houses have become genuine social centers where neighborhood groups may be found any evening of the week; where the "regulars" stroll up and down the aisles between acts and visit friends, and where the farsighted proprietor has learned the names of the children and remembers them with a friendly pat on the head.

This suggested to Palmer that the movies had a mission, as a true "people's theater," to reunite the family and reintegrate the neighborhood.[24] Many of the reformers repeated this theme in the years that followed. Orrin Cocks even paid homage to the film on those terms as a "great silent social worker" in fostering neighborhood spirit.[25] From a prewar reformer that was the ultimate accolade.

Unfortunately that silent social worker had a penchant for projecting material that reformers often found morally objectionable, and in that assessment they had company from watchdog organizations all over the country. Resentment had begun to press on the nerve centers of government early in the century, resulting in a wave of censorship laws that empowered local authorities to review and suppress films prior to any public exhibition. By 1915 cities from Atlanta to Seattle, as well as the states of Ohio and Pennsylvania, had passed such laws, and the Supreme Court had recently upheld them as a legitimate exercise of the police power to protect the morals of the public.[26]

The Supreme Court decision, however, left wide areas open to controversy and probable future litigation (for example, precisely what material constitutes a threat to public morals?), so that most reformers looked for some way to tone up the content of movies without resorting to formal censorship. They found it in the National Board of Censorship, which was established in 1909 by the People's Institute of New York to act for an unlikely coalition of movie exhibitors, movie producers, and reform-minded civic and religious bodies. The film exhibitors wished to placate local authorities in New York, who had recently tried to close down all the nickelodeons in the city. The producers, for their part, were fishing for some way to protect themselves from the whims of public censors, who stood as a constant, but unpredictable, threat to confiscate their costly products. The civic and religious organizations wanted to influence the substance of films without opening the pandora's box of constitutional and ethical issues that lurked in prior censorship. On the common grounds of expediency these groups joined forces to support the board.

The National Board of Censorship consisted of representatives from several reform organizations and was served by dozens of volunteers who screened thousands of films annually, passing most of them without change, recommending deletions from some, and condemning a few outright. But it had absolutely no legal standing or power of any sort to prevent movies from being shown. Instead it mailed out a weekly bulletin of its recommendations to hundreds of individuals and agencies in the nation and relied upon the fact that it was the only clearinghouse that acted on a national basis to pass moral judgments on films. Because local authorities were likely to act upon the information in these bulletins by using their licensing power to close a theater *after* it showed a condemned film, the movie producers usually made an effort to comply with the board's standards and decisions.[27] The object was to force the industry to censor itself, a *"subtly compulsory"* technique, noted John Collier, that was more effective than legislated prior censorship (Collier's emphasis).

From time to time the board was tempted to overreach itself. The furor over the D. W. Griffith film, "The Birth of a Nation," for instance, forced it to confront a very sensitive question: Should the board take a stand on controversial social issues? At first it recommended only that a few scenes of sex and violence be toned down. Griffith made the required cuts, but instead of approving the film at that point the board split bitterly over its social content, with several members flatly determined to condemn it because of its sectional bias and blatant racism. Finally by a vote of 15 to 8 the general committee allowed the film to pass (without the standard form of approval), insisting that the board had no business making judgments on social or political issues.[28]

The real tension arose between film producers and the board over questions of public morals. On the one hand, the board was eager to press forward the frontiers of morality and sought to suppress sensational material; on the other, the producers were eager to press forward the frontiers of profit and sought to exploit it. Then, as now, sensationalism was defined by sex and violence, and that is where the board chose to draw the line.

Summarizing the board's policies in 1914, Orrin Cocks reported that it opposed "close dancing," suggestive clothing, and (quoting from a board statement) "prolonged love scenes which are ardent beyond the strict requirement of the dramatic situation." It was permissible to portray prostitution as a loathesome institution, but never as a mode of sexual gratification or a path to easy money. Where it was integral to the story line, violence was acceptable, but the less detail, the better. Similarly, crime was a legitimate subject if it was followed by punishment and if it avoided "gruesome and suggestive details."[29]

In practice it was not easy to apply these standards, because the board was made up of people with different levels of tolerance for sex and violence, as well as different religious, social, and esthetic commitments. The result was a series of erratic compromises that never reached the level of predictability desired by the producers. Many of the reformers were quite content with this situation. John Collier, a cofounder of the board, argued that inconsistency was actually a blessing, since the unbending application of rules in these cases almost always led to overcensorship. In fact, he continued, the flexibility of the board was its most attractive feature. Since it could only inform and advise, it provided the widest possible scope for the application of local standards. A French love triangle that might seem perfectly innocent in New York might be totally unacceptable in a North Carolina village. Thanks to the board's bulletins, he said, the film could be seen in New York and banned in North Carolina without flouting local norms in either case. Thus the board's list of standards, which ran on for twenty-three pages, was intended more as a statement of loose policy guidelines than as a set of commandments. According to Collier, that was why the board was usually less restrictive than state and local authorities.[30]

In almost every form of commercial recreation the new professionals perceived a new and open sexuality that upset them terribly. It is not at all unlikely that they were reporting the origins in the working-class districts of a sexual revolution that is ordinarily attributed to the middle- and upper-class "flaming youth" of the 1920s. However that may be, it would be a mistake to dismiss their prewar anguish over this development as nothing more than a blue-nosed resentment at the possibility that someone out there was having fun. The reformers did not try to deny the pursuit of pleasure, which they believed was a natural, healthy impulse, but they were afraid to give it free rein lest they send it plunging into the "base passions." In a way, their fear was confirmed by the merchants of pleasure who catered to those very passions—by the owners of dance halls, amusement parks, and nickelodeons whose interest was not in common decency but common profit. Operating in an open marketplace of recreation, they were perfectly free to invest in wholesome forms of recreation—in gymnasiums or folk-dance pavilions—but they didn't because they knew it would not pay. Instead, they continued to put their money into the "lowest" forms of recreational ventures, which of course only added to the frustration and fears of the reformers.

Apprehension at the social unrest and immorality in the urban slums was as much a part of the reform ethos in that era as outrage over oppressive living and working conditions. This apprehension betrays some lingering doubts among the reformers about human nature, for in spite of their avowed environmentalism, they were not yet able to shed the conviction that behavior without institutional direction would gravitate naturally toward socially unacceptable patterns. Apparently human beings were not infinitely malleable after all. Liberation *from* social oppression was necessary, to be sure, but without firm guidance *toward* desirable modes of conduct and belief it would accomplish little over the long haul.

For that reason the reformers embarked upon a course of moral regeneration to complement their pursuit of social reform. For a start, they proposed to seal off some of the outlets for objectionable behavior. That was what lay behind their actions to have the street trades supervised closely by city inspectors, to police prostitution out of existence, and to place most forms of commercial recreation under the licensing authority of the cities.

Since this regulatory approach was supported by legislation, it carried the power of the state behind it and was to that extent coercive. In addition, it could easily be justified under the police power in terms of the need to protect public morals. At the same time, it had a certain broad appeal because it offered a convenient moral analogue to the rhetoric of economic regulation that was so widespread at the time and because it had a respectable ancestry in the laws passed to govern the moral implications of social behavior since early colonial times.

At best, however, legislation was a negative means of controlling behavior. It could direct people what *not* to do, but with the reformers' misgivings about unguided behavior that was plainly not enough. Traditionally the family had assumed primary responsibility for teaching people how to behave properly, but a fundamental tenet of the reformers was that the family in industrial society was disintegrating. It could no longer be trusted to prepare its members for society. That presented these social visionaries with a problem, for they could not simply pass a law forcing the immigrants to comport themselves in a socially sanctioned fashion; they could not command the poor to be more attractive. To accomplish that, and thus to restore a measure of order and decency to the cities, the reformers needed a more subtle approach.

II

The strategy they adopted was implicit in the ideas of the new specialists in recreation. Because these people were forced to compete with the seductive forms of commercial recreation, they had to devise activities that were, at the same time, interesting enough to win over recruits of all ages, and thoughtful enough to educate them.

One group—the play reformers—moved to accomplish this by working primarily with children. Guided by the axiom that the child is father to the man, they believed that any serious attempt to reform American society must begin just out of the cradle. A leading figure in this movement was that proper Bostonian, Joseph Lee, a man of wide-ranging reform interests (including immigration restriction) and a gift for extravagant historical generalizations.[31]

Lee discerned three stages in the socialization of boys. In the first, from ages two to six, they learned to relate to one another as individuals and as a group through such games as "ring around a rosey." At the same time they learned about family relationships by imitating the activities of their parents. In this way they absorbed "the two great sources of the civic sense, the two forerunners of the State—the family and the group of equals, the paternal and the democratic social organization." The second stage, from six to eleven, was the "big injun period," when the boy learned to become a "single, confident, aggressive, and wholly self-satisfied and self-sufficient atom in the animal world." The competitive impulse to win emerged strongly during these years, but was tempered by a survival of the cooperative spirit from the earlier period. The child was now beginning to perceive his personal interests in relation to a larger social unit. In the third stage, beginning around age eleven, the boy began to join others in team sports, where he discovered that his individual abilities contributed to a sense of common purpose and that he must adapt continuously with his teammates to the flow of the game. For Lee this represented a maturing of the "team instinct" and was proof that man was a political animal. Significantly, Lee associated each of these stages of play with some characteristic of adult life. Therefore proper training in games was essential to prepare the child for participation in government as an adult.[32]

Lee's colleague in the playground movement, Luther Gulick, also believed that play should be designed to produce good adult citizens. In learning about relationships on the playground, he said, children soon discover that "the social unit is larger than the individual unit . . . and that the most perfect self-realization is won by the most perfect sinking of one's self in the welfare of the larger unit—the team." The need to impose controls did not inhibit democratic tendencies because it was "control by opinion, rather than control by either force or fear." If the child did not like it, he could leave. If he decided to stay and play by the rules, he was exercising self-control, which, in its deeper meaning, was an expression of freedom—"self-control of [the] higher type," as Gulick called it.[33] Like John Collier's wish for self-censorship by movie producers, Gulick's conception of self-discipline was meant to be a "subtly compulsory" method of exercising social control without force.

Lee and Gulick reflected some of the major impulses of the Progressive years in their thinking about the meaning of play. Both of them were trying to reconcile the competitive individualism of the nineteenth century with the emerging collectivist tendencies of the twentieth. Both were wrestling with the primal American problem of balancing freedom with social control. Even the era's growing emphasis on specialization found an outlet in team sports, where, according to Lee, the team was defined by "differentiation of function, each boy being assigned to his own particular job and trained for it." For these men play was a serious way to train children for proper adult behavior and for a style of democracy which they felt to be appropriate to the needs of modern urban life.

Just as the problem with children was to give proper direction to the "play instinct," so the problem with adolescents and young adults was to give proper direction to the "rhythmic instinct." Joseph Lee again supplied the framework for discussing the situation.

Like many of the reformers, Lee was of two minds about the craze for the new style of social dancing that was sweeping across the nation. As an expression of the rhythmic instinct it pleased him, but it had an explicit sexuality to it that troubled him and colored his thinking about it. As usual, he devised an elaborate historical metaphor to make his point. He recounted the tale of Bacchus, "the god of the great primal forces that well up in us," who avenged his imprisonment in Thebes by driving his captors mad when they released him. For Lee this was the mythic statement of a cyclical pattern in history according to which human behavior swung back and forth between self-denial and sensualism, between puritanism and license. Just now, he said, after long years of confinement by the forces of puritanism, Bacchus was once again breaking free in his "cruder form" and threatening to avenge himself by driving Americans as mad as the Thebans.[34]

This Bacchus was a troublesome god for the Progressive social reformers. They knew that it was unwise to suppress him altogether, but they were equally certain that it was imprudent to release him outright. For Lee the solution was to strike a balance between puritanism and license—Bacchus in moderation, as it were. His aim was to encourage rhythmic creativity without triggering an erotic response. The newer forms of social dancing did just the opposite, he felt, with their elemental, pulsing rhythms that narrowed one's consciousness down "to a pinpoint of attention, while the emotion generated keeps piling up until it reaches the bursting point or overflows." Yet within even the simplest rhythms, he said, there lay the potential for infinite expression, like the complex variations on a single theme in music. Both moral safety and human enrichment depended upon developing this rhythmic potential in its most intricate forms and not in succumbing to it in its simplest.

Properly trained, then, the rhythmic instinct would bring a measure of refinement into the lives of the poor. More than that, it could be cultivated to serve civic purposes as well. Lee pointed out that dance and song had been instrumental in the growth of social consciousness through the ages and saw no reason why rhythm should not still perform that service. What he had in mind specifically was crew rowing, which he described as the perfect blend of rhythm and sport in team play, and therefore an ideal activity for training in democracy. It was no accident, he said with his customary historical sweep, that the Greeks, the Saxons, the Danes, and the Norsemen—"the great rowing nations . . . with their training in rhythmic cooperation, have been the great democratic nations of the world."[35]

For the movies many reformers had even grander dreams. Sniffing at the crudeness of a Charlie Chaplin, they aimed to have the entire industry overhaul itself to produce "worthwhile" films that educated as they entertained. Many of the reformers discussed this point, but John Collier developed it best in a remarkable series that he wrote for *The Survey* in 1915–1916. Most of these essays centered on live theater, but he made it clear that motion pictures were only "the newest mechanics of drama," a marriage of pantomime and technology that would eventually perform the same functions as theater.[36]

Collier's esthetic required that true theater be "a means for advancing social action and social consciousness" at the same time that it put people of limited experience in touch with "the wellsprings of life." Thus in a well-integrated society theater should be both a broadly humanizing and a more narrowly socializing agency. Industrial society, however, had never been well integrated and consequently had never produced decent theater. Moreover, the impulse to produce it had been stymied in the United States by the enormous cost of producing a single play or movie. In the face of this hard commercial reality, theatrical and movie producers had chosen to play things safely by cranking out mass products for a mass audience.

For Collier the relationship between the theater and its audience was crucial. Broadway producers merely catered to a crowd of tourists and tired businessmen with a gruel of musical comedy, trifling melodrama, and farce. What went on before the footlights was not theater, and what sat down behind them was not an audience. Genuine theater could only thrive in harmony with "a coherent, continuous public" and had to engage the services of a certain number of nonprofessionals from its public to cement this organic bond. He cited the folk theater of Ireland as an example of amateurs and professionals that had produced in Synge a genius who wove the humble folk materials of his native Aran into plays that spoke simultaneously to the local community and the whole world beyond it—the narrowly social and the broadly humanistic.

The United States had not produced its Synge yet, but Collier saw promising signs of true indigenous theater springing up in everything from ethnic productions on Manhattan's East Side to repertory companies on the Great Plains. A man of impressive culture and erudition, he nevertheless explicitly rejected the idea that theater had to be, in the usual sense, cultured or erudite in order to be good. He was enthusiastic, for instance, about a five-hour pageant produced recently by the Polish Alliance in New York for Polish victims of the Great War. Its author was an East Side unknown; the customers were simple Polish women; the producer was a barber; and the theme was the biblical flight from Egypt, "the dream of group autonomy, of nationalism." Here, for Collier, were all the elements of genuine theater. It established an intimate relationship with its audience; it enlisted talented amateurs in the project; and it addressed an immediate social issue in timeless terms.

Movies presented him with a somewhat different problem. Made for a mass audience to turn a large profit in a short time, they had a life expectancy of no more than six months; during this time they passed from theater to theater and then on to oblivion. That annoyed Collier. Books were not printed to circulate and disappear in six months, he pointed out, nor phonograph records to fall silent after a single hearing. Why should movies not be made for the ages as well? His answer was to propose a network of film rental libraries to be set up in cities and towns all over the nation. The existence of these repositories would permit producers to make movies for specific audiences instead of for a faceless mass and even to make their customary profit, though in smaller amounts over a longer span of time. Eventually, he predicted, these libraries would build up special collections for discrete audiences in schools, clubs, churches, and community centers, would elevate public taste, and would eliminate the need for censorship. In this way movies would join with theater to create and animate different audiences, and to serve society and humanity by educating people through art.[37]

From dance halls to music halls, from playgrounds to movies, the recreation movement had a remarkably broad appeal in the Progressive era. At the beginning it was shapeless enough to draw Social Gospelers, playground specialists, single taxers, child-welfare experts, city planners, settlement workers, and many of the irrepressible gadflies who shuttled freely from one cause to another in those years. All were intrigued with the idea of remaking the city by remaking the people who lived in it. Characteristically they researched the problem of commercial recreation to a fare-thee-well and then suggested ways to direct the use of leisure into what *they* thought would be constructive channels. Their expertise expanded rapidly, which helped them to tighten their control of the situation. Some of them even calculated precisely, and with dense mathematical formulae, how many square feet of play space per child were necessary to prepare children for useful citizenship, which they defined as democratic action that subordinated individual desires to collective needs. Others worked to steer theater, movies, and the "rhythmic instinct" toward similar ends. Their approach to recreation was relentlessly, almost grimly, reformist. Not a rhythmic twitch without social purpose; not a frame of film without social content; not a moment of play for the sake of playfulness. In this way they gradually fashioned the public recreation movement into a loose field of specialization related to the new profession of social work.

The recreation movement was part of the larger moral purpose of the new professionals, which was to unify a badly fragmented society by persuading everyone to share the same system of values. Robert Woods marked out this position early in the century when he discussed the attitude that settlement workers should take toward laborers in their district. The objective of the reformers was to reconcile the clashing elements in society, he said, and their chief target must be the middle levels of labor, by which he meant unskilled workers. Below them were the paupers, who were either unable or unwilling to work, and therefore beyond help; above were the aristocracy of labor (skilled workers) who didn't need help. Woods advised the settlement workers to abandon their naive belief that they would be able to communicate easily with these laborers, because the two groups were so badly divided by ethnic and religious differences. The challenge was for the settlement workers to break down these barriers, and "to build up new standards, new bulwarks of character and family life." While sympathizing with the larger aim of trade unionists, they must remain alert for union blunders, and be prepared to advise their clients against "wrong or hasty action" in this sphere.[38] In this way, Woods concluded, by tutoring immigrants in Americanism and laborers in patience, settlement workers could help to eliminate friction between immigrants and natives and between workers and bosses.

The dreams of the new professionals did not stop with social reconciliation. As important as that was, it would have seemed pointless if it did not fit into some larger image of the good society. Perhaps paradoxically, in view of the sad state of urban affairs, that image was fixed on the city.

Of course there were still those whose imaginations were rooted nostalgically in memories of village America, where life had been more leisurely, human contacts more personal, families more stable, morals more wholesome, and society more manageably of one piece. This outlook characterized the "summer outing" movement, in which charity and church reformers sent youngsters from the urban tenements on brief, revitalizing vacations to nearby farms and villages before returning them to the suffocating slums of the cities; and it was palpable in the quixotic proposal to include farming as a subject of study in the curriculum of New York City schools.[39]

This pastoral escapism was more a survival of the charity past than a harbinger of the welfare future, however. It had some devotees at the beginning of the era, but it lost ground steadily in the years that followed. The great majority of the new public-service elite were involved in reality, not reverie, and sought to improve the city, not to flee from it.

In the forefront, a worldview apart from the village memorialists, stood a confident and growing body of philo-urbanists, whose profound significance lay in the simple fact that they tried to view the urban future on urban terms. No one better represented this outlook than Charles Mulford Robinson. Robinson began his career as a journalist and was drawn by his love for cities toward urban improvement and finally into city planning.[40] A graduate of Rochester University, he had already received many commissions and written extensively on municipal improvements when in 1908 he wrote *The Call of the City* (the title was no doubt a mocking reference to Jack London's recently popular *The Call of the Wild*), an appreciation of urban life that boldly reversed the clichés commonly attached to city and country. Robinson took an almost perverse delight in asserting his preference for the abrasive energy of the city to the fresh air of the countryside, and for city lights to starlit nights. He even spoke caressingly of "the loveliness of the urban sunset, when the dust- and smoke-laden air throbs with rich color."[41] He characterized the city as "the highest social expression" and promised that "the American city of the future . . . [would] be the most splendid city of the world.[42]

Although few of the reformers were as yet prepared to sing odes to polluted air, most of them did share Robinson's enthusiasm for the city on other terms. They were especially attracted to the concrete advantages of urban life, and they took a nasty delight in discussing them alongside rural deficiencies. Thus the city was alive with economic opportunity, the farm, a dead end. Paul Kellogg used Turner's frontier hypothesis to set this view in historical perspective. "The edge of settlement," he said, "is no longer open as a safety valve for foot-loose rebels against the fixity of things." Henceforth Americans would look to the city—"the frontier of today"—for advancement.[43]

In proclaiming the economic superiority of the city, of course, the reformers were serving up a warmed-over idea. Many rural apologists had long since conceded that much to the bustling urban areas. But the idea that the city was a healthier place to live than the village or the farm in spite of recurrent epidemics was novel, and health officials were delighted to broadcast the news. They noted smugly that country districts were turning constantly to city health departments for advice, and they praised the new systems of medical inspection that gave clear superiority in health matters to urban schools.[44]

In the same mocking tones Frederick Almy discussed the dramatic improvements in urban conditions when he gave his presidential address to the National Conference of Social Work in 1917, and he attributed the improvement specifically to the new expertise in such fields as public health and social work. He remarked that a baby now had a better chance to survive its critical first few years in a New York slum than in some remote village, and it was no accident that he chose the most notorious slums in the nation to drive his point home. Nor was that all. Food and water, he said, were purer and more wholesome in the cities nowadays than in the country. His evaluation of the fabled one-room schoolhouse of the rural districts? By and large, he said, prisons, stables, and pigpens were more suitable for educating children. With Almy, as with many of the reformers, the note of self-congratulation was unmistakable. If professional expertise could cut into the problems of urban life, he concluded triumphantly, then it could do almost anything.[45]

Apart from these specific advantages, some of the reformers were fascinated simply by the dense texture of urban life. Edward Devine was one of these, a man who had gravitated from the charity movement into the orbit of social work during his long career in public service. Like many of the charity workers, Devine was never able to conceal his distaste for the squalor of city slums, for the immigrants who lived in them, and for the social conflict that festered in them. Yet in spite of these feelings he rejoiced at the sheer richness of life that resulted from the concentration of population in the city, at the superior schools, lectures and press, the brilliant show windows and counters of the retail stores . . . the opportunity to buy furniture on the installment plan and to pawn it when necessary, the hospitals and dispensaries, the hotels and restaurants and lodging houses, the parks and theaters, and music halls and the opera, but above all the crowds of people, the entertainment of innumerable kinds that the crowd insures, and the possibility among large numbers of finding somewhere congenial company.[46]

The problem was to find a way to enjoy the fruits of population concentration without suffering the curse of population congestion. The solution, he suggested, would most likely be worked out through planning and controls in smaller cities.

The more visionary among the new professionals looked beyond practical advantages in economic and health matters and beyond the excitement of cosmopolitan variety to a future in which the cities would reactivate lapsed ideals and serve as the core of a new national culture. William Kent, who began his public career as a reform alderman in Chicago, was typical of many who saw national renewal in urban terms. Kent believed that cities had been such a dismal failure in the past because they had come "unwelcomed and unprovided for into our national culture." The founding fathers and their successors had simply "failed to realize that the city, historically and inherently, is the most important and permanent political unit." Only recently had Americans begun to perceive this fundamental truth. Moreover, he added, "it is in the cities where all that is best and highest in human life flourishes, and has always flourished." His conclusions flowed smoothly from these perceptions:

The struggle of and for Democracy must be primarily an urban struggle. Out of the congested masses of men, through their own voice in representative government, will come humanity, opportunity, and justice that will bless the individual, ennoble the city and make more glorious the nation.[47]

The city, the hope of democracy! Frederic Howe had put it that way a year earlier in his classic treatment of urban problems and prospects. He returned to the theme some years later when *American City* invited him to comment on a proposal to make separate states out of the nation's largest cities. He did not think much of the idea, as it turned out, because the needs of urban and rural areas were too intertwined to make urban autonomy feasible. On one hand, the cities were at the mercy of rural areas for food, milk, and water. On the other, the city was now "the most forceful agency of democracy" in the nation. "To deprive the country districts of this democratic impulse," he observed wryly, "would undoubtedly retard the state and also the nation."[48]

Robinson, Kellogg, Almy, Devine, Kent, Howe, and others were setting down the principles of a new philo-urbanism in the United States. First of all, there was the belief that cities had moved ahead of the country districts in health, education, and economic opportunity. Second, there was a growing feeling that the cosmopolitan virtues of the city—its cultural, social, and esthetic diversity—were their own reward. Finally, many of the professionals viewed the city as a source of inspiration to revitalize old ideals and ultimately to revitalize the nation. Against these precepts they held a counterimage of farm and village which served to sharpen their urban vision. In song and story the countryside had long been glorified as the wellspring of America's greatness. Now the professionals were beginning to see it more as a backwater than a wellspring, a spot to rest perhaps, but not to grow; in short, it was a nice place to visit, but they wouldn't want to live there. This philo-urban impulse expressed an arrogant reversal of the principles set out in the nineteenth century as the natural order of things and summarized by William Jennings Bryan's famous "cross-of-gold" oration in 1896. "Burn down your cities and leave our farms, and your cities will spring up again as if by magic," he had cried: "But destroy our farms and the grass will grow in the streets of every city in the country." Little more than a decade later the new professionals were more disposed to follow the prophet who proclaimed that the city "makes the towns; the towns make the villages; the villages make the country. He who makes the City makes the world."[49]

But what kind of city? The problem for the reformers was to scale down the viciousness of urban life and expand the attractions at the same time. Over the years they devised three different solutions to this problem, each of which projected a different image of the city. In the Progressive era that image was dominated by the neighborhood.

Like so many of the commitments in those years the neighborhood ideal originated in the settlement houses and spread from there into all of the new policy professions. Once again it was Robert Woods who set the terms of this ideal and who remained its most dogged proponent through the years. Woods saw the neighborhood in organic terms as "an elaborate plexus of interests, relations, needs, ambitions, largely determining the lives of those within it," and insisted that the settlement house should act as its nerve center. Because its horizons were limited without being parochial, the settlement had the capacity to soothe the social wounds in a community and to build new cultural traditions as the old ones broke down in the New World.[50] All of Woods's familiar themes—the organicism, the primacy of the settlement, the mission of social reconciliation and moral regeneration—were fused here in an image that put the neighborhood at the center of the universe.

Dwight Davis developed these ideas a few years later when he discussed the relationship between the neighborhood and city planning. Davis, a member of the St. Louis Civic League, believed that the ideal city was made up of harmoniously related neighborhoods, much like the cells of a healthy organism. The nucleus of each of these cells would be the neighborhood center, by which he meant "the grouping of all the various public, semi-public and private institutions which have as their aim the mental, moral, or physical up-building of the neighborhood." Such a grouping of community-oriented institutions would be immediately beneficial to immigrants, he pointed out. At present the only public institution they were likely to encounter was the police station, where they were painfully apprised from time to time of their transgressions against the civic order. The neighborhood center would be a constructive force in their lives by teaching them that government existed for their welfare rather than for their punishment. In addition, the center would create a sense of community feeling and identification by involving the local inhabitants in neighborhood affairs. He implied that reform efforts were doomed without this spirit.[51]

The idea of neighborhood or community centers to organize and focus local activities spread rapidly among the reformers. Many of them believed that the modern school was ideally suited to integrate community life after the children went home each day. The recent innovations in design that provided schools with gymnasiums, auditoriums, playgrounds, and indoor plumbing opened up marvelous opportunities to provide cultural and recreational services to the neighborhood. Many of the reformers began to visualize the local community center as a kind of department store of constructive activities. Games and sports for the children; wholesome music and social dancing for adolescents; lectures, discussions, and library facilities for adults; proper theater, educational films, and decent sanitary facilities for the entire family—the neighborhood center would have something for everyone as an alternative to the destructive forms of commercial recreation that normally befouled the slum districts.[52] With the right kind of supervision these centers had the potential to bring out all of the latent cultural resources of the immigrant poor.

The right kind of supervision—there was the crux of the matter. What did the new professionals mean? For a few of them it was enough apparently to let the poor supervise themselves. In that spirit Frederic Howe saw the community center as a ''people's clubhouse'' and suggested that ''autonomous neighborhood administration . . . be developed, through which the people [would] work out their own recreational and cultural desires.''[53] Most of the professionals, however, were skeptical of the autonomous organization of recreation. For one thing, such doings had an air of café camaraderie that smacked of lounging around when there were more important things to do with leisure time. For another, they implied that the recreational expertise of the reformers was unwanted and, worse still, unnecessary. The professionals were willing to give local residents a voice in limited committee decisions or to have them schedule the next dance or basketball game, but control over broad policy questions was another matter. Mary McDowell, for example, saw great possibilities for community development through recreation and culture in Chicago's field houses, but she insisted that these local centers be run by professional social workers. Only on those terms were most of the reformers willing to endorse Lee Hanmer's definition of the community center as ''an organizing center for the life of the neighborhood.''[54]

By 1909 neighborhood thinking had spread to the point where the NCCC created a new section on Families and Neighborhoods. The participants in this session spoke of neighborliness as if it were some sort of primordial urge, a "primitive possession" that was under assault by the forces of industrialization. Specialization, uprootedness, ethnic cleavages, irregular employment—all conspired to alienate individuals from one another and caused them to "lose their sense of belonging to anything or anybody." But the reformers were encouraged by the recent emergence of individuals and institutions bent upon tackling urban problems at the neighborhood level. If the battle against evil could be won there, it could be won anywhere. Paul Kellogg pointed out that cities were already too enormous to be apprehended in their entirety. But they could be grasped through their neighborhoods, which were more compact, more homogeneous, and less amorphous.[55]

By its more ardent proponents, the neighborhood ideal was visualized as something more than just a way to set the cities straight. To these people it was the key to reconstructing the entire nation. George Hooker helped to work this idea out when he described a scheme to rest the entire structure of American politics on a foundation of urban neighborhoods. The traditional units of state, county, and town had served a rural nation well enough in their time, he said, but they were no longer adequate to the needs of an urbanizing society. To replace them, he advocated a system that would link local to national needs through ascending levels of authority—city, metropolitian district, and state. At the base of this pyramid was the neighborhood government, elected to provide planning for the physical, social, and cultural needs of the local district and by engaging the "common folk," to create a sense of community that would stabilize local populations by "making neighborhoods more worthy of permanent residence." At the apex was the federal government, for which he recommended a Department of Urban Life to deal with any urban affairs that spilled across state lines and to make city planning a matter of national policy.[56]

The neighborhood ideal was even expressed in response to developments in New York's garment industry. The industry had already spread into some established mercantile areas and by 1916 was beginning to creep up Fifth Avenue. This so alarmed the merchants of Fifth Avenue that they formed a "Save New York Committee," which aimed to drive the industry out and preserve the avenue for a higher class of people. Noting this, The Survey reported on the plan of an industrial engineer to establish the garment industry in its own self-contained neighborhood. With 1,500 small factories and 200,000 workers, along with the warehouses, stores, and other facilities needed to serve all these people, the industry would form a city within the city. This was not the village writ large; it was the city writ small. Similar industrial communities could be spaced elsewhere throughout the city. In time, as these neighborhoods demonstrated their efficiency in improving local health and sanitary conditions, the present system of organizing the city along functional lines—residential districts, commercial areas, and so on—would be replaced by a system of communities, each of which would be integrated around a specific industry.[57]

On the eve of World War I the language of these proposals was becoming guardedly professional in its coloration. It was often more impersonal and less infused with moral and emotional fervor than had once been the case. The moral substance, however, remained much the same. Fifteen years earlier these neighborhood reformers had been trying to cut the metropolis down to size by carving it into small communities, which would restore a sense of human proportion to things. They were still trying when America entered the war. Thus Robert Woods could close out the era as he had begun it, with a call to "the most spirited participation of all . . . citizens to regenerate the city through its neighborhoods." His tone, appropriate to the beginning of the century, now sounded a bit stilted, but the organic localism of the "cluster of interlacing communities" that he spoke of fitted the assumptions at either end of the era.[58]

Fully worked out, the neighborhood ideal offered a comprehensive solution to the social and moral problems that bedevilled the reformers. It hinged on the neighborhood center, which they portrayed as an institutional cluster to serve the poor in terms of their own values. It would Americanize the immigrants, educate their children, school their families in proper conduct and values, and provide an opportunity to express suitable recreational, cultural, and fraternal impulses, which would also be part of the educational process. To the extent that the family had lost its traditional functions, the center would replace it as a means of guidance, recreation, and creativity and beyond that as a source for defining the individual's very identity. In this way it would work to close the cultural gap between the poor and the rest, and thus to relax social tensions. In addition, it would restore the feeling for community consciousness that had been lost in the blind rush to industrial growth, without sacrificing any of the economic and cultural advantages of the wider city around it. In time, as the network of such centers spread, the fragmented city itself would draw together, fulfill its great promise, and serve as a model for rebuilding the nation.

And yet the neighborhood plan for urban reconstruction never really took root. After the war it virtually disappeared. What happened? After all, the idea grew from a reasonable perception of city life at the time. Mother and children were indeed walled in by the tenements day and night. Men did commonly work in or near the neighborhood. Family life, education, religion, shopping, and recreation were all carried on close to home. The neighborhood ideal grew quite simply from the neighborhood reality.

The flaw in the reformers' vision was not in what they saw before them but in what they did not see before them. They were aware that modern urban life was a dynamic process, but they failed to foresee the consequences of changes that were already in the air. Better public transportation, shorter work days, new patterns of leisure and consumption (which related closely to the commercial recreation they deplored), the beginning of an automobile culture, mass education, and the new mass media of communications were already modifying urban life before the war. In the next decade these processes would spread and batter down the confining walls of the neighborhood, expanding human awareness and activities to the city's boundaries and beyond. Most important, they would open minds to new sources and forms of manipulation. In the meantime, as Flavel Shurtleff said of city planners in 1915, most of the public-service professionals preferred to address the city as "a strongly-knit federation of neighborhoods," and to reform it on those terms.[59]

All this illustrates an important point about these new middle-class policy professionals. At no time during the Progressive era did their interest in new bureaucratic means blind them to the ends they sought. They knew what was wrong with American cities, and they knew what they wanted to do about it. Throughout they were guided by a powerful moral vision, and that, more than anything else, established their identity as a demi-class in American society.

NOTES

1. Clinton Rogers Woodruff, "A More Beautiful America," *Charities* (August 1, 1903):101–105.

2. Robert A. Woods, "Social Work: A New Profession," *Charities and The Commons* (January 6, 1906): 469–476.

3. Jane Addams, "The Chicago Settlements and Social Unrest," Ibid. (May 2, 1908):155–166.

4. Graham Taylor, "City and Church Reapproaching Each Other," *The Survey* (August 3, 1912):625–628.

5. Lawrence Veiller, "The Social Value of Playgrounds in Crowded Districts," *Charities and The Commons* (August 3, 1907):507–510.

6. Raymond Robins, "The One Main Thing," NCCC, *Proceedings* (1907):326–334.

7. Joseph Lee et al., "Immigration" (Report of the Committee on Immigration), Ibid. (1906):282–285. Genetic assumptions also shaped Edward Devine's views on the immigration problem. As editor of *The Survey* he was a leading evangelist for the new professional ideals. At the same time he feared that the current flood of "inherently" inferior immigrants would inevitably produce "a mongrel and degenerate breed" in America. Not surprisingly, he supported restriction. See Edward T. Devine, "The Selection of Immigrants," *The Survey* (February 4, 1911):715–716.

8. Johanna Von Wagner, "Inspection of Tenement Houses," *Journal of the Massachusetts Association of Boards of Health* (July 1903):41–45. This journal was a forerunner to the *American Journal of Public Health*.

9. Antonio Mangano, "The Associated Life of Italians in New York City," *Charities* (May 7, 1904):476–482.

10. Alice G. Masaryk, "The Bohemians in Chicago," Ibid. (December 3, 1904):206–210.

11. Lillian Brandt, "A Transplanted Birthright," Ibid. (May 7, 1904):494–499.

12. Jane Addams, "Immigrants" (Report of the Committee of Immigration), NCCC, *Proceedings* (1909):213–215.

13. George A. Bellamy, "Recreation and Social Progress: The Settlement," Ibid. (1914):375–382.

14. Ibid. See also Lee F. Hanmer, "Organizing the Neighborhood for Recreation," Ibid. (1915):70–75.

15. All the professionals were concerned about prostitution. For a sampling of their

feelings about it see the following: Graham Taylor, "The Police and Vice in Chicago," *The Survey* (November 6, 1909):160–165; George F. Butler, "The Report of the Minneapolis Vice Commission," *Journal of the American Public Health Association* (December 1911):897–898; J. H. Landis, "The Social Evil in Relation to the Health Problem," *AJPH* (October 1913):1073–1086; James B. Reynolds, "War Against the White Slave Traffic and Commercialized Vice," NCCC, *Proceedings* (1914):211–217; "Church Crusade on the Barbary Coast," *The Survey* (March 17, 1917):694–695.

16. Attitudes toward the street trades are revealed in the following few among many such articles: Everett W. Goodhue, "Boston Newsboys, How They Live and Work," *Charities* (June 7, 1902):527–532; Lettie L. Johnston, "Street Trades and Their Regulation," NCCC, *Proceedings* (1915):518–524; Bernard J. Newman, "The Home of the Street Urchin," *National Municipal Review* (October 1915):587–593.

17. Jane Addams, "Some Reflections on the Failure of the Modern City to Provide Recreation for Young Girls," *Charities and The Commons* (December 5, 1908):365–368. See also Addams, "Public Recreation and Social Morality," Ibid. (August 3, 1907):492–494.

18. Louise De Koven Bowen, "Dance Halls," *The Survey* (June 3, 1911):383–387.

19. Belle Lindner Israels, "The Way of the Girl," *Charities and The Commons* (July 3, 1909):486–497, and "The Dance Problem," NCCC, *Proceedings* (1912):140–146.

20. Beulah Kennard, "Emotional Life of Girls," Ibid., pp. 146–148.

21. *The Survey* (May 6, 1916):163–164; Ibid. (May 27, 1916):218; Belle Lindner Israels, "The Way of The Girl," *Charities and The Commons* (July 3, 1909):486–497.

22. Sherman C. Kingsley, "The Penny Arcade and the Cheap Theater," Ibid. (June 8, 1907): 295–297.

23. Some of the social implications of the movies in these years are discussed in Robert Sklar, *Movie-Made America* (New York: Random House, 1975).

24. Lewis E. Palmer, "The World in Motion," *The Survey* (June 5, 1909):355–365.

25. Orrin G. Cocks, "Moving Pictures as a Factor in Municipal Life," *National Municipal Review* (October 1914):708–712.

26. A brief survey of the early censorship laws and of the efforts to enforce them may be found in John Collier, "Censorship in Action," *The Survey* (August 7, 1915):423–427.

27. The structure and methods of the board are discussed in Orrin G. Cocks, "Applying Standards to Motion Picture Films," Ibid. (June 27, 1914):337–338, and John Collier, "Censorship; and the National Board," Ibid. (October 2, 1915):9–14. For a discussion of the National Board and early efforts at censorship see Lary May, *Screening Out the Past: The Birth of Mass Culture and the Motion Picture Industry* (Chicago: University of Chicago Press, 1980).

28. "Films and Births and Censorship," *The Survey* (April 3, 1915):4–5.

29. Orrin G. Cocks, "Applying Standards to Motion Picture Films," Ibid. (June 27, 1914):337–338.

30. John Collier, "Censorship; and the National Board," Ibid. (October 2, 1915):9–14. Still, Collier was disturbed by a growing rigidity of outlook on the Board which could "ultimately limit (its) own freedom of action and even of debate and may discourage the creative producer of films."

31. Lee's role in the playground movement is discussed in Dominick Cavallo, *Muscles and Morals* (Philadelphia: University of Pennsylvania Press, 1981). The general

drift of the rest of this chapter parallels Paul Boyer's discussion of "positive environmentalism." See Paul Boyer, *Urban Masses and Moral Order in America, 1820–1920* (Cambridge: Harvard University Press, 1978), pp. 220–283.

32. Joseph Lee, "Play as a School of the Citizen," *Charities and The Commons* (August 3, 1907):486–491.

33. Luther Halsey Gulick, "Play and Democracy," Ibid., pp. 481–486. See also Henry S. Curtis, "The Playground," NCCC, *Proceedings* (1907):278–286.

34. Joseph Lee, "Rhythm and Recreation," Ibid. (1912):126–139.

35. *Ibid.*, and Lee, "Play as a School of the Citizen."

36. There were nine articles in the series. I have based this discussion of Collier's ideas upon the following from among those essays: "Back of Our Footlights," *The Survey* (June 5, 1915):213–217; "Before Our Footlights," Ibid. (July 3, 1915):315–317; "The Theater of Tomorrow," Ibid. (January 1, 1916):381–385; and "For a New Drama," Ibid. (May 6, 1916):137–141.

37. John Collier, "A Film Library," Ibid. (March 4, 1916):663–668.

38. Robert Woods, "The Success of the Settlement as a Means of Improving a Neighborhood," *Charities* (September 6, 1902):225–229.

39. For expressions of village nostalgia see "Summer Philanthropy," Ibid. (October 5, 1901):279–288; Henry Barker, "The Park in its Relation to Physical Geography and the City Plan," *Charities and The Commons* (February 1, 1908):1506–1512; "Gardening for City Children," *Charities* (August 9, 1902):143.

40. A good, brief summary of Robinson's career and ideas may be found in Park Dixon Goist, *From Main Street to State Street* (Port Washington, N.Y.: Kennikat Press, 1977), pp. 121–130.

41. Ibid., p. 124.

42. Charles Mulford Robinson, "The City of the Future," *Charities and The Commons* (November 5, 1906):189–190.

43. Paul U. Kellogg, "The Pittsburgh Survey," Ibid. (January 2, 1909):517–526.

44. Francis E. Fronczak, "Health Work Progress in America," *AJPH* (March 1913):197–201; "Should Rural Schools Be Closed?" Ibid. (May 1914):436–437.

45. Frederick Almy, "The Conquest of Poverty," NCSW, *Proceedings* (1917):6–7.

46. Edward T. Devine, "Congestion of Population," *Charities and The Commons* (March 14, 1908):1739–1740. For Devine's views on social conflict see "Is Our Social Ideal Bourgeois?" *The Survey* (December 18, 1909):369–370; on immigrants, "The Selection of Immigrants," Ibid. (February 4, 1911):715–716; on congestion and squalor, almost anything he wrote in his years as a reform editor.

47. William Kent, "The American City Electorate," *Charities and The Commons* (November 5, 1906):209–211.

48. Frederic C. Howe et al., "Shall Our Great Cities Be Made States?" *American City* (February 1914):142–144.

49. Henry Drummond, quoted in John Nolen, "City Making," Ibid. (September 1909):15–19.

50. Robert A. Woods, "The Success of the Settlement as a Means of Improving a Neighborhood," *Charities* (September 6, 1902):225–229. For a schematic view of neighborhood thinking since 1880, see Zane L. Miller, "The Role and Concept of Neighborhood in American Cities," in Robert Fisher and Peter Romanofsky, eds., *Community Organization for Urban Social Change* (Westport, Conn.: Greenwood Press,

1981), pp. 3–32. See also Robert Fisher, "From Grass Roots Organizing to Community Service: Community Organization Practice in the Community Center Movement, 1907–1932," Ibid., pp. 33–38.

51. Dwight F. Davis, "The Neighborhood Center—A Moral and Educational Factor," *Charities and The Commons* (February 1, 1908):1504–1506.

52. Jens Jensen, "Regulating City Building," *The Survey* (November 18, 1911):1202–1205; Henry S. Curtis, "The Neighborhood Center," *American City* (July 1912):14–17; Clarence Arthur Perry, "Why Recreation in the Schoolhouse?" NCCC, *Proceedings* (1914):382–385; Lee F. Hanmer, "Organizing the Neighborhood for Recreation," Ibid. (1915):70–75; George A. Bellamy, "Municipal Recreation—A Review of Recent Literature," *National Municipal Review* (January 1917):49–56.

53. Frederic C. Howe, "Leisure," *The Survey* (January 3, 1914):415–416.

54. Mary McDowell, "The Field Houses of Chicago and Their Possibilities," *Charities and The Commons* (August 3, 1907):535–538.

55. Paul U. Kellogg, "The Neighborhood and the Municipality," NCCC, *Proceedings* (1909):163–178; Graham Taylor, "The Neighborhood and the Municipality," Ibid., pp. 156–163.

56. George E. Hooker, "City Planning and Political Areas," *American City* (February 1917):122–125. See also Robert A. Woods, "The Neighborhood and the Nation," NCCC, *Proceedings* (1909):101–106.

57. "Garment Town: A City Within a City," *The Survey* (November 11, 1916):140–143.

58. Robert A. Woods, "The City and its Local Community Life," NCCC, *Proceedings* (1917):455–458. Woods's argument was supported by Mary McDowell's experiences "back-of-the-yards" (the meat-packing neighborhood) in Chicago. See her paper, "The Significance to the City of its Local Community Life," Ibid., pp. 458–462.

59. Flavel Shurtleff, "Six Years of City Planning in the United States," NCCP, *Proceedings* (1915):33–44.

3

The Perils of Professionalism

In the early years of the century the reformers drifted toward professionalism more through the internal dynamics of their chosen fields than by any conscious efforts on their part. The process ordinarily followed a line from theory and method through research to the accumulation of vast stores of information, and then to specialization and organization, though not always precisely in that order. Somewhere along the line a sense of special identity always emerged, and at that point the reformers became increasingly aware of their occupation as a profession. The more conscious they became of it, the more they worked to cultivate both the image and the reality of professionalism. That created some problems, however, for many of them pictured the professional essentially as they pictured the scientist—rational, objective, dispassionate, and generally disengaged socially—and that did not sit well with those who insisted upon the primacy of reform and the need to adapt professional standards to social goals. At the same time there was an uneasy awareness in the new policy fields that the rapid expansion of knowledge was creating a serious problem of communication between the professionals and the lay public. Thus the process of professionalization itself was generating tensions in the public-service occupations. By the 1920s this was a nagging theme running through all of them.

The problem was especially acute among social workers, who appeared to feel less secure than others about their professionalism and who therefore spent more time agonizing about it. That insecurity dominated a session on professional standards at the NCCC in 1915, where social workers demonstrated that they were quite aware of how far professionalism had proceeded in their field, yet extremely uncomfortable with how far it had still to go. The papers on social work education agreed that standards were unacceptably low in this area. To raise them, they urged that course work be expanded to two years, that it include work in "applied psychology," that it be patterned after the sciences, and that fieldwork training be integrated into the curriculum, much as it was in medical education, where students did their training in hospital wards in the later stages of their education.[1] The angles of approach differed in these various papers, but they all converged on the same point: social work education was still not nearly rigorous enough to meet the kind of standards laid down for other professions, especially medicine.

The real bombshell at the conference was dropped by Abraham Flexner, and Flexner was a difficult man to ignore on the subject of professionalism. A few years earlier he had played a vital role in separating medicine from quackery by helping to set up the high standards of modern medical education. In the process, he had established and codified the canons of professionalism for other occupations as well. Thus when Flexner was invited to address the conference, it was not as an expert on social work, but as an expert on professionalism. He was the first specialist in specialization.

Flexner laid down several criteria for determining professionalism. Above all, he felt that an occupation had to be essentially intellectual in character and that its practitioners had to initiate activities for which they were directly and personally responsible. Beyond that a profession had to center on expertise or knowledge that was not immediately accessible to the general public; it had to aim at practical results, to have techniques that were communicable only through a highly specialized education, to express its self-awareness in an organization, and to proceed from altruistic motives. Flexner measured social work against these standards and found it wanting. The fundamental flaw was that it did not even begin to solve problems on its own. "Let me explain as concretely as I can," he said:

The social worker takes hold of a case, that of a disintegrating family, a wrecked individual, or an unsocialized industry. Having localized his problem, having decided on its particular nature, is he not usually driven to invoke the specialized agency, professional or other, best equipped to handle it? There is illness to be dealt with—the doctor is needed; ignorance requires the school; poverty calls for the legislator, organized charity, and so on.

Thus according to Flexner, the social worker always identified the problem in terms of some other area of specialization and almost always called in some other profession or agency to solve it. Responsibility, too, was usually passed along to that agency. The social worker was at best a mediator in the problem. But Flexner's sniping did not stop there. He had reservations because social work did not have a clear and concrete object and because it relied so heavily upon the expertise of other fields. He even questioned whether it had enough substance to sustain a "purposely organized educational discipline." In short, he did not believe that social work had a soul of its own. He conceded that the motive of altruism ran more strongly in it than in most professions, that it had a vibrant "professional spirit," and that it was absolutely necessary. But he would not budge on the question of its professionalism.[2] Failing four of his six tests, it did not even come close.

It was not by chance that this soul-searching among social workers took place when it did. Physicians, engineers, architects, lawyers, and teachers were also striving for higher professional standards at the time. What's more, they wanted to be *seen* striving for higher professional standards because that was the high road to public acceptance. To social workers these standards offered a way to shed the label of "do-gooder." Of course, what all the new professionals professed more than anything else was their wish to do good, but somehow only social workers were forced to bear the term as a stigma. That was unfortunate because "do-gooder" evoked the image of a person who was perhaps well intentioned, but was otherwise muddle-headed, impractical, ineffective, and generally wrong. People did not pay much attention to a do-gooder. The professional, on the other hand, was not only well intentioned, but was also clear-minded, practical, detached, scientific, and generally right. People listened to the professional.

In view of their wish to be listened to, it is surprising that social workers concluded in 1915 that they were not yet very professional. With Flexner, the outsider to their field, that conclusion was firm and explicit. With the others, insiders all, it was implicit, an inference to be drawn from their discussions of the shortcomings of social work education. Otherwise outsider and insiders were in complete harmony on the point.

But there was one issue on which their difference was profound and irreconcilable. The insiders were concerned to make social work completely professional, and toward that end they laid down a barrage of recommendations, almost all of which emphasized techniques rather than substance. But Flexner's questions went much deeper than that, went to the very core of social work, or rather to what he considered its lack of a core. The deficiencies he saw could not be remedied by improving techniques. His assessment of social workers as mediators among *real* professionals made them out to be little more than errand boys and girls in the world of social altruism. As a result, he not only denied that they were professionals, but he implied strongly that they would never be professionals because social work was inherently nonprofessional. This conclusion was demeaning and it was devastating. What is surprising is how seriously social workers took Flexner. His judgments haunted them for years.

These prewar discussions foreshadowed a serious split in the 1920s over the meaning of social work and, for that matter, of professionalism as well. In its formative years social work had been inspirational, almost devotional. In the hands of such people as Jane Addams and Florence Kelley it had been charged with moral energy and, in spite of its ambiguities, had been associated with a broad program of social reform in the communities and at all levels of government. That was already beginning to change by the time America entered the war. For one thing, the marriage of casework to psychology narrowed the vision of many social workers from society to the individual. For another, a new generation of social workers was maturing, and many of them were frankly embarrassed by the moral heat generated by their predecessors. It was unscientific; it was unprofessional; it was almost indecent. And therein lay the basis for the conflict. Some social workers wished to purge the field of moral commitment in order to gain professional credibilty. Others refused to abandon the old commitments and insisted that social work, morally neutered, was simply not social work.

In 1920 Neva Deardorff commented on these trends as she had observed them at the recent New Orleans meetings of NCSW. Reporting on the meetings in *The Survey*, she described a side trip that many of the workers had taken to a nearby bayou to see one of the "sociological phenomena" of the area, a faith healer known locally as "Brother Isaiah." Deardorff was not taken by the man's healing power—she had witnessed "no miraculous cures," she said— but she was fascinated by the intensity of emotion that flowed between the preacher and his followers and wondered why "scientific methods so often fail to arouse in the beneficiaries this white flame of yearning and faith." Perhaps, she mused, social workers had doubts about their own "rational methods" and somehow communicated these doubts to their clients.[3] Acting simultaneously as clinical observer and moral critic, Deardorff reflected the confusion already visible in social work by 1920.

Deardorff should not have been so puzzled at the emotional distance she detected between practitioner and client, for it was what many social workers had been working to achieve ever since Flexner's comments five years earlier. By 1925 many of them began to feel that they had finally put Flexner behind them, or so William Hodson concluded in his triumphant survey of the field that year. Patiently Hodson explained that social workers now met all the conditions for professionalism that Flexner had set down in 1915. For that reason he was pained at the continuing reluctance of the general public to accept social workers at last as professionals.[4]

Trends in social work education seemed to confirm Hodson's observations. From a bare handful before the war, schools of social work had multiplied until there were more than three dozen by the late 1920s. For admission all of them required at least a secondary school diploma, many required some prior work at the university level, and a few now required a university degree. Influenced by recent trends in legal education, most of these schools used the case-study method to sharpen the techniques of their students. Now under the sway of psychoanalytic theory, casework was already as popular as community work as a field of specialization, and would soon surpass it.[5]

The growing emphasis on form and technique in social work education was a perfect match to the temper of new recruits to the field. All reports in the 20s indicated that the current crop of university students scoffed at the idea of "service" and had little faith that they might change things in any fundamental way. It was the style of the decade. At one time this cynicism would have been inconceivable in social work; now it was considered an asset. "To be sentimental," Beulah Weldon said of the students, "is taboo; to be hard-boiled a matter of course and pride." To Weldon this toughness demonstrated the superiority of contemporary students, whom she praised because they were more likely to answer the call of science than that of self-sacrifice.[6] Teacher and students were in apparent agreement that there was no room in professionalism for passion.

Porter Lee summed it all up at the end of the decade when he spoke as president to the NCSW. Lee described two distinct historical phases in the development of social work. In the early years, he said, it had been a *cause*, by which he meant a reform movement aimed at rooting out entrenched social evils. In recent years, however, it had become a *function*, which he defined as an organized effort to administer the programs created in the reform stage. He used such phrases as ''the emblazoned banner and the shibboleth,'' ''devoted sacrifice,'' ''flaming spirit,'' and ''embattled host'' to characterize the cause. A function, by contrast, offered ''the program and the manual,'' ''standards and methods,'' and ''efficient personnel.'' A cause inspired ''zeal''; a function required ''intelligence.'' At bottom Lee was describing the difference between a crusade and a bureaucracy, and he made it clear that his preference now was for the bureaucracy.[7]

This new bureaucratic professionalism did not go unchallenged in those years. There were still many social welfare theorists who struggled to preserve the crusading spirit, and there were quite a few more who looked for ways to reconcile the old social work with the new. Such people as Eduard Lindeman, John Lapp, and Isaac Rubinow rejected the bland new technicians and worked to keep the reformist ethos alive in the 1920s.

More reflective than many of the others, Lindeman moved from social work into academic life in the 20s and devoted himself to working out a philosophical framework for social work that was flexible enough to accommodate a profession in transition. Specifically, Lindeman wished to infuse the cool new expertise with some of the heated old compassion. The trouble was that expertise was an expression of modern professional standards, which demanded a degree of moral and psychological detachment that left little room for compassion. Lindeman brooded over this problem because he felt that it was leading social workers into a dangerously imperious relationship with their clients. They were practicing manipulative techniques that prevented the clients from sharing in decisions that affected their lives. They were losing the common touch, he said, and edging perilously close to autocracy. At a time when many social thinkers were striving to give democracy a modern meaning, that was a serious charge.

Lindeman had identified one of the fundamental problems in social work, but his attempt to solve it did not carry him very far. The best he could offer was the limp hope that the values of social workers and the values of the lay community would ''interpenetrate'' as the two groups mingled in the future. The expert would somehow educate the community and the community would somehow humanize the expert.[8] It was an act of faith that defied the logical contradiction between traditional reform and modern professionalism but did nothing to resolve it. Like Deardorff, Lindeman did not merely isolate the problem; he embodied it.

Other leaders in social work were less concerned with the interplay of expertise and democracy than with the erosion of reformism they detected in the land. These leaders had the qualities that Porter Lee attributed to the participants in a Cause. Proud of their crusading spirit, they were the standard bearers of the old social justice movement who sought to roll back what they perceived to be the armies of reaction that threatened to sweep over society and government. In the 1920s they certainly qualified as Porter Lee's "embattled host."

John Lapp spoke for all of these unreconstructed reformers in his presidential address to the NCSW in 1927, when he insisted upon the primacy of social justice over personal adjustment in social work. Lapp blamed the war for snuffing out the flame of reform, and he bitterly rebuked the "special interests who profit by letting things alone" for keeping it out. He laid the blame at their feet for the prevailing "philosophy of the jungle" in social affairs and for the appalling revival of the "heathen doctrine" of Social Darwinism. "No previous time in our history," he said angrily, "has seen such a concerted movement to break the confidence of the people in their government as an instrument for social betterment." Well, Lapp said, it was not going to work. Social justice was as much a human right as life, liberty, and the pursuit of happiness. The people had begun to assert that right in the social legislation of the Progressive era, and they would not be put off from completing the job by the "anarchistic cant" of the day or thwarted by the predatory interests who hid behind the "bogy of paternalism." [9]

Lapp's militant reformism might not have been in the mainstream of social work in the 1920s, but there was nothing quixotic about it. From one end of the decade to the other there were important figures in the field who rejected the chilly impersonality that many thought necessary for professionalism and reaffirmed social work as social commitment. Many of them were by now old hands in the field, people like Paul Kellogg who had been one of the first to argue for the fusion of professionalism and reform, and who refused to concede that there was anything antipathetic between them. His journal, *The Survey*, for instance, was the first to rediscover the "Negro problem" in the 20s as a significant area for social action. Others were younger and quite different in demeanor from the pioneers. Such a person was Harry Hopkins, who had absorbed the ethos of social reform as a young man before the war and mastered the techniques of social work after it. A prototype of the reformer-professional first envisioned by Paul Kellogg, he was at the same time the image of hard-boiled realism described by Beulah Weldon.

For the time being, Hopkins's voice was, perhaps uncharacteristically, restrained in the profession, but his day would come soon enough. In the 1920s Isaac Rubinow commanded a much wider audience than Hopkins. Rubinow was a veteran of the social justice wars of the Progressive era and the nation's leading expert on social insurance. In 1929 he wrote a lengthy and, as it turned out, prophetic essay on the inadequacy of private charity in the face of public poverty. In the process he fired off some wicked shots at casework and the community chest movement, revealing just how deeply divided the profession was.

With the community chest Rubinow was merciless. He observed derisively that its campaign opened each year with a pathetic poster—a child on crutches perhaps, or a young widow clinging pitifully to her baby—and was then run through a maze of budget committees, auditors, publicity departments, and campaign managers before it was driven to its frenzied climax by an "army of energetic, well-meaning team lieutenants, captains, and generals." In the brief period of ten years it had "created its technique, its literature, its authorities and leaders, its traditions and principles, perhaps its chairs of instruction in colleges and professional schools." Rubinow had given a savage description of the bureaucratization of pity. The only positive accomplishment of the community chest, he said, was to relieve the donor of guilt feelings. It did almost nothing to relieve the problem of poverty. Rubinow was not ordinarily a malicious person, but there was more than a trace of malice in the gratitude he expressed toward the chest for at least confirming that poverty did exist, no matter what anyone else might claim about the wondrous march of prosperity in America's New Era.

In all fairness to them, the spokesmen for the New Era did not claim that poverty was gone, but only that it was going. They did not ask just how widespread it was at the peak of prosperity, however. Rubinow did, but he could not find the systematic data necessary to answer such a question accurately. For that he blamed a government that could proudly announce an annual production of 22,958,940,000 eggs without having the slightest interest in counting how many people could not afford to eat any of them. So Rubinow made his own estimates based upon the fugitive fragments of evidence that did exist. He calculated that perhaps 10 percent of the population lived in dire poverty and that several million people were currently unemployed. Before the war, he said, this information would have surprised nobody, but recently developments had conspired to obscure the truth. The financial euphoria of the late 1920s was partly to blame, but he looked primarily to social work itself for the sources of ignorance about poverty.

That brought Rubinow around to a discussion of casework, with its emphasis upon personal inadequacies and maladjustment rather than social problems. Rubinow described how research into poverty had given way to studies of the psyche in recent years and how the specialists were now putting all their newfound expertise into "hypotheses and experiments [about] him or her in order to make him or her adjust, and often that means conform." He did not deny that casework had produced significant results on occasion, but he fretted over its relentless drive to "influence attitudes" and "change character." The applicant who went for assistance was given adjustment. Meanwhile, caseworkers simply ignored the fact that "poverty is still here and relief is still necessary."

Although the substance and direction of Rubinow's essay were altogether different from Lindeman's, there was a striking similarity between the manipulative behavior he witnessed in casework and the cultural imperialism that Lindeman observed in professionalism.

For Rubinow the point of all this was that poverty was still a critical social problem, that too many social workers were content to sweep it under the rug, and that private charity would never be able to cope with it. Indeed, he said, public posturing to the contrary, all signs now indicated that the public's willingness to tax itself voluntarily for the poor had reached its limit. The community chest, which had never more than scratched the surface, would grow no more. His conclusion was that government had to step in.[10]

City planners in the 1920s were almost as shaky in their professionalism, and as divided over their goals, as social workers. In 1917 they finally gave themselves an organizational focus in the American City Planning Institute (ACPI) and then promptly forfeited all claims to professional exclusivity by opening it to anyone with two years experience in any activity relating to city planning. Having cast such a wide net, they made a predictably motley catch. Engineers and landscape architects made up half the charter membership of the ACPI; the remainder included attorneys, housing experts, architects, publishers, realtors, educators, and tax specialists. The chances for a clear sense of professional identity and purpose emerging soon from that occupational grab bag were very slim.

In fact, when the ACPI was founded, city planners were in much the same position that social workers had been in at the time of the Flexner critique two years earlier. Without a discipline or a special body of knowledge that was uniquely their own, they acted for the most part as mediators among a variety of concerned urban groups that did have some claim to special, often professional status. The city planner was likely to come from any one of these groups—architects, landscape architects, engineers, land speculators—and to borrow cheerfully from all the others. But did that make him a professional or only an intellectual magpie?

That question troubled Henry Hubbard when he returned from the Washington meetings of the NCCP in 1927. Certainly there were few people better qualified to wrestle with it. A charter member of the ACPI, Hubbard taught city planning at Harvard University, he edited the major journal in the field, and he became the founding director of the nation's first School of City Planning, which was established at Harvard in 1929. Hubbard discussed the arguments over professionalism that he had heard at the conference and appeared to be especially disturbed by those people who had insisted that city planning was not a profession at all, at least not "as a thing distinct from architecture, engineering, law, or some other already existing and recognized profession." Hubbard rejected this argument out of hand. The city planner, he said, was indeed a professional, but with a difference. Part specialist and part generalist, he needed sufficient training in one discipline to give him depth and sufficient familiarity with others to give him breadth.

Like a forest in a fog, Hubbard's version of professionalism in city planning was identifiable, yet somehow vague and elusive. He knew that the planner had no chance to master all the specialized fields that fed into city planning, but he knew also that a professional had to be more than just the classic jack of all trades. And so he concentrated on that rapidly growing body of knowledge that was neither architecture, nor medicine, nor law, nor engineering, but which drew from all of those professions and others. The specialist who could absorb enough of that general knowledge to apply to a broad range of urban problems could legitimately consider himself a professional city planner.[11]

Hubbard put a proud face on city planning by stating that it synthesized "all the fields of human endeavor that concern themselves with the bettering of the surroundings of civilized humanity." Perhaps. But it was still a field without a shape of its own. No matter how Hubbard dressed him up, the city planner still looked suspiciously like Flexner's mediator, the man whose function it was to refer problems to other professionals. And yet, perhaps Hubbard's real contribution was to ignore Flexner's criteria and hunt for other guidelines. After all, why should the generalist-mediator not be considered a professional?

Hubbard also believed that city planning should be imbued with the old sense of social reform, but on this issue he did not carry the day with most city planners in the 1920s. In that respect they were similar to many of the young social workers, and like the social workers they devised a professionally sanctioned alternative to social commitment. For social workers it was casework; for planners it was zoning. For those who rejected social reform the great advantage of zoning was that it could be used like a laser to target a limited, concrete objective without disturbing the wider network of social relations around it. The proposal to widen a street did not have to be part of a package to save mankind. All it had to do was move traffic more efficiently from Point A to Point B. Many planners argued that zoning without broad planning was apt to do more harm than good, but the plain fact was that by 1927 the great majority of cities with zoning ordinances had no master plan at all. For many in the 1920s—city planners as well as community leaders—the urban vision never got beyond Point B.

Public health had already negotiated the narrow early stages of professionalization before the war. To the populace at large, it was on firmer footing in claiming professional status than either social work or city planning. For one thing, it was closely related to medicine, the profession against which most others were measuring their professionalism by the 1920s. For another, it could point to monumental results instead of making monumental promises. In living memory smallpox, typhoid fever, yellow fever, and cholera had all virtually disappeared from North America; tuberculosis was being brought under control; infant and child mortality had declined dramatically. Since the middle of the nineteenth century life expectancy for the average American had risen by eighteen years, four of which had come in the preceding decade alone. The achievements were truly remarkable, and health reformers could be excused their occasional uncontrollable spasms of self-congratulation.

Although public-health workers did not simply rest on their laurels in the 1920s, most of them did seem content to stabilize their discipline and to sharpen both their self-image and their public image. Like the other policy professionals, they found the community survey—in their case, a health survey—to be a useful adjunct in that task. The Harvard School of Public Health considered these surveys to be so important that it required all of its students to complete one as a normal degree requirement. The purpose of the surveys was to provide information on health conditions in urban areas everywhere and at the same time to stimulate public interest in health work. In the process, of course, they would also bind cities of all sizes more tightly than ever to the technological imperatives of modern society.[12]

Another means of stabilizing the profession was to centralize control into fewer hands. The very act of establishing qualifications for membership in the APHA had been a first step in that direction years earlier. Effectively it prevented green grocers, plumbers, musicians, and other well-meaning amateurs from having much influence in the field. Sooner or later all the professions took some such action. In 1922 the APHA centralized control even further and put public health "on a truly professional basis" by limiting all voting and policy making in the association to a handful of fellows selected from the general membership.[13] Now it was to be run by an elite within the elite. Among other things, that would make it easier for the association to establish standards for the entire profession. By the mid-20s public health workers were coming to have a fairly sophisticated understanding of how standards might not only give their efforts direction, but give them protection as well. As "an expression of group judgment" a standard might thus suggest to the health worker what course of action to follow in a given situation. But it might also provide a defense if he came under attack when things went wrong. After all, he could not be held personally responsible for what amounted to a judgment made by the entire profession. In addition, a standard—this "group judgment"—might come in very handy if the health officer chose to go on the attack against some "special interest" group that had only a "partial" or defective view of a given situation.[14] In general, then, by rallying around official standards, practitioners could clarify the contours of their profession, could determine, for example, that immunization was a proper approach for health workers to take toward smallpox but that snake oil and prayer were not.

One of the problems that public health officials encountered in promoting their professional image was the widespread indifference outside the profession to distinctions between public health and private practice. To the general public it was all simply medicine, no more, no less. To public health personnel, however, it was a matter of identity and pride. In recent years they had built their profession on a foundation of medical knowledge, but now they wanted to put as much distance as possible between themselves and the general practitioner. Even before the war one could occasionally detect an air of superiority in the attitude of some public-health doctors toward the private practitioner. By the 1920s the attitude had soured into a palpable hostility. John Robertson expressed the anger that many of his colleagues felt toward the "obstructionism" of private physicians after the war when he attacked the American Medical Association and its journal for opposing public health in the interest of personal income. He warned the AMA that if general practitioners did not begin to practice preventive medicine soon, their worst fears about state intervention would be realized.[15] Like all the new professionals, public-health workers derived great satisfaction from knowing that they worked in the public interest at some cost to their own.

At a symposium on public health training in mid-decade, C. E. Turner went still further to establish an identity for public-health personnel that was separate from private physicians. To him the differences between the two fields were fundamental. The growing importance in public health of such special areas as sanitary biology, public health law, and vital statistics proved those differences beyond question. Turner said that it was only a matter of time before "the medical sanitarian [would] secure most of his public health training *after* instead of *during* his medical course."[16]

Several of the participants in that symposium, along with others throughout the decade, proved that the medicobiological approach, while dominant in public health, had not completely obscured all other perspectives on the field. A social worker and a bacteriologist both emphasized the enduring importance of the social environment in health and disease.[17] Others kept alive the specific issue of housing in health and explored the implications for public health of such issues as "mental hygiene," air pollution, and even noise.[18] As in city planning and social work, so too in public health, the flame of reformism flickered in the 1920s, but did not die out.

II

Among themselves the new professionals were divided over their goals in the 1920s and still not fully certain of their professionalism. To the public at large, however, they radiated a picture of unity and confidence, acting at times like a priesthood shepherding their flocks toward a higher truth and a greater common good. The trouble was that their professionalism kept getting between themselves and the sheep.

The heart of professionalism was its expertise, its special knowledge and skills. And that was the problem. On the one hand, the professionals were formulating schemes that were best understood and implemented by an elite equipped with their own kind of special knowledge and skills; on the other, they had to bring their schemes before voters who were innocent of their theories, ignorant of their data, and often suspicious of their motives. This tension between politics and expertise first showed up in the Progressive era, and it led the reformers to experiment with various methods of exerting political leverage in order to put their programs across.

Historians have shown how the professionals met this situation by working directly on the seats of power,[19] or by aligning themselves with economic elites to insulate the mechanisms of decision making from grass-roots pressures.[20] But these explanations concentrate on the institutions of power and do not reveal how the public-service elites confronted the deepest level of their dilemma: the instability that was built into the system itself and indeed was necessary to it. There was simply no assurance that today's friendly decision makers would not be turned out at tomorrow's election, leaving the professionals and their programs at the mercy of a hostile new government.

The designs of reform were impressive enough to the designers, but they were not always warmly received in the urban slums. Public-health officials, for instance, who worked constantly among the immigrant poor, were often frustrated by cultural barriers. They had difficulty persuading the immigrants that garlic water was no match for measles and that the evil eye would not ward off diphtheria. Nor was that all. In 1910 a visiting nurse told of a Syrian couple in Cleveland who could not afford to buy a much-needed ten-cent yarn truss for their baby because they were already literally starving themselves to save fourteen dollars for the infant's christening and for the celebration that would follow. The nurse could not understand the parents because she was acting on a professional commitment that called for technical solutions to pathological conditions. The parents resisted the nurse because they proceeded from priorities that were deeply embedded in their cultural heritage. Uncomprehendingly she was asking them to shame themselves in the eyes of their fellow Syrians, and they would not have been able to live with that shame. There was no way to reconcile these viewpoints.[21]

The economic problems of the poor did not help matters either. There were many tubercular patients who felt that they could not afford to leave work for bed rest; yet, in the eyes of health officials, who were at war with a contagious killer, prolonged isolation and bed rest were minimal prescriptions. And then there were those families that took in lodgers to supplement meager incomes, while housing reformers grew livid at the way this practice compounded all of the problems that were related to population congestion.[22]

Behind these specific problems of outlook and income lay the more general problem of a political system in which short-term elections threatened to disrupt long-term projects. This is what happened when the Los Angeles Health Department demanded that tuberculin tests be given to the cows that supplied milk for the city. The issue came to referendum locally in 1912, and when it was defeated, the editors of the *AJPH* were incensed. They condemned a system that permitted "agitators" to mislead an ignorant public on vital health issues. The need to shield an educated elite from political sniping was a recurrent theme among the professionals. They longed for autonomy but knew they would have to settle for less. A New Jersey health official proposed a compromise in which health programs would be coordinated under a single executive with full power to hire and fire his subordinates. Yet even that system, he noted, might run afoul of democratic impulses. He granted that popular rule was "fundamentally desirable," but he warned that where health matters were concerned, "democratic government carried to its extreme" placed the most ignorant naturalized immigrant on the same level as "the physician, the engineer and the sanitarian who has given all his mature years to the study of measures for the conservation and prolongation of human life." The only way to protect the public from "sinister influences," he concluded, was to proceed through a broad program of health instruction.[23] One way or another, all reformers reached the same conclusion.

For that reason they set out to build a reservoir of support for their programs by educating the public. At first few of them had a clear idea what they meant either by "educate" or "public," and so specific suggestions did not usually push beyond such time-honored methods as press campaigns and school programs. These techniques played a significant role over the years, but given the urgency of urban problems, they seemed agonizingly slow to the reformers.

Gradually they began to experiment with other modes of influencing public opinion more rapidly and effectively. One method they exploited was the public exhibition. A landmark of its type was New York's famous "Congestion Show" of 1908. The brainchild of several New York social reformers, the show sought to build sentiment for population decentralization by dramatizing the evils of congestion in a wide assortment of graphic displays. Mel Scott describes how the reformers used bits of shot on a large map of New York to bring the problem home: "On the lower part of Manhattan the shot was heaped up and running over the fences used to hold it in place, whereas in great areas on the outskirts it was scattered thin as flowers in meadows."[24] The Metropolitan Parks Association at the time used this imagery of flowers scattered in the meadows, and it suggests precisely the visual impact that the map was intended to have.

The following year a group of businessmen formulated a plan for the civic and social regeneration of Boston. Concerned initially with the future prosperity of the city, they worked through business, civic, and professional organizations and soon enlisted the support of such reform leaders as Edward Filene, Louis Brandeis, and Richard Cabot in their efforts to educate the public to support the "Boston—1915" movement. The campaign was launched with an exhibition designed to draw large crowds to its colorful displays. One of these displays reproduced a North End tenement apartment with its "rusty, partly broken stove, dirty floor . . . rickety beds with noticeably soiled coverings," and all the other accoutrements necessary "to present a truly vivid picture of actual slum life." Next to this horror was a model apartment with a bathroom. It was "all clean and decent" and could be built, according to the reformers, to rent for very little more than the slum flat. One stands in awe here at the way a change of venue stimulated the tenants to scrub the floors, launder the sheets, and repair the furniture. The show was filled with similar exhibits "of real interest to the people—to everyday folks who don't care a toothpick about statistics and deep sentences."[25]

The Congestion Show and the Boston—1915 exhibition marked the direction in which the professionals were taking their educational campaign to sway the public. Issues whose deepest implications were often too complicated to explain to the average citizen and too important to expose to counterpressures, were presented in symbolic forms to reach behind consciousness and stir a favorable emotional response.

The reformers worked out many of their early ventures in publicity on a trial-and-error basis, but from time to time they were given instruction by experts in advertising theory. In 1908 Edward Shaw, the managing editor of the Washington, D.C., *Times*, advised the social and charity workers gathered at the NCCC that their appeals for popular support would be more effective in the form of human interest stories aimed frankly at the emotions. Charity workers, he said, should learn from advertising men how to use the principles of modern scientific psychology, because the average person was simply not interested in dull facts or technical procedures.[26] The social workers were abreast of him, as it happened, for at that same conference they set up a section on press and publicity to advise people in the profession on just such matters.

Almost immediately this new section set out to spread the gospel of advertising as a means of softening the public for social programs. In 1909 John Kingsbury informed the NCCC that social publicity differed from commercial advertising only in its need to be moral and truthful, and he blurred even that distinction when he encouraged the social workers to emphasize "the harrowing human details," which he said were the essential truth of a case, whenever they prepared a human interest release for the press.[27]

In the next few years health officials moved ahead of the other professionals in the sophistication of their approach to publicity. What was the purpose of employing advertising techniques? According to a New York physician, it was to persuade people to live a sanitary life "of their own accord."[28] What was the best way of going about it? According to a New Jersey health official, it was by applying the lessons that advertising men had learned from the new science of psychology. The advantage of modern advertising was that it eliminated the need for elaborate explanations. Indeed, he said, "the most effective advertisements of the day are those which rely upon a single phrase or even a single apt word for their effect."[29] In other words, health workers could put their message across more forcefully with slogans than with information.

Late in the Progressive era these developments were summarized by Edward Moree, a charity worker writing in the *AJPH*. Moree claimed that "publicity properly applied will save more lives than any other single agency employed by health workers." The goal was to "change the lives and habits of the people or to focus or re-focus public opinion." First, however, the health worker would have to "get [people] to think in the right way," which is where advertising entered the picture. At this point Moree likened the health worker to a businessman with a new brand of baked beans to sell. Obviously no modern merchant would market his beans without first hiring an advertising expert to prepare the public for them. The health official, who also had a new product to sell, would be wise to adopt the same strategy and employ a professional advertising agency to cultivate the public for his own ends, which was to "get them to think in the right way."[30] Moree took ideas that had been implicit in the notion of publicity and worked them into a system explicitly designed to engineer consent for public projects and ultimately to regulate human behavior so that people would "think in the right way."

Under the tutelage of people like Moree, the new professionals were discovering how to cope with the gouging tactics of the political cockpit. They learned that it paid to advertise; they learned that modern advertising was based upon a new psychology that emphasized the nonrational sources of human behavior, and above all they learned that influencing the public, like protecting it, was too formidable a task to entrust to amateurs.[31] In time they came to believe that they could make democracy work for them through professionally calculated appeals to unreason, that they could effect social control through psychological manipulation as well as through legislation and outright coercion. The political implications of this lesson emerged more clearly in the next decade.

Before that, however, the war intervened, much to the advantage of the professionals. In the past they had been forced to struggle for recognition of their plans and to beg for the meager public funds available to carry them out. Now their services were suddenly in demand to design army camps and housing projects and to implement crash programs in health and sanitation for the new military and industrial armies. Above the turmoil stood the federal government, approving projects and dispensing funds. Free at last from the need to justify their ideas to an ignorant public, sanitation and housing experts, health workers, city planners, architects, municipal engineers, and social workers all pitched in with great enthusiasm, and with growing hopes for this model of cooperation between the federal government and the professional elites.

Parallel to this development was the major contribution made to the war effort by the advertising industry. Overcoming his distaste for advertising men, George Creel eventually used them with striking success in his Committee on Public Information to whip up popular support for wartime policies. As a result they had grown in public regard as well as self-esteem and came out of the war with the firm conviction that they could sell practically anything to practically anybody.[32]

The success of advertising in the war confirmed what the professionals had learned about it earlier in the decade. Thus when the war ended and they returned to the massive problems of the cities, when their federal benefactors faded from the scene and they were forced to bid anew for public support, education once again became an integral part of their activities, and advertising more than ever represented their guideline to education.

In addition they began to perceive the awesome potential of the new electronic media of communications after the war. Actually they had been dabbling with films since about 1910, when health publicists had produced "The Acrobatic Fly" for distribution to nickelodeons around the Chicago area. Now they plunged ahead with characteristic thoroughness. In 1921 the NCCP set up a Committee on Moving Pictures and was soon promoting films that demonstrated how a dismal "before" could be transformed into a utopian "after" by planning. At the same time, the APHA began to sponsor colloquia on the use of films in health publicity. The participants regularly cautioned publicists about the ignorance of the people who saw health movies and urged them to produce films with that in mind. They recommended the use of animation, for example, to hold the attention of audiences that would otherwise be alienated by filmed sermons on health.[33]

By the mid-1920s the NCSW was also beginning to address systematically the problem of educating the public. In 1926 it turned over an entire section of the meetings to "Educational Publicity." The recurrent theme at these sessions was the need to sway public opinion and stimulate a favorable "crowd psychology" by working on the emotions of the audience. The director of the St. Louis Community Fund summed it all up by describing a soap manufacturer who had suffered severe losses some years earlier because he had failed to advertise. "Social service, like soap," he said, "must keep itself continually before the public." The important thing is to "keep our product 'sold.' "[34] That was the basic message that ran through these sessions.

Even as they worked at their apprenticeship in publicity methods, the professionals were beginning to initiate information programs all over the nation. City planning publicity matured as cities large and small adopted plans and then devised programs to sell their plans to concerned citizens. In 1921 the Chicago Planning Commission deluged the city's clergymen with "Seed Thoughts for Sermons," a pamphlet that described how city planning would benefit church social work. Leaders of the Kessler Plan Association of Dallas, aware of the volatility of democratic politics, in 1927 sought to create a source of perpetual support by authorizing a civics textbook for the schools that would "establish the right mind set" for planning in future generations. School officials in Cincinnati followed a bolder plan when they decided that the best way to teach children about city planning was to let them *do* some city planning, and the younger the better. At one school the kindergarten children built an entire town. They learned how to group houses; they learned how to direct the flow of traffic by building viaducts over the boulevards and bridges over the river; they learned how to make the town more pleasing by adding trees, flowers, shrubbery, benches, and boulevard lighting. In this way these five-year-olds were introduced to some of the principles of both the "City Beautiful" and the "City Functional." The justification for assigning the project was quite plainly that today's schools mold tomorrow's citizens, which is precisely what the Kessler Plan leaders assumed in their bid to set the minds of Dallas school children.[35]

In health education some of the basic precepts were established at a Cleveland clinic in 1923, where an advertising executive, an art teacher, a printer, and an editor were asked to evaluate a range of printed and graphic matter on health publicity. The comments of the advertising man, William Feather, were particularly instructive for the health publicists. He observed, first of all, that too much of the health material beamed to the public was depressing. It portrayed sickness when it should have projected health and was thus negative when it should have been positive. Second, he said, too much of the material was dull and failed to engage the attention. He contrasted the advertisements for commercial health products with those for public health and declared that it was no contest. " 'Avoid sickness, visit our clinics and use our facilities,' " said the public health notices. How dull! " 'Eat our yeast, raisins and breakfast foods; be beautiful and youthful,' " promised the commercial ads. Beauty and youth! The attention was immediately captured. The implication was that people were more interested in their looks than their health and that health publicity should be framed with that in mind. For instance, smallpox posters featuring scarred and unsightly victims would be especially effective if they included the warning, " 'Do Not Endanger Your Beauty with Smallpox—Vaccination Will Prevent It.' " Finally, Feather was disturbed by the vocabulary in much of the printed matter. This material was aimed primarily at plain people, he pointed out, and words like "malnutrition," "migration," and "prenatal" were likely to be lost on them. In short, his advice to health publicists was to keep it happy, keep it pretty, and keep it simple. On the whole, that is just what they did in the years that followed.[36]

In general, health officials approached publicity with more flair than planners and social workers. They produced increasingly sophisticated screen plays through the decade and made extensive use of animated cartoons such as "Jinks," which told the story of an unemployed worker who dreamed one night that "Mike Robe" was about to infest his lungs because he had been careless in his health habits. He awoke in a sweat and vowed to turn over a new leaf in personal hygiene. This was not an isolated or exaggerated example of health films but only one of many like it in the 1920s. The *AJPH* commented that "the film is an excellent example of happy treatment of a subject which has too often been made morbid."[37]

In order to get through to the nation's youth, health reformers found it useful to exploit a variety of contemporary trends. In a strange but timely metaphor, the Indiana Board of Health proclaimed to school children that "Your Body is the Automobile of Your Soul," and then drew long parallel lists between people and cars: good gasoline/good food; clear headlights/good eyes; sound brakes/self-control. Two years later the Indianapolis Tuberculosis League assisted the local Y.W.C.A. in drawing up a series of posters to publicize the merits of a good diet. One of the posters recommended prunes and oranges for good complexions; another praised onions as "Eye Sparklers"; a third pre-scribed celery and radishes as "Vanity Brushes for the teeth." By far the most effective of these "Beauty Hint" posters showed graphically how beets act as a natural lipstick. Officials were ecstatic as they watched beet sales soar at the "Y" cafeteria in the next few days. The fruit and vegetable crusade proved to be a mixed blessing, however, because as beet sales climbed, meat sales plunged. Alarmed at this development, one of the cooks, who had clearly caught the spirit of the campaign, proposed a sure-fire corrective: simply turn out a series of meat posters.[38] The purpose of this publicity effort was to promote good health through sound nutrition, yet nothing in the posters spoke either of health or nutrition. Instead they advertised food as cosmetics; the appeal was to van-ity, not health.

The career of Herman Bundesen in the 1920s illustrates many of the prob-lems encountered by the professionals and some of the solutions they worked out. Dr. Bundesen, who was the director of the Chicago Board of Health, fused the zeal of a missionary with the talent of a carnival barker in this trailblazing crusade to publicize health methods. He was already well known locally and in the profession for his radio talks on public health when he concocted a stunt in mid-decade that opened eyes all over the country. He wanted to teach the public a lesson about the food value of milk and hit upon the startling idea of fueling a locomotive entirely with milk and having it pull a five-car train for six miles. The deed was picked up by over one hundred newspapers across the nation and was perhaps the most successful single stroke of health publicity in the decade.

Public-health officials were jubilant over this kind of publicity. One of them used it to support his plea for more "salesmanship" and "advertising" in health matters, advertising of the same sort, he said, that sold cars, chewing gum, cigarettes, and soap.[39] Of course the stunt had no more to do with the growing body of expertise in the young field of nutrition than the vegetable posters at the Indianapolis "Y," but that is exactly the point. Its whole purpose was to popularize milk without bringing technical information before the public. It was precisely what health publicists were striving for. They looked upon Bundesen as a genius.

In the next few years Bundesen's fortunes veered sharply back and forth. In 1926 he received the Beneficial Action award of the Chicago *Daily News* for his work on behalf of clean milk. A year later he was out of a job, the victim of a political purge by Mayor "Big Bill" Thompson, who had only recently been called back to office by the forgiving voters of Chicago. The incident infuriated professional health workers and brought home to them once again the folly of mixing politics with science. In 1928 Bundesen gained some sat-isfaction when he was elected president of the APHA. In his presidential ad-dress he acknowledged that science would probably continue to "outstrip pub-lic knowledge" and proposed that his colleagues meet the situation with an all-out effort to "sell" public health by any means available—by the "motion pictures, the radio, slogan and poster, or in any other way you will. But *sell* it."[40] (Bundesen's emphasis.)

By the end of the decade the professionals were reasonably confident that they knew how to educate and were working out a more refined notion of whom to educate as well. Above all they learned to pitch their appeals not just at "the public," but at the many publics that were out there, especially in the form of organized community forces. Virginia Wing, of Cleveland's Social Work Publicity Council, carried out the entire publicity campaign for a new hospital with that in mind. "Moving people to action," she said, "means separating the basis of the campaign into its parts, and organizing each part so that it will appeal to the motor nerves of the general public." It turned out that she was not talking about the "general public" at all but about a variety of discrete publics. Her organization had made separate appeals to the Chamber of Commerce in terms of business that would be generated, to labor unions in terms of jobs that would be created, to women's clubs in terms of civic improvements that would be made, and to politicians in terms of votes that would be won, although the object of the campaign had nothing to do with business, or jobs, or civic improvements, or votes. A committee was formed that included "all the sources of power, nationality groups, etc., so that the letterhead has someone on it from every force." The committee directed a campaign that used all kinds of printed materials, newspaper publicity, radio propaganda, and stunts, such as having a blimp fly over the city to advertise the project. The campaign was a smashing success, and Cleveland got its hospital.[41]

Many of these themes were orchestrated near the end of the decade by H. A. Overstreet in a paper that he presented to the NCCP. Overstreet asserted that "most people do not act from their reasoning power but from their emotions," and that the emotions can be harnessed by appealing to such instincts as self-preservation, acquisitiveness, and competition. Since the average person visualizes ideas better than he thinks them, pictures should play a major role in channeling these instinctual needs. Moreover, he pointed out, people can be conditioned to accept what they might otherwise question:

Advertisers have long since learned that mere repetition has an almost compelling effect. . . . The same thing should be true in matters of public welfare. Say "city planning" enough times and people will take it for granted that city planning is one of the accepted procedures in our civilization.

Once these principles are mastered, said Overstreet, the city planning publicist must learn to apply them through the voluntary associations that abound in American society, for it is in them that power is centered. "When an individual is purely an individual," he said, "he is about as powerless as any being can possibly be." Organizations as different as Tammany Hall and the League of Women Voters knew this, and it was time that city planners profited from the experience of such groups.[42]

As the twenties drew to a close, people like Wing and Overstreet were bringing Edward Moree's prewar suggestions up to date with the latest thinking and research about opinion formation, and were beaming the message clearly and often to new professionals across the land.

It is tempting to explain these developments as an expression of the ethos of a business culture and let it go at that. Certainly such an observation would not be off the mark for the 1920s. But they reveal a different aspect, and a larger meaning, if we view them as an American variant of *modernization*. Not without reason, historians are wary about the way in which this notion tends to obscure differences of time and circumstance, but, applied prudently, it can be a useful concept. Although theorists differ over how to define the term, most of them would agree that it embraces urbanization and the vast expansion of new kinds of knowledge, and that when modernization challenges the established institutions and beliefs of a society it generally leads to political dislocation and readjustment, as new groups reach out for power and older ones fight to hold on.[43] We recognize this process readily enough in younger or rapidly developing nations, where it so often erupts with volcanic force, but in the United States, where post–Civil War modernization unfolded without the dramatic intensity of revolutionary upheavals, its wider implications went unnoticed for decades. Only in recent years have some historians begun to use this concept in discussing twentieth-century America. The tension between democracy and expertise, and the adjustment they made to each other, seem clearly to have been a phase in this process.

Democracy, after all, had matured in the nineteenth century as the political framework of a diffuse agrarian society. It was rooted in egalitarian values, guided by a chronic fear of centralized power, and regulated by periodic elections in which candidates debated issues with information that was accessible to everybody. That was the theory at any rate, and if realities never fulfilled the ideal, they never completely lost contact with it either.

The new professionals, on the other hand, were the product of an urban crisis. In a society that believed that democratic politics depended upon democratic information, they trafficked in knowledge that was inscrutable to the general public. Nothing had prepared common people to believe that sickness and death were caused by plants and animals that were present everywhere but visible nowhere. Nothing had prepared them to grasp the dense mathematical formulae that determined the amount of open space necessary, so the planners said, to end urban congestion. The experts might lay out the arcane facts and theories of their programs to an upper tier of civic leaders, but they knew that they could not get through to the urban masses on those terms. On the whole, their activities would have been better served by protection *from* periodic elections than by exposure *to* them, but that was out of the question. Instead they would have to bend the system somehow to their own needs.

Thus it was a political imperative born of their professionalization that sent the new public policy specialists out to woo the public. Early in the century they felt their way toward a strategy designed to engage the feelings more than to inform the intellect. That was the hidden implication of the splashy Congestion Show of 1908, and the Boston—1915 exhibition, where they used the symbolic *representation* of issues to evade the systematic *presentation* of issues. In that respect the publicity efforts of the professionals broke completely from their own commitment to the rational evaluation of scientific data.

Soon they began to absorb ideas from other new areas of expertise quite unlike their own. Technicians and tinkers were experimenting with new modes of communication; psychologists were probing for the roots of human behavior; advertising men were discovering how to manipulate vast numbers of people with the new media and the new psychology. Even before the war the professionals had begun to adapt their publicity campaigns willy-nilly to these developments.

As they refined their methods in the 1920s, they committed themselves increasingly to the communications revolution and commercial ethos that reached far out into American society at the time. Their efforts to influence the public moved rapidly toward the manipulation of nonrational drives. They wrapped their messages in bright packages—cheerful tuberculosis films, happy smallpox posters—and marketed them as if they were peddling chewing gum and cigarettes. They did this consciously and without a trace of embarrassment or cynicism.

At the same time, they worked out a more complex notion of the public. For years they had perceived it as a more or less shapeless mass of individuals, but that perception yielded before a growing appreciation of group dynamics in an organizational society. After that their strategies for group persuasion only reinforced the manipulative aspects of social publicity, since the message was no longer inherent solely in the information, but now as well in the groups at which the information was directed. Thus to round out his professional training the publicist had to familiarize himself with social research, so that he could frame his message effectively in different ways for different groups.

This process proceeded along similar lines in all of the new public-service professions. It was not isolated, it was not random, it was scarcely even controversial. On the contrary, it became an integral part of the efforts to move public opinion and was treated with respect in the various professional organizations. By the 1920s each of the associations had added, under one name or another, a separate section of publicity. In the professional journals and at annual meetings these agencies furnished articles, papers, and colloquia on publicity methods, reported on the publicity campaigns that were under way all over the country, and designed courses on social publicity that were to be added to the professional training programs at universities everywhere. Ironically the professionals had come full circle. Their efforts to spread technical knowledge in nontechnical terms had grown into a whole new field of expertise with its own cadre of technicians to administer it. They had discovered that specialization created its own problems, and that the only cure was more specialization.

And so the abrasive impulses of democracy and expertise were gradually reconciled by the new marketing techniques of business enterprise in the early decades of the century. The professionals did not have things all their own way, of course, for if they found in advertising a means of access to power, they found also that it would be wise to use that power cautiously and with an eye on the next election up the road. Herman Bundesen was one of those who learned this lesson the hard way in his futile clash with Chicago's Mayor Thompson. In the end, however, the new professionals succeeded in making a nineteenth-century political institution more responsive to their own vision of a twentieth-century America.

NOTES

1. Jeffrey R. Brackett, "The Curriculum of the Professional School of Social Work," NCCC, *Proceedings* (1915):610–612; George B. Mangold, "The Curriculum of Schools of Social Service," Ibid., pp. 612–615; Edith Abbott, "Field Work and the Training of the Social Worker," Ibid., pp. 615–621; Porter R. Lee, "The Professional Basis of Social Work," Ibid., pp. 596–606.

2. Abraham Flexner, "Is Social Work a Profession?" Ibid., pp. 576–590.

3. Neva R. Deardorff, "The National Conference of Social Work at New Orleans," *The Survey* (May 8, 1920):212–214.

4. William Hodson, "Is Social Work Professional? A Re-examination of the Question," NCSW, *Proceedings* (1925):629–636.

5. Earle E. Eubank, "New Horizons in Professional Training: Social Work," *The Survey* (June 1, 1928):284–285.

6. Beulah Weldon, "Training for Social Work," Ibid. (September 1, 1927):510–511.

7. Porter R. Lee, "Social Work: Cause and Function," NCSW, *Proceedings* (1929):3–20.

8. Eduard C. Lindeman, "The Social Worker and His Community," *The Survey* (April 15, 1924):83–85. See also Kenneth L. M. Pray, "Where in Social Work Can the Concept of Democracy Be Applied?" NCSW, *Proceedings* (1926):625–636.

9. John A. Lapp, "Justice First," Ibid. (1927):3–13. On the persistence of reform sentiment in the 1920s see Clarke A. Chambers, *Seedtime of Reform: American Social Service and Social Action, 1918–1933* (Minneapolis: University of Minnesota Press, 1963).

10. I. M. Rubinow, "Can Private Philanthropy Do It?" *Social Service Review* (September 1929):361–394.

11. Henry V. Hubbard, "The Profession of City Planning," *City Planning* (July 1927):201–203.

12. Murray Horwood and Jules Schevitz, "The Value of the Public Health Survey in the Public Health Campaign," *AJPH* (February 1921):113–117.

13. "Toward a Profession of Public Health," Ibid. (December 1922):1040–1041.

14. W. S. Rankin, "The Fly in the Ointment," Ibid. (October 1924):819–825.

15. John Dill Robertson, "The Health Officer's Challenge to the General Practitioner," Ibid. (January 1923):1–5.

16. C. E. Turner, "Forward to A Symposium on Public Health Training," Ibid. (June 1924):467–470. Author's italics.

17. Homer Folks, "Social Service Training," Ibid., p. 479. I. S. Falk, "The Place of Vital Statistics in Public Health Training," Ibid., pp. 474–476. See also Thomas D. Eliot, "Sociological Prerequisites for a Public Health Curriculum," Ibid. (June 1925):522–525.

18. On housing see George H. Shaw, "Housing Problems in Philadelphia," Ibid. (May 1924):401–403, and "Municipal Housing," Ibid. (February 1925):145–146; on mental health, "The Mental Hygiene Campaign as Seen by an Inside Observer," Ibid. (April 1923):308–309, and "Man's Last Specter—Mental Disease," Ibid. (July 1928):902–904; on foul air, Abel Wolman, "Some Special Problems in Atmospheric Pollution," Ibid. (March 1930):243–245, and Jerome Meyers, "Cancer Death Rates, Smoke and Topography," Ibid. (June 1930):581–588; on noise pollution, "Noise," Ibid. (March 1929):304–305. Allen Freeman, a physician who taught at Johns Hopkins University, observed that the student of public health was inevitably more aware of the social causes of disease than the student of medicine. He looked forward to the day when public health workers would be guided by "a real social program." See Allen W. Freeman, "The Growth of the Social Point of View in Medical and Health Education," NCSW, Proceedings (1923):58–61.

19. Samuel P. Hays, Conservation and the Gospel of Efficiency (Cambridge: Harvard University Press, 1959); Roy Lubove, The Progressives and the Slums (Pittsburgh: University of Pittsburgh Press, 1962), pp. 124–126; August Cerillo, Jr., "The Impact of Reform Ideology: Early Twentieth-Century Municipal Government in New York City," in Michael H. Ebner and Eugene M. Tobin, eds., The Age of Urban Reform (Port Washington, N.Y.: Kennikat Press, 1977).

20. Samuel P. Hays, "The Politics of Reform in Municipal Government in the Progressive Era," Pacific Northwest Quarterly (October 1964):157–169; John F. Bauman, "Disinfecting the Industrial City: The Philadelphia Housing Commission and Scientific Efficiency, 1909–1916," in Ebner and Tobin, The Age of Urban Reform.

21. Harriet Leet, "The Problem of Many Tongues," Visiting Nurse Quarterly (July 1910):30–39. The problem of clashing priorities between professionals and ethnic minorities had had important consequences a few years earlier in San Francisco. Given an opportunity to rebuild the city "rationally" after the earthquake and fire of 1906, Chinese and Irish voters went to the polls and voted heavily to reject Daniel Burnham's plan for the city, because they felt that it threatened their economic and cultural interests. See Judd Kahn, Imperial San Francisco: Politics and Planning in an American City, 1897–1906 (Lincoln: University of Nebraska Press, 1979).

22. Mary Buell Sayles, "Housing and Social Conditions in a Slavic Neighborhood," Charities (December 3, 1904):257–261; Lawrence Veiller, "Room Overcrowding and the Lodger Evil," AJPH (January 1913):11–23.

23. M. N. Baker, "The Municipal Health Problem," National Municipal Review (April 1913):200–207. On the referendum in Los Angeles see "The Referendum in Public Health," AJPH (July 1912):535–536.

24. Mel Scott, American City Planning Since 1890 (Berkeley and Los Angeles: University of California Press, 1969), p. 85.

25. Everett Mero, "An Exposition that Mirrors a City," *American City* (November 1909):95–101.

26. Edward E. Shaw, "Publicity in Charitable Work From the Newspaper Point of View," NCCC, *Proceedings* (1908):267–275. Roy Lubove suggests that social work publicity developed so that welfare could "compete with business for the consumer's dollar." See Roy Lubove, *The Professional Altruist* (Cambridge: Harvard University Press, 1965), pp. 202–206.

27. John A. Kingsbury, "Right Publicity and Public Health Work," NCCC, *Proceedings* (1909):333–338. See also Claude C. Hopkins, "The Psychology of Advertising as Applied to Social Publicity," Ibid. (1910):547–558.

28. Woods Hutchinson, "Publicity in Public Health Work," *AJPH* (August 1913):777–779.

29. J. Scott MacNutt, "Publicity: Some Observations on Its Uses and Misuses," Ibid. (February 1914):108–112.

30. Edward A. Moree, "Public Health Publicity: The Art of Stimulating and Focusing Public Opinion," Ibid. (February 1916):97–108.

31. The relationship between advertising and the new psychology in the Progressive era is explored in A. Michael McMahon, "An American Courtship: Psychologists and Advertising Theory in the Progressive Era," *American Studies* (Fall 1972):5–18.

32. The role of advertising in the war is discussed in Otis Pease, *The Responsibilities of American Advertising* (New Haven: Yale University Press, 1958), p. 17, and in James P. Wood, *The Story of Advertising* (New York: Donald Press, 1958), pp. 354–357.

33. E. G. Routzahn et al., "Symposium on Motion Pictures," *AJPH* (April 1922):269–279.

34. Robert W. Kelso, "The Need of Educational Publicity in Social Work," NCSW, *Proceedings* (1926):637–641; Donald Vance, "Importance of Educational Publicity from the Angle of the Federation," Ibid., pp. 645–648; Paul S. Bliss, "Interpreting Professional Standards of Social Work to the Public: From the Standpoint of the Community Fund," Ibid., pp. 669–678; Mary Swain Routzahn, "Available Channels of Publicity," Ibid., pp. 643–645; Elwood Street, "The Proper Form of Organization for Federation Publicity," Ibid., pp. 648–655.

35. C. J. Hamlin, "The Buffalo City Plan," NCCP, *Proceedings* (1922):191–197; Charles L. Sanger, "Activities of the Kessler Plan Association of Dallas, Texas," *City Planning* (October 1925):173–174; Justin F. Kimball, "Spreading the Gospel of City Planning," NCCP, *Proceedings* (1928):137–141; Randall J. Condon, "How the Public Schools Cooperated with a City Planning Commission," *City Planning* (January 1927):32–36.

36. E. G. Routzahn, "Health Education and Publicity," *AJPH* (March 1923):248–250.

37. "Health Films Committee of the National Health Council," Ibid. (July 1923):597.

38. E. G. Routzahn, "Education and Publicity," Ibid. (July 1925):668.

39. Philip P. Jacobs, "The Health Workers' Point of View," Ibid. (February 1925):125–128.

40. Herman N. Bundesen, "Selling Public Health—A Vital Duty," Ibid. (December 1928):1451–1454.

41. Virginia Wing, "Arousing Voters to Action: A Story of a City Campaign," NCSW, *Proceedings* (1929):620–627. See also P. L. Brockaway, "Study Your Public, Mr. City Engineer," *American City* (May 1929):91–93.

42. H. A. Overstreet, "Arousing the Public Interest in City Planning," NCCP, *Proceedings* (1928):125–136. See also Virginia Wing, "Some Psychological Experiments in Health Publicity," NCSW, *Proceedings* (1929):258–263.

43. C. E. Black, *The Dynamics of Modernization* (New York: Harper and Row, 1975) is the standard general introduction to the concept of modernization.

4

The Imagined City

The war was in some ways an exhilarating experience for the new professionals. The federal government funded their experiments, gave them a nation for a laboratory, deepened their already profound sense of mission, and lent an air of legitimacy to their professional aspirations. At the same time, their participation in the war effort confirmed their suspicions about the seriousness of the national pathology. Public-health workers discovered that one-third of the nation's youth were unfit for military service, and city planners found out just how bad the housing situation was for the urban working class. The whole experience whetted their appetites for the reconstruction of American cities, which they were certain would mark the postwar era. Influenced by various legal and technological innovations, they turned their imaginations loose on urban alternatives in the 1920s, modernizing some of their earlier views and fashioning others that were strikingly new.

Except to note that time had made things worse, their diagnosis of the situation had not changed significantly since before the war. The immediate problem in the Progressive era had been congestion, the cause, unchecked speculation. In these matters the war had changed nothing. Congestion was still the problem, speculation still the cause.

For health workers the problem was particularly vexing. They felt that the progress they had made in the laboratory had been cancelled in the city, because congestion acted to spread disease rapidly and to induce "mental disorders." Haven Emerson, a leading public-health official in New York, dipped into his own area of expertise for an apt metaphor to describe the lethal effects of population congestion. Bacteria, he noted, "begin to die out at the center of the mass" when they multiply out of control, because they are victimized by the poisons of their own body waste. So it must be with people also if they continue to crowd greedily into the centers of the great cities. As an alternative he offered the organizational model of ants and bees, which he described in terms of "orderliness, system, division of function [and] sacrifice of individual rights for the good of the swarm."[1] The way of the bacterium or the way of the ant—chaos, congestion, and death, or planning, order, and vigor. The metaphors expressed the new professional impulse perfectly.

More than health officials like Emerson, and more than the welfare reformers who had initiated the outcry years earlier, it was city planners who led the attack on congestion in the 1920s. The special target of their wrath after the war was the mania for skyscrapers. Like everything else in city building these slender towers had been thrown up in bunches with no thought to planning and had succeeded only in magnifying a problem into a crisis. Health officials blamed them for causing an increase in respiratory diseases; fire officials blamed them for increasing the danger to life from conflagrations; and everyone blamed them for making difficult traffic conditions impossible. The city planners directed this chorus.

Early in the decade some of the planners still hoped that skyscrapers would level off at reasonable heights, regulated by the very economic forces that had sent them climbing in the first place. George Nimmons described the way in which high land values had forced builders upward to maximize the return on their heavy investments. Then with elaborate mathematical calculations he proved beyond a doubt that the rate of return on investment was progressively lower beyond the twentieth floor. The higher the building, the lower the return. For sound economic reasons, he concluded cheerfully, the skyscraper craze would soon pass.[2]

As it turned out, foresight was not one of Nimmons's strengths. Uninformed of his arithmetic, investors proceeded to soar confidently above the twentieth floor, and then the thirtieth and the fortieth. In the metropolis, which was their natural home, skyscrapers were making city planning into a three-dimensional occupation, forcing planners to double- and triple-deck midtown streets where parking space was already at a premium.[3]

To make matters worse, the relentless economic logic that pushed skyscrapers up from the city floor often forced congestion outward from the city center. C. A. Dykstra, a Los Angeles utilities administrator, blamed it all on the "centralization complex" of downtown businessmen. In their eagerness for more customers and higher sales volumes, he said, these merchants managed to drive up land values, thus forcing rents to rise until only skyscrapers could carry the values without placing impossible rental burdens on the tenants. Naturally, the new skyscrapers increased congestion, which put still more pressure on the land, which set off another round of mounting values and buildings—and congestion. Sooner or later, he continued, sensible people broke out of this circle and moved away from the city center. But that only led the merchants to demand transit lines to bring the expatriates back for shopping. Inevitably the new transit routes attracted new housing, which drove up land values, which meant that still taller buildings must be built to house still more people. In this way the mad process fed on its own energy, forcing congestion outward along transit routes until it threatened, cancer-like, to destroy the entire urban organism.[4]

In the end it all came down to greed. For Dykstra it was the specific greed of downtown merchants. Most of the planners, however, identified the problem more generally as a legacy of unregulated speculation in land values. That argument, given substance decades earlier by Henry George, had played a major role in late nineteenth-century reform thought and in shaping the doctrine of community rights among pioneer professionals in the Progressive era. After the war it became more or less conventional wisdom and was most forcefully expressed by the innovative men who gathered around the regional planning movement. The villain in their analysis was the landlord, the man who neither created any wealth nor performed any work, yet reaped the profits from land values and rents that rose solely because the population increased.

Thomas Adams showed how unchecked speculation had created a crisis in urban housing. Adams, a transplanted Scotsman who became a leading figure in regional planning in both Canada and the United States, pointed out that there was a difference between values based upon productive use and values based upon speculation alone. Unfortunately the two types of value had become entangled in the American system. As a result, rampant speculation acted as a sort of tax on productive use, driving up costs and rents and creating congestion of the sort that eventually produced slums. Even before the war, he said, speculative values had outrun the capacity of land to generate profits from housing, and had forced capital to flow into other areas of investment. Thus as urban populations continued to expand, the quantity of urban housing remained stable and the quality deteriorated. Paradoxically, he concluded, "we have a system which lives by taxing industry, art and life and then drives away the capital needed to maintain these things."[5]

Unless corrective action were taken soon, the professionals feared for the very survival of the metropolis. Clarence Stein, a prominent New York architect and one of the founders of the regional planning movement, summed it all up with his vision of "dinosaur cities." The city of our dreams, he said, "is the sum of all our possible aspirations" to beauty, excitement, pleasure, variety, learning, culture, and opportunity. For a few fortunate people that dream was a reality. For the vast majority, however, the dream city was hidden "in another city which could occur to a sane mind only in a nightmare." Such a city was New York, whose glittering facade masked its nightmarish realities. Its housing was abominable; its water was a health hazard; its streets were impassable. Nothing functioned properly. The city was in a perpetual state of breakdown. Such was the nature of New York's "greatness." Such would be the fate of any city that tolerated congestion as the price for that kind of greatness.[6]

The new professionals agreed substantially on the source and nature of urban problems, but they were deeply divided over how to treat them. Inevitably their recommendations were founded in some image of the ideal city. These images fell broadly into three categories. First there were the neighborhood communitarians, who carried the localistic spirit of an earlier era into the 1920s. Next there were the philo-urbanists, who looked beyond the neighborhood to the city as a whole. Critics on the periphery before the war, they were now perhaps the dominant voice in urban thought. Finally there were the regionalists, a group of innovators who looked beyond the city to a broad area of farms, towns, and cities, all organically integrated and conceived as a single unit.

The prewar interest in neighborhood life and community values had been intimately bound up with the settlement house movement. At one time or another such notables as Jane Addams, George Bellamy, Mary Simkhovitch, Graham Taylor, and Robert Woods made significant contributions to it. As long as the settlements served as "spearheads for reform," this neighborhood ideal played a vital role in urban thinking. Time and the impact of war, however, took their toll on the prewar reform impulse and many of its leaders. Jane Addams's opposition to the war tarnished her reputation somewhat, and after the war her continued attention to international problems kept her away from Hull House much of the time. Robert Woods was getting on in years, and before his death in mid-decade he spoke with little authority to reformers when he spoke at all. Other reformers were attracted to different realms of activity, such as casework, or were influenced by the war to move their gaze from the neighborhood to the nation. At the same time many of the wealthy patrons of the settlements were reassessing their own priorities in the chilled reform climate of the 1920s and finding causes that were more attractive and less controversial to invest in. Plagued with financial problems, bereft of revered leaders, and forced to compete with more recent conceptions of social work, the settlements began to appear anachronistic after the war. They lost their position at the center of a wavering reform movement, and the neighborhood outlook declined as a factor in the urban vision.

But it did not disappear by any means. Throughout the 1920s there were always individuals dedicated to keeping the communitarian spirit alive in the neighborhoods. They remained loyal to the original spirit of professionalism in neighborhood affairs, but they became increasingly aware that specialization and professionalism were hobbling their intentions. Community centers had begun to face this situation before the war and had been trying ever since to keep lines of communication open between laymen and experts. During the war the federal government acknowledged the problem and asked Newton Baker's Council of National Defense to work on a solution. John Collier served in this agency on the Community Council of New York, was impressed with the job it did, and vowed to carry it on after the war.

Always a thoughtful participant in urban affairs and social welfare work during those years, Collier had been concerned with the crisis of democracy in the cities since the Progressive era. Others equally concerned had fixed on the commission and manager systems as the panacea for urban ills, but for Collier they were not enough. He had no quarrels with these forms of government for getting public work done efficiently, but he flatly rejected the argument that they were sufficient in themselves to revive democracy, except perhaps as a hollow platitude. Real democracy, he argued, could only be realized by putting the common man in touch with the technical processes of municipal affairs, and that could not be done by having the common man submit to the superior knowledge of trained experts as some urged. The day of the upper-class reformer was passing, said Collier. "Demos is contra-suggestible to that sort of prestige, [and] votes men out of office, not into office, when politics becomes a business of trusting not of doing."[7]

There was a fundamental difference here between Collier and many of his colleagues in the new professions who did not have his feeling for localism. For them the problem was to modify democracy so that it did not interfere with the new expertise on urban policy. For Collier it was to reconcile democracy and expertise without modifying either in any important way. That could only be done by involving plain people in public affairs at the community level. As an example, he described how a local health district in New York had worked through community centers "to make possible a give-and-take between the people organized in groups, on the one side, and the expertness of society . . . on the other side."[8] He was advocating a kind of "modernized town meeting" where the people would not be manipulated by expert knowledge.

Expertise acted in other ways as a barrier to social integration, as Hyman Kaplan demonstrated with his portrayal of a slum-ridden, immigrant family in an eastern city. The father, recently out of the hospital, was confined to bed; the illiterate mother was ignorant of American ways and generally a poor housekeeper; the adolescent daughter, torn between the world of the immigrant inside the house and the world of the native outside, was already classified as "troublesome"; the twelve-year-old son was a truant; a bright seven-year-old daughter was beginning to reveal "psychopathic" tendencies; and there were two younger children, including an infant. Enter the social agencies. A relief society was providing financial assistance, supplemented by regular visits from a caseworker; the Home Economics Association often sent a housekeeper to help the mother manage the household; a local settlement worker looked in frequently just to keep in touch with things; one visiting nurse appeared weekly to care for the husband and another to advise the mother in pediatric matters; the Big Sisters sent out a worker to counsel the delinquent girl, and the Big Brothers sent out one to counsel the delinquent boy; finally, the local psychiatric clinic had assigned a worker to the troubled little girl. Ignoring the appearance of occasional irregulars—a medical social worker when the father was released from the hospital, a maternity nurse during the mother's recent pregnancy—there were eight experts supervising a family of seven people. The only thing missing was an expert in traffic management. Moreover, Kaplan, who was the head of Cincinnati's Jewish social agencies, assured his readers that the case, far from being extreme, "may be said to typify fairly, both in composition and in social disabilities, a large proportion of the families which come to the attention of social agencies."

With that many workers fluttering about the household, confusion and annoyance were inevitable. As Kaplan noted, the confidence that might have been inspired in this family by an intimate relationship with one advisor was impossible to achieve with eight, especially since the problems overlapped and predictably brought out different viewpoints and conflicting advice among the visitors. Social work had emerged in the first place as a solution to the problems of fragmentation in family and community life. But the unexpected growth of specialization had led to the vertical organization of uncoordinated social agencies, each of which tended to stake out a segment of the family as its own domain and thus to perpetuate the disease of fragmentation in the name of treating it. By the 1920s the solution had become a part of the problem.

The partner of functional overspecialization, Kaplan continued, was administrative overcentralization on a citywide basis by narrow groups that had neither representation from the neighborhoods nor any feel for them. Founded in the name of efficiency, these bureaucratic agencies were implicitly antidemocratic and fostered a pervasive apathy in the communities toward social agencies and a general atrophy of neighborhood forces.

Still, Kaplan was not discouraged by these trends in social welfare. On the contrary, he was optimistic about the possibilities he perceived in certain countertrends. Specifically he praised the initiative of a lower-middle-class Jewish neighborhood in Baltimore for taking charge of its own welfare and recreation problems. The overall direction of this endeavor was provided by a council elected largely by and from the neighborhood and was centered in a community house directed by a secretary who was responsible for all clubs, classes, recreation, and welfare work.

The immediate goal of such a program was to restore human feeling to social policy by coordinating on a local basis the social services that were already distributed randomly throughout the city and placing them in the hands of a generalist who would act as a buffer between client and technician. That much was primarily a mechanical problem and did not worry Kaplan. The ultimate goal was to make democracy more effective by restoring it to its original community context. Now that was essentially a normative problem and much more difficult, according to Kaplan, because the breakdown of the communitarian spirit had resulted in widespread ignorance and apathy, the nemeses of intelligent participation in local affairs. Drained of substance, only the constitutional forms of democracy had survived into the twentieth century. To pour content back into those forms, Kaplan recommended that plain people be educated in public issues by involving them directly in their own local affairs. On those terms, he believed, "the re-creation of the community is the task of the century."[9] Facing the same problem, John Collier had pleaded for a "modernized town meeting." Both were pressing for something similar to what a later generation would call "participatory democracy."

Of course, there were institutions that already did serve to integrate people at the local level, but they had evolved without the guiding intelligence of the new professionals and all too often had an uncertain moral quality about them. For the reformers the challenge was to improve the character of these institutions without destroying their function. A case in point was the urban saloon.

Unlike the leaders of the Anti-Saloon League, who tended to articulate the anxieties of village America, the community reformers had been in constant contact with the urban poor since the 1890s and perceived subtleties in the problem that eluded the militant drys altogether. Without apologizing for the saloon, which they faced daily as a bitter rival after all, they asked why, if it was so evil, the poor patronized it at all. The charity workers of an earlier era might have waved this question off with a reference to moral depravity, but that answer was plainly not congenial to the environmental assumptions of the new neighborhood workers. Instead they perceived, even before the war, that the saloon served a very positive social purpose in the absence of attractive alternatives for recreation and conviviality.

The matter was discussed sympathetically by Frank Laubach in 1913, when prohibition was spreading through the states. If men wanted only to quench their thirst or get drunk, he said, they could do it easily enough and cheaply by drinking their fill at home. The reason they went to the saloon instead was not to satisfy a craving for alcohol but to satisfy "one of the finest cravings of the soul, the craving for human fellowship." The saloon welcomed them with cheerful informality and friendship at almost any hour. It had pool tables and card games to entertain them, and for the price of a five-cent beer it offered them a free lunch that would cost up to five times as much in a restaurant. "In a word," he said, "the saloon is the poor man's club. To him it seems the purest form of democracy in America." No one had to preach piously to him about the evils of alcohol, because he saw its evil effects about him all the time. What he needed was a substitute for the saloon that would satisfy his normal needs for human discourse and relaxation without beer or booze. When that institution appeared, the power of the saloon over the urban poor would be broken.[10] Laubach thought that the church-sponsored clubhouse was the appropriate substitute. Most of the community workers preferred one form or another of the neighborhood center. Denominational or secular, each alternative had a strongly moralistic cast to it in the Progressive era.

By 1919 national prohibition was imminent, and finding a substitute for the saloon was an urgent matter for the communitarians. John Collier pondered the problem and echoed Laubach's appraisal of the saloon's institutional meaning. But Collier had a shrewder understanding of the ambiance of the saloon. He observed that the moderate use of alcohol which characterized most saloon behavior tended to create a fairly boisterous atmosphere in which argumentation, histrionics, and a certain amount of aggressive confrontation were commonplace. He found these to be relatively harmless ways to release feelings which could be explosive if they were bottled up. With the saloon now about to disappear, the problem at hand was to devise some way—not a place, but a method—to dislodge these feelings without the stimulus of alcohol. What Collier proposed was to stimulate the nervous system and alter consciousness— basically to loosen buried feelings—by engaging people in "combat games," in drama, and in oratory. It was more like group therapy than casual recreation. Collier imposed two conditions upon his scheme. First of all these dramatic substitutes for the saloon had to engage people actively as participants and not merely passively as observers. Second, the activities must not be directed toward specific ends. "The saloon," said Collier,

is a place of unequivocal freedom. It tolerates idiosyncracies. . . . This freedom is basic to all successful leisure institutions. Most leisure interests are and should be ends in themselves; the ulterior product, in terms of civic education or public work, should result from the way in which spontaneous leisure is organized, and should not be obtained thru [sic] a Calvinistic forcing down of utilitarian considerations upon the pleasure interest.[11]

Frank Crane, a public-health doctor, showed the same reluctance to moralize about the saloon. He saw it as a place where rich and poor could mingle on equal terms "in that true communion of human beings that comes only from eating and drinking together." Of course, the rich did not ordinarily eat and drink with the poor, but that only emphasizes Crane's raffish-romantic view of the saloon. Part of the lure of the saloon, he continued, was precisely the roughish lack of respectability that many reformers deplored. Now that the saloon was about to become a relic, Crane warned do-gooders that any substitute conceived to "elevate the poorer classes" was doomed to fail. "People do not want a place to be 'improved,' " he said. "They want a place for self-expression, a place to be bad if they choose."[12] Only on those terms was he willing to contemplate a replacement for the saloon.

In their approach to the problems of leisure and community life, Collier and Crane abandoned the customary attitudes of reformers. Just a few years earlier, when the professionals first recognized that leisure might have serious social implications, they had tried to give recreational activities a moral framework and social content. Collier himself had contributed to this movement. Now they were beginning to speak of spontaneity and idiosyncratic behavior with an admiration that would have been unthinkable—or at least unspeakable—for them just five years earlier. That does not mean that all restraints were off. Combat games in raucous surroundings were one thing; unbuttoned hedonism and barroom brawls were quite another. But it does suggest that people like Collier and Crane were beginning to adapt the communitarian outlook to the more relaxed moral spirit of urban life in the New Era.

For the neighborhood communitarians the idea of community involved a web of social relationships that gave shape and meaning to life by integrating individuals, families, and neighbors with their work, their leisure, and with each other in a local context. They agreed with other reformers that the source of urban alienation was congestion, but unlike many of these other professionals they made almost no contribution to contemporary thought about how to decongest the cities. Because their professional lives usually immersed them in the demoralizing day-to-day crises of the urban poor, they did not link their activities to some distant, abstract image of the city. Their conception of community had a strong and concrete sense of place to it. It reached out through the neighborhood but not beyond it. It was geographically finite, it was familiar, and it was palpable. But it was also a vision that was fading into the background of reform in the 1920s.[13]

The neighborhood communitarians had always had a love/hate relationship with the city. Part of them embraced urban life, part clung to preurban values. Others among the new professionals were less ambivalent toward urban culture. Indeed an alternative vision had begun to emerge with the philo-urbanists of the Progressive era. These reformers looked beyond neighborhood boundaries to city limits, and were generally more attuned to the rapid, often clashing rhythms of urban life. That is not to say that they were oblivious to urban problems. On the contrary, they often proceeded from the same perceptions of congestion as the communitarians, but they were more inclined to accept the city on its own terms and to work for improvement from there.

In the past the evangelists of urbanism had been embarrassed by the congestion and anonymity of cities but had accepted those conditions as the price one had to pay for the cultural and material advantages they offered. By the 1920s some of the philo-urbanists were becoming less defensive about the liabilities of the city, and in some cases even converted the liabilities into assets.

In this spirit Mary Bonner saw the city as the real source of American values. Why, wondered Bonner, did the flight from farm to city continue? Surely it was not for the bright lights and easy work, as some still claimed, since rural amusements were now much the same as urban, and city work—even desk work—was not easy. No, she said, what drew people away from farms and villages was the egalitarian nature of urban society. In the small town one's family status marked one for life. Class lines were rigid, failure was a matter for cheap gossip, and eccentricity a matter for ostracism. In contrast, the tumultuous impersonality of the city permitted people to choose their own paths and proceed at their own pace. Failure was not terminal because nobody paid attention to it, and one could always start again. If people wished to "improve themselves," no one asked about their family background. And even if one did not rise in society, there was no stigma in belonging to the vast working class. It was only in the cities, she concluded, that one found the truly American virtues, only in the cities where conditions were "crowded enough for true equality," and one could finally "feel free and independent and his brother's equal."[14]

Freedom, independence, equality—the hallmarks of urban life! Of course, Bonner was not the first to expropriate the traditional country virtues and put them to work for the city. A few of the philo-urbanists had enjoyed tweaking traditionalists in that manner before the war. Bonner's contribution was to take some of the most widely condemned characteristics of the industrial city—its impersonality, even its congestion—and establish them as the very conditions for freedom and equality.

Charles Beard, on the other hand, was prepared to concede that Jeffersonian precepts about liberty and yeomanry had had "some elements of truth" in them at one time. But he was plainly unconcerned with traditional American virtues when he assessed "The City's Place in Civilization" in a widely reprinted 1928 essay that he prepared originally for the National Municipal League.

In the decade since his departure from Columbia University this renowned political scientist and historian had become one of the preeminent urbanists in American life. Now he impatiently dismissed critics on both sides of the Atlantic who wished to return to the self-sufficient agrarian community. "Whether we like it or not," he said, "the machine drives relentlessly forward, crushing the old order to earth." To emphasize this point he cautioned Americans in that election year not to succumb to the cultivated image of Herbert Hoover as just a simple country boy. Hoover was an engineer and a business promoter who embodied the spirit of the age perfectly, he told them. As for those who preferred to dream of cities past, he observed savagely that the glories of Athens had been sustained by slavery, that Cicero had been a slumlord, and that the "heaven-searching spires" of medieval cathedrals had hidden wretched masses in the shadows below. So much for the idealized past, rural or urban. Beard was more concerned with transforming the present into an idealized future.

The dominant reality of the present for Beard was the machine, for it was the machine that defined the prevailing "culture of urbanism," and it was the culture of urbanism that would inevitably shape the future. He said this not with resignation but with enthusiasm. He assured his readers that "the city is not inherently a menace to civilization, as Jefferson believed." Quite the contrary, it was the nursery of human creativity. "What great book, painting, imaginative work, or invention has ever come from the country?" he asked. He agreed with the "European esthetes" who portrayed America as a mass culture, but he ridiculed them for condemning it on those terms. Nevertheless, it was to Europe that Beard looked for the imagination to fuel the machinery of mass culture. He had great admiration for Le Corbusier's dream of "a Paris Taylorized" and boundless enthusiasm for the way in which European planners were adapting new materials and techniques to urban design. Moreover, he admitted frankly that he found the socialist-inspired housing projects of Vienna "more beautiful than most of the old Hapsburg piles" that architects slavishly copied, gingerbread trimmings and all, from other civilizations.[15]

Eclectically Beard took the technological imperative of Le Corbusier, the architectural innovations of the Bauhaus, and the social inspiration of Vienna and set them in a broad American landscape of urban-dominated regions that would be unified eventually by national planning. It was a bold and comprehensive vision shaped by Beard's belief that "if radicals are usually wrong, it must be confessed that the conservatives who suppose things will never change are always wrong."

Although Beard meant his suggestions to be a practical point of departure for urban planning, there was a tinge of futurism about them that hinted at some of the more fantastic schemes advanced by urbanists in the 1920s. For instance, Samuel R. Lewis, a Chicago engineer, drew up a blueprint for building half-mile-square urban sections ten to fifteen stories high and enclosing them under panels of glass roofing hinged for summer removal. His plan included artificial rain showers to regulate temperature, humidity, and dust, and rooftop truck gardens to supply inexpensive vegetables. One $16 million section, he said, would soon pay itself off in fuel savings, would provide a clean environment, and would bestow a benign year-round climate upon even such a city as Chicago.[16] It was a primitive and soon-forgotten effort to introduce solar heating into urban thinking.

Harvey Corbett, a New York architect, had a scheme that was more down-to-earth, or at least closer to earth. Like all of the new professionals, Corbett was disturbed by urban congestion, not only of people, but now as well of automobiles, which were becoming a critical problem by mid-decade. After sardonically weighing several possibilities—thinning out pedestrian traffic by attrition through accidents; eliminating traffic jams by paving over the entire city; solving the population problem by chaining farmers to trees in the fresh air of their beloved countryside so they could not migrate to the cities—he got down to cases. Basically, he said, there were three forms of traffic tying the city in knots: foot, wheel, and rail. The most rational way out of the present mess was to separate them onto different levels. The street level would continue to carry wheel traffic, and only wheel traffic; rail traffic would all be moved underground; and foot traffic would be elevated one level above the street, along with all shops, onto covered walking arcades with bridges crossing over at every corner. This system of layering traffic would cure one of the major headaches of urban life by providing more space for parking, unsnarling traffic, facilitating commerce, and brightening the hopes of pedestrians to survive from day to day.[17]

If three tiers, why not more? After the middle of the decade, with New York beginning to drown in its own traffic, the layered fantasies of some urbanists reached epic dimensions. John Hencken, a New York engineer, drew up the plans for a structure that varied along its length from six to twelve stories high, and extended without a wrinkle for more than fifteen miles from lower Manhattan to Yonkers. In effect it was a linear city. In addition to an elaborate distribution of traffic, the "Henckenway" included shops, light industry, restaurants, apartments, hotels, even schools, churches, and theaters, all strategically located according to the type of neighborhood through which it was pass-

ing. Its most inspired feature was a moving pedestrian way on the second level.
A two-way thoroughfare, the level was divided into fourteen enlongated strips,
seven proceeding in each direction the entire length of the structure at speeds
graded in regular increments from three to twenty-one miles per hour. At maximum capacity the walkway would carry 200,000 people past a given point in
one hour.[18] Hencken thus proposed to solve the problems inherent in building
upward by building outward. Like the other adventures in futuristic fantasy of
those years, the Heckenway was technically feasible but practically preposter-
ous. And yet its central assumption—that congestion could be eased by using
technology to siphon off excess population and commerce—was dogma among
the new professionals in the 1920s.

Occasional attacks of this planner's delirium seem to have afflicted many of
the new public-service professionals in those years. Even men of such conservative temperament as Frederic Delano were not immune. Delano, a New
York architect-planner, expressed his alarm at the "growing menace of high
buildings" mindlessly built in the great cities. Not only that, he lamented, but
the plague was now spreading to the smaller cities as well. Every city that
aspired to metropolitan greatness, it seemed, wanted a skyscraper of its very
own, "one that can be illustrated on a picture postcard and sent far and wide
as an evidence of modernity and a go-ahead spirit." Skyscrapers were becoming mere symbols of the booster spirit and were blinding cities to the rational
modes of growth that were now available. Still, Delano was not a Luddite
when it came to skyscrapers. On the contrary, his remedy was a perfect expression of those rational modes of growth. All that was necessary, he said, was
that cities plan for a specific maximum of population per acre, then ascertain
the average height of buildings required to service that population, and then
simply build accordingly. That could be done by spreading the average out
evenly over the entire acre, and eventually over the entire city, much like Paris;
or it could be done by doubling the average building height on only half the
land, or by quadrupling it on a quarter, and so on, as long as all unbuilt land
was used for parks. In that way the taller the building, the more ground space
would be turned over to park land. The ultimate expression of Delano's plan
was portrayed in one of the drawings that illustrated this essay, a depiction of
architect Raymond Hood's futuristic city of towering skyscrapers isolated in
vast parks and laced together by broad boulevards. It was an almost surrealistic
vision of lofty spires standing, desolate, like lonely sentries with nothing to
guard.[19]

The men who whipped up these confections were a reflection of the engineering imagination in its triumphant ascendancy after the war. They viewed
the overload of people and the derangement of traffic in cities as purely mechanical problems, and so they took up slide rule and T square to devise purely
mechanical solutions. They knew that their ideas were extravagant; yet they
considered them in all seriousness to be practicable or at least to point in the
direction of practicality. Radical problems called forth radical solutions. What

mattered to them was that their projects were technologically feasible. The truly impressive potential for mechanical breakdown and human chaos that lurked in such a contraption as Hencken's multispeed walkway was perhaps better suited to the imagination of a Charlie Chaplin than to that of the new professionals, but they were not deterred. The only obstacles they foresaw were financial, and their lofty fantasies enabled them to hurdle those with ease. The bramble of politics and the maze of bureaucracy were situated somewhere beneath their gaze. Still, while their fancies were excessive in whole, they proved eventually to be practical in many of their parts. Solar heating, pedestrian arcades, covered shopping malls, graded road separations, even moving walkways, are all direct, if sometimes mutated, descendants of these ancestral urban visionaries.

Most of the philo-urbanists of the 1920s dreamed no grand dreams, however. They were caught up in the day-to-day tumble of city life and were content to think in terms of piecemeal solutions to concrete problems. For them zoning appeared to be the ideal method.

Zoning fell into two broad categories. *Bulk* zoning was designed to control the size and distribution of buildings in a given area. Applicable anywhere in new construction, it was of particular interest in the 1920s to planners in the large eastern cities where skyscraper congestion threatened to reshape narrow streets into urban canyons forever shut off from the light of day. Thus in New York bulk zoning principles required that as buildings increased in height, they be set back from the curb line in regular stages according to a set formula, which accounts for the vaguely pyramidal shape that characterizes the skyscrapers of midtown Manhattan. *Use* zoning aimed more ambitiously to dictate the character and tone of an area by laying down the terms of its land use. It enabled planners to decide that one area should be given over to commerce, another to industry, another to housing, and still another to some mix of these. It even authorized them to limit residential areas to specific types of dwellings—apartment blocs here, single-family houses there. Ideally use zoning and bulk zoning were perfectly complementary. Planners could designate an area for commercial *use* and control its *bulk* by setting height limitations on the buildings and space allocations between them.

Morris Knowles traced the origins of zoning in America to the time before the war when New York's garment workers began to spill over onto nearby Fifth Avenue, "crowding out the shoppers and the hotel population" from morning till night. He reminded his audience that Fifth Avenue merchants at that time had formed a "protective association" to keep the garment industry at a distance and preserve the avenue for its more exclusive clients. It was an early example of use zoning, and, by the way, of the recurrent class overtones that so often antagonized the opponents of many zoning plans in the years that followed.

Knowles, a civil engineer and planner, was a supremely practical man who had no time for urban dreamers. The only test of a zoning plan for him was whether it worked, and it could pass this test of practicability only by settling for something less than a theoretical ideal. He proposed, therefore, that zoning commissions recruit representatives from all of the major functions and service occupations in the city—from industrialists and workers, politicans and lawyers, architects and engineers, economists and social workers, builders and realtors, bankers and insurance agents.[20] Any zoning plan that emerged from that crowd was bound to be a compromise, which was essentially how Knowles and the other advocates of zoning defined workability.

Zoning appealed to planners above all for its flexibility. It could be adapted to almost any purpose from decongesting the traffic on a city block to implementing a comprehensive city plan. It could be used next year or next generation with equal ease. It permitted planners to target a specific problem in the urban maze without disrupting the larger pattern of physical or social relationships around it. In addition, it interested planners because it interested the movers and shakers of urban politics, the businessmen organized in chambers of commerce who saw in zoning a means to achieve their own ends. In difficult situations the political muscle of these organizations could be decisive.

As adaptable as it was, zoning gave planners a useful approach to the housing situation, which they all agreed was the most pressing problem in the cities by the end of the war. Charles Cheney, a West Coast planner, set the tone for the early postwar era when he described how residential zoning could act as a nostrum for all the ills of the city. It would make industrial investment safe and thereby prevent the flight of industry from the cities; it would protect residential areas, thereby stabilizing real estate values and the mortgage-loan market; it would stimulate home ownership, thereby soothing labor discontent and increasing productivity. In Cheney's eyes it had something for everyone and was the first prerequisite to intelligent city planning.[21] At one end of his vision stood property values; at the other, labor productivity. The efficiency-oriented planners stressed these ideas repeatedly in the 1920s.

Unfortunately the planners were unable to agree on the type of housing that was needed to ease the crisis. The drift in the cities after the war was unmistakably toward apartment buildings, but early in the era planners still held out for the single-family dwelling. More than just a place to shelter people, it represented to them a way of life. Such planners as Charles Cheney and John Ihlder thought of the private house as the bulwark of the family and "the backbone of our nation." Reluctantly they granted that apartment buildings were necessary, but they insisted on zoning them into confined districts. Otherwise they would drive out private dwellings "just as Oriental labor can under-live and drive out white labor." They spoke of apartment buildings as if they were a communicable disease and of planning as a kind of quarantine to contain the contagion.[22]

This commitment to detached housing was useful up to a point, but in their single-minded devotion to it the planners of the early 1920s proved to be rather less the practical realists than their self-image suggested. Consider some of their perceptions: (1) there was a desperate housing shortage in most cities right

after the war; (2) while the shortage existed at all levels, it struck with dispro-
portionate severity in the poorer districts; (3) because the urban poor lived in
housing that was both qualitatively and quantitatively inadequate, the cities
were in a state of crisis characterized by inefficient productivity, labor unrest,
generalized squalor, and social disorganization. That analysis had been shared
for years almost universally by the new professionals. The zoners agreed with
the analysis and then virtually ignored it for a strategy of dealing with urban
problems by relieving the pressures on middle-class housing. The cure did not
fit the disease. Detached housing was simply irrelevant to the problems of Manhattan's Lower East Side or Chicago's expanding Black Belt. The zoners acknowledged that with a perfunctory nod to apartment blocs for the slums before
turning their attention and their training to the more affluent neighborhoods.
Here at least their treatment was thoughtful and thorough, including suggestions for financing, for low-cost construction, and for eliminating speculation
by the imposition of controls, usually at either the city or state level. To be
sure, the strain on middle-class housing was real enough, and by the end of the
war it was severe. Unfortunately most of the zoners abandoned their own analysis
and acted as if it were the only trouble spot in urban housing. It wasn't.

There were exceptions among the planners, of course, and as the decade
matured, they grew bolder and more numerous until, on the eve of the depression, they were no longer exceptions. There were several reasons for the change
of emphasis. First of all, there was the fact, noted with dismay by some of the
professionals, that more and more people actually did prefer to live in apartments. Second, builders ignored the values and wishes of planners and were
erecting apartment houses because they were a more profitable way for them
to develop available tracts of urban land. As a result, there was a dramatic
change in urban housing patterns. After the war the preference for detached
housing continued for a while. As late as 1921 starts on detached housing in
the cities exceeded the construction of new apartment units by a margin of
more than two to one. Only five years later, according to the Bureau of Labor
Statistics, starts on apartment units outnumbered those on single-family dwellings for the first time.[23] Urbanites were becoming a race of what the bureau
called "cliff dwellers" in spite of the wishes of planners, and so the planners
began to yield to the inevitable.[24]

But there was more to it than mere resignation. Most of the reformers came
to see apartment buildings as the only realistic way out of the housing crisis.
Eventually many of them even saw the multifamily dwelling as a positive contribution to urban life.

One of the first signs of this change in attitude was given not by an American, but by a German architect, Walter Behrendt. In 1923 Behrendt published
a paper in the *Journal of the American Institute of Architects* on recent German
thinking about skyscrapers. In it he spoke enthusiastically of the skyscraper and
of how other German architects now perceived it "as a new and attractive
problem of monumental architecture" for housing as well as for commercial

purposes. Behrendt expressed his admiration for this American contribution to world architecture, but he made it clear immediately that his mission was not to shower praise on American ingenuity. As a feat of engineering, he said, the American skyscraper was impressive, but as a work of architecture it was lamentable. He and other German architects deplored the way that Americans used land, shutting out light and air in the name of efficiency by filling up lots to their very edges with rectangular structures; and they deplored the way that Americans foolishly imitated a Beaux Arts esthetic that led to the erection of "tremendous piles of stone" garnished ridiculously with an "empty pompousness of architectural ornamentation." Architecturally, he said, it made no sense for commercial buildings to look like outsized Renaissance palaces.

Behrendt then described recent trends in Germany where skyscraper competitions had brought forth a number of strikingly original entries that solved these problems. In particular he singled out several that were variations on the same theme—a central service core with wings jutting out, opening every room in the structure to a flood of light and air. Two of these designs, one star-shaped and the other curvilinear, were conceived by the young Mies van der Rohe and dramatically applied a new esthetic to skyscrapers. No more gingerbread ornamentation. These were soaring spires of iron and glass whose esthetic was expressed in form and proportions rather than cornices and pilasters. Behrendt then chastised the Americans for building skyscrapers promiscuously instead of adapting them to the "general scene of the city" in order to preserve "beautiful urban compositions." He ridiculed academic city planning with its "sentimental talk of sky-line effects and of 'architectural accents' " and insisted that planning "according to purpose and practical requirements [was] capable of originating new architectural forms." Applied to skyscrapers, these principles would create "an artistic urban unity."[25]

Housing in the sky, curved buildings, walls of glass, function dictating form, beauty in austerity. At first it was too much for the arbiters of American architecture, and they stormed back in protest, charging that the whole idea was "contrary to the human housing instinct," dismissing the designs as monstrous "birdcages," and ridiculing the curved structure for resembling "A Picture of a Nude Building falling down stairs."[26] So much for Duchamps; so much for van der Rohe; so much for the Bauhaus and its esthetic of form and proportion.

In the next several years the controversy over the Bauhaus ideal became what one architect called a major "undercurrent" in the profession. It surfaced again in a debate before the San Francisco chapter of the AIA in 1928. Speaking on behalf of modernism, Irving Morrow condemned the atavistic principles of most American architects. Like any other living art, he said, architecture ought to express the spirit of the society that creates it. Unfortunately American architects, who were more or less abreast of social needs (he conceded that they did all right with bathrooms), were committed to hopelessly archaic notions of weight and bulk. The result was a "devastating dualism" in which they tried to satisfy present needs and obsolete ideals simultaneously. The history of all the arts proved them wrong, proved that beauty was not a matter of immutable principles, as traditionalists claimed, but of habit. With that in mind, Morrow urged American architects to change their habits and move on to an esthetic of "lightness and elasticity" based upon new materials and machine technology. The automobile was a perfect example of this modern esthetic. If its design had been left to architects, he said, we would still be lumbering along at fifteen miles per hour in heavily gilded coaches "reverently copied from the most authentic examples at Versailles." Fortunately its creators had long since recognized that the automobile was not just a horseless carriage and, by keeping pace with technological change, had conceived a design that was perfectly tailored to its function. It was time now for architects to do the same thing.[27] The seeds planted five years earlier by Walter Behrendt had taken root in American soil.

By 1929 a sizable corps of urbanists stood ready to refashion American cities from parts contributed by all of the new professions: a broadly social outlook in matters of health, housing, and recreation; increasingly sophisticated approaches to planning; a new architecture. They even had before them a plan to use assembly-line techniques for prefabricated housing.[28] But they still had some major obstacles to overcome. For one thing, as Harold Buttenheim pointed out, the existence of a city plan did not guarantee its implementation. Many cities had plans, but most of them were content to display the blueprints as a symbol of progress and ignore them otherwise, except for building the boulevards necessary to carry the "Rotary boys" from their offices to their country clubs. Building these boulevards for the rich without executing the rest of the plan, Buttenheim said, was like "putting diamond crowns upon leprous brows."[29]

That, of course, raised the much broader question of who was to finance and administer these plans. The urbanists were at no loss for suggestions here. Some recommended private investors, others philanthropic foundations; many favored intervention by local or state authorities; a few looked to the federal government. Yet these suggestions were usually made without reflection as casual asides in essays on substantive issues. The professionals were still more concerned with elaborating and justifying their plans than with implementing them.

The most impressive contribution to urban thought in the 1920s was regional planning. Born of the same combination of despair and hope for the urban condition as neighborhood communitarianism and philo-urbanism, regional planning fired the imaginations of new professionals in the postwar decade as no other approach to urban design.

Regional planning was inspired originally by the garden-city movement of Victorian England. The garden city was the brainchild of Ebenezer Howard, who, like most Victorian reformers, recoiled from the multiple horrors of industrial society. Howard had a vision of an organic community of 30,000 people protected from the encroachment of large industrial cities by an encircling belt of greenery. In theory it would integrate agricultural, industrial, and cultural endeavors and provide an alternative to the inhuman metropolis. The incarnation of this ideal at Letchworth proved perhaps to be less an alternative to industrialism than a refuge from it, but it was nonetheless influential. Transplanted to the New World, the garden-city idea won some converts among American reformers late in the Progressive era and was beginning to have a serious impact on urbanists by the end of the war.

More than anyone else, the man responsible for adapting it to North American realities, and thus for transforming it into regional planning, was Thomas Adams, a Scot who had emigrated to Canada in 1909 and who moved to the United States in the 1920s. Trained in town planning and seasoned in the administration of Letchworth itself, Adams was already preaching about garden cities to American planners during the war. His insistence upon the need to curb speculation, regulate land use, and stabilize the social structure guaranteed him a sympathetic hearing.[30]

The trouble with the garden city was its fortress mentality, symbolized by the greenbelt that it wished to erect as a barrier against the intrusion of heavy industry and metropolitan sprawl. Perhaps in a land as densely populated as England that isolation was necessary to the vision. In North America it was not. Thus by 1921 Adams had opened the garden city outward to include the metropolis and its hinterland. He agreed with the prevailing analysis of urban development, lamenting the scourge of land speculation and the economic system that encouraged it and attacking the sort of zoning whose purpose was to preserve real estate values and class distinctions. But Adams was a temperate man who was inclined to work with things as they were. Unlike some of the regionalists, he did not use his energy to curse industrial capitalism. It was the system that prevailed, and that was that. As for zoning, the problem was not intrinsic to the technique but to the people currently using it. In the proper hands it could be a force for positive social change. The real challenge was to apply zoning to rational ends within the system that existed.

To Adams that meant conceiving of city and suburbs as a continuum from dense core out to countryside. In the past zoning had been applied to the central city alone, most often badly. Now, he said, "the worst evils of bad development are occurring in the outer suburbs where new industrial development is taking place." In the future zoning must aim to coordinate the planning of developed, semideveloped, and undeveloped areas.[31] That idea pointed directly to regional planning.

What made regional planning more than just an intellectual plaything for professionals was the astonishing development of technology after the war, especially in the field of electric power. As a source of light for urban housing and of power for industry, electricity was no longer a novelty by the 1920s, but its potential for social reconstruction was not yet widely grasped. *Survey Graphic* undertook to correct that by discussing the implications of electricity for planning in nontechnical terms for reformers across the nation.

In an issue devoted entirely to "giant power" Joseph Hart set matters in perspective by tracing the historical relationship between energy and culture. In the process he reflected many of the anxieties and some of the hopes of the regionalists. He described steam as the "great centralizer," an inflexible mode of power that had torn people loose from their local roots in a culture of artisanry and sucked them into grim new industrial cities by the millions. Adapting to the artificial environment of the industrial city, said Hart, man was now completely alienated from nature. Electricity, on the other hand, had the potential to reverse this process. Unlike steam, which did not carry power away from its energy source, it was flexible. It had the capacity to transmit power over great distances, and thus to decentralize industry and population, revive the local community, and put people in touch again with nature and each other.[32]

Although Hart shared many of the assumptions of the regionalists, his rejection of urban culture was so absolute that he never really entered their inner circle. Members of the Regional Planning Association of America (RPAA) had broader horizons. Founded in 1923, the RPAA, somewhat more modestly than its title suggests, consisted of a handful of self-proclaimed "insurgents" led by such men as Clarence Stein, Lewis Mumford, and Frederick Ackerman, who were convinced that the megalopolis was afflicted with terminal congestion, which made it economically insupportable and generally unlivable. Most of them lived in New York City.

The controlling image of the metropolis for these regionalists was death. Mumford called it a "necropolis"; Stein likened it to the dinosaur; Charles Whitaker consigned it, like the great cities of the past, to oblivion in a grave of its own digging. Death, burial, extinction, oblivion. Nuts-and-bolts city planners, they said, were like doctors treating an incurable disease with "pills and a lotion"; they might relieve some of the suffering, but the patient was still doomed.[33]

The reason why mere tinkering could not work was that a profound disjuncture had developed in American society between man's instincts, which tend to unify him with nature, and his present economic institutions, which alienate him from it. Echoing Veblen, Ackerman argued that human instincts had been conditioned originally in the neolithic age, and then bred over millennia to the imperatives of that epoch, a process in which natural selection had favored "those best endowed to live under neolithic conditions." Now, in just a few generations, American society had torn people loose from their neolithic moorings. Guided entirely by "pecuniary motives" toward the elaboration of giant cities, it had imposed "alien conditions" upon man's "genetic background." Even city planning had fallen victim to these conditions and was concerned these days only with how much abuse people could tolerate and how much money they could pay. With questions such as those now paramount, America was rapidly approaching the day when its cities would be uninhabitable. That prospect hardly dismayed the acerbic Ackerman. In their present distended condition, he felt, they had absolutely nothing to recommend them. Deserted, they would at least serve as monuments memorializing "a people who, worshipping their monstrous institutions, failed to hear the small voice of their own rebelling instincts and who thus became the sacrificial offerings to their own institutional gods." [34]

All of the members of the RPAA subscribed to this analysis of a gap between human institutions and human nature, between what is and what ought to be. Generally they used a shorthand of paired opposites to describe it: commercial interest/community interest; engineering values/human values; metropolitan barracks/home life; insanity/serenity; robots/humans; death/birth. Inevitably the metropolis was savaged in these comparisons. The preference of the RPAA, always expressed as a necessity, was clearly for a mode of social organization that would put people back in touch with their instincts.

At first glance this preference seemed to point directly toward the small town which, mythically at least, was the classic source of communitarian values in America. But small-town America was not the answer for the regionalists because their tastes were too cosmopolitan. What they called the "Ladies' Social of Gopher Prairie" was not their idea of a cultural utopia. They needed a place like Clarence Stein's dream city, a place that offered excitement, pleasure, varied foods, great libraries, museums, universities, opera, and symphony. Indeed, according to Mumford, only in the city could "man . . . enter most fully into his social heritage." [35] But metropolitan America, where these things abounded, was not the answer either, because its culture did not compensate for its thousand daily assaults upon the spirit.

That put the regionalists in something of a quandary. Torn between their values and their tastes, they wanted the communitarian wholeness of the small town without its cultural sterility, and they wanted the broad culture of the metropolis without its dehumanizing alienation. This dilemma was the source of their inspiration. Since no such place existed, they had to invent it. What they devised was a kind of intellectual mutant—the regional cell without its metropolitan nucleus. The metropolis would no doubt continue to exist—Mumford conceded that "nothing short of famine or poison gas" could eliminate it—but it played no serious part in their calculations; they virtually ignored it. The unit they dealt with instead was an enhanced version of the garden city, ranging up to 100,000 people. The region they envisoned consisted of many such cities nestled organically amid farmlands and recreation areas, connected by modern roads, unified by the automobile, and powered by giant electricity. It was a fusion of Renaissance Tuscany (Mumford's ideal) and twentieth-century technology.

How was it all to come about? On that question the ingenuity of the RPAA associates faltered. They knew precisely where they wanted to go, but they had no concrete strategy for getting there. They realized, for instance, that a fundamental change in values and institutions was a necessary precondition to their regional society—they stressed this repeatedly—but they did not really confront the issue, except for occasional wan references to government cooperation. They seemed to assume that as soon as enough of the right kind of people recognized the atavistic character of the metropolis, they would rebuild the nation around regional units. Somehow.

But "somehow" begged the question. Indeed their entire approach begged the question, for in their search for an ideal solution they lost contact with the problem. The metropolis was a dominant force by the 1920s and was bound to remain so as far ahead as anyone could reasonably project. All other urbanists, including Thomas Adams and his associates with the Regional Plan of New York, agreed on that much. For them the big cities were seriously ill and needed treatment quickly. For Mumford and his colleagues the cities were fatally ill and beyond treatment. Consequently these visionary regionalists turned their backs on the present and put their imaginations to work on a utopian future that was no more serviceable in the 20s than the doodling that produced the Henckenway.

Serviceability, however, is too rigid a standard to apply to visionaries. To be sure, by almost any standard the proposal to rebuild the nation around garden cities was frivolous by the 1920s. But the idea of breaking through the traditional dichotomy of city and country to the region was not. That notion joined with others and emerged unexpectedly a few years later as the Tennessee Valley Authority.

Meanwhile a different approach to regionalism was taking shape in the 1920s. It was characterized by Thomas Adams's hard-nosed realism and was embodied in the "Comprehensive Regional Plan of New York and its Environs." The Regional Plan of New York was funded by the Russell Sage Foundation in 1922. A private undertaking with no political authority whatsoever, it aimed nevertheless to inspire political action by the public through the soundness of its proposals. Thomas Adams directed the project and imparted the flavor of his practical genius to it.

The most daring quality of the plan was the scope of its organicism. City planners and other professionals had proceeded from organic assumptions for years, but always their vision had been limited by the streetcar tracks that bounded the neighborhood or the political tracks that bounded the city. The New York planners pressed their organic postulates outward to the entire region, which they saw as a geographically and economically coherent nexus of communities, all of which were affected by each other and above all by the great city at its center. Accordingly, effective planning for any one community was not possible without intelligent planning for the entire region. For that reason the New York plan boldly ignored established political jurisdictions and spilled over state lines into Connecticut and New Jersey, including more than 300 cities, towns, and villages, as well as all of the open space in the region.[36]

What emerged in 1922 was really only the plan for a plan, but that was enough for Paul Kellogg, who announced it to reformers across the nation almost immediately. Kellogg informed his readers that the initial phase of the plan would be a four-part survey of economic, physical, legal, and social conditions that would be several years in the making. Armed with the information in this survey, economists, businessmen, lawyers, artists, and public-service professionals would then be able to cooperate in drawing up a comprehensive plan to develop the entire region rationally for years to come.[37] Kellogg had been instrumental in formulating the survey idea years earlier and in fostering cooperation among different professionals before the war. Now the New York plan promised to codify the aspirations of service professionals in a regional-planning framework much as the Pittsburgh Survey had done in a social-welfare framework early in the century, but on an infinitely grander scale. His enthusiasm is understandable. It was also infectious. In the next year the idea swept over the nation as cities from Boston to Los Angeles gave serious consideration to regional planning.[38]

After the initial flurries of excitement over the plan, fanfares gave way to a more subdued air of expectancy as research on the survey got under way. Because of the conflicting strains in urban thinking at the time, there was still some uncertainty among the new professionals over the shape that the plan might take, but all doubts were removed near the end of the decade when the volumes of the survey began to appear. In stark contrast to the dour prophets of the RPAA, the survey concluded surprisingly that New York was a reasonably efficient city economically. Through a process of trial and error over the years, businessmen had created a rational economic entity by concentrating the large supplies of capital and labor necessary for consumer-oriented production and by lowering transportation costs to facilitate distribution.[39]

Of course the committee did not spend more than a million dollars and the better part of a decade just to produce ten volumes of praise for the economic status quo in New York City. On the contrary, it concluded that inner-city traffic congestion was becoming an economic liability, that health and housing were below acceptable standards, that the recent flight from the city was creating new strains by removing people from proximity to the workplace, and that the rise of unplanned suburbs was already duplicating the problems of unplanned cities, as well as creating new ones in the surrounding countryside. Perhaps the invisible hand had done its job in the past, but now, it seems, it was becoming palsied, if not yet paralyzed.

The solution to these problems lay not in ignoring New York, as the RPAA seemed inclined to do, but in perceiving it as the heart of an organic metropolitan region and planning comprehensively for the whole. In practice this would mean not the decentralization of population, which was generally understood to mean an exodus to bedroom suburbs, villages, and beyond, but the "diffused recentralization" of industry, housing, and commerce into noncentral parts of the metropolis and into complex, new satellite cities.[40] That was a far cry from the garden city.

In 1928 with the survey well under way, Thomas Adams laid out the principles and promise of regional planning to the American Society of Civil Engineers. The essence of the problem, he said, was to recognize the difference between concentration and congestion. Concentration of enterprise and large populations—the very definition of urban life—were necessary and valuable. Without planning and regulated land use, however, concentration was likely to thicken into congestion, which inevitably impaired health, safety, and business. Perhaps the harm already done in the great cities could never be completely undone, but it could be lessened by the planned recentralization of residential and industrial areas in a region that integrated metropolitan core, satellite cities, and vast parklands. With comprehensive planning of this sort, he said, there was no reason why the area within a thirty-mile radius of central Manhattan could not accommodate a population of 26,000,000 comfortably.[41] In some ways the New York regional plan was an effort to apply zoning principles to an entire metropolitan region.

The 1920s were intellectually adventurous years for new professionals trying to visualize the ideal city. Most of them were unaffected by the deep despair that characterized so many of the literary figures of that decade and remained reasonably confident about the future. They often expressed reservations about the mass culture that was taking shape in the nation, but on the whole they saw more potential in it for good than for evil, providing only that their expertise be allowed to guide technology toward social goals. On that much there was accord among them.

Beyond that there was intellectual disarray, as they got caught up in the swirling currents of the era. Some of the urbanists were animated primarily by the new values of order and efficiency, and were concerned above all with how well the city functioned. Others were fixed more on the older values of democracy and community, and were more concerned with the human implications than with the mechanical processes of urban life. Still others were inspired by the promise of technology and searched out new shapes and contexts for urban life. Some were unable to look beyond the neighborhood, others unwilling to look beneath the region. Some were utopians, others eminently practical.

To an extent, of course, categorizing the professionals in this manner is an artificial exercise that tends to exaggerate the differences among them. The urbanists who stressed order and efficiency, after all, were not devoid of human feeling or human goals any more than the communitarians were ignorant of the need for efficiency and order in urban life. The utopians did not deal in science fiction, but confined their thinking to what was at least technically possible. And the practical realists who settled for compromise through zoning were neither grumpy reactionaries nor mere tools of greedy real estate interests. The differences were as much of degree as of kind.

In the end, however, these differences generated a tension among the various factions of urbanists that was more significant than the hopes they held in common. There really was no urban vision in the 1920s. There were only separate, sometimes fragmented, and often conflicting alternatives.

NOTES

1. Haven Emerson, "The Robust City," *Survey Graphic* (November 1925):121–124.

2. George C. Nimmons, "The Passing of the Skyscraper," *Journal of the American Institute of Architects* (November 1922):356–361.

3. Frederic A. Delano, "Skyscrapers," *American City* (January 1926):1–9.

4. C. A. Dykstra, "Congestion De Luxe. Do We Want It?" *National Municipal Review* (July 1926):394–398.

5. Thomas Adams, "City Planning and City Building," *Journal of the American Institute of Architects* (June 1921):195–197.

6. Clarence Stein, "Dinosaur Cities," *Survey Graphic* (May 1, 1925):134–138.

7. John Collier, "Community Councils—What Have They Done and What Is Their Future?" NCSW, *Proceedings* (1919):476–479.

8. Ibid.

9. Hyman Kaplan, "Federating from the Bottom Up," *The Survey* (March 15, 1924):681–685.

10. Frank Charles Laubach, "What the Church May Learn From the Saloon," Ibid. (September 27, 1913):751–753.

11. John Collier, "What Shall We Substitute for the Saloon?" *American City* (February 1919):163–165.

12. Dr. Frank Crane, "A Substitute for the Saloon," Ibid. (August 1919):77. Many community workers continued to evaluate local politics in functional terms and to praise local bosses for their intuitive grasp of neighborhood customs and needs, including jobs, as much as they condemned them for their corruption. See Jane E. Robbins, "Bureaucratic and Political Influences in Neighborhood Civic Problems," NCSW, *Proceedings* (1925):391–395.

13. A few people searched for some principle other than geography to define community in the 1920s. Viewing the neighborhood ideal as an anachronism, they looked instead to functional groups—labor unions, medical societies, bar associations—for a rebirth of the community spirit. See, for instance, Allen T. Burns, "The Effects of Modern Industry on Community Life," Ibid. (1922):77–82.

14. Mary Bonner, "The Freedom of the City," *The Survey* (November 15, 1926):198.

15. Charles A. Beard, "The City's Place in Civilization," Ibid. (November 15, 1928):213–215. This was originally an address delivered at the convention of the National Municipal League and was reprinted in the *National Municipal Review* (December 1928):726–731.

16. "Will Future Cities Be Under Glass?" *American City* (April 1924):383.

17. Harvey Wiley Corbett, "Different Levels for Foot, Wheel and Rail," Ibid. (July 1924):2–6.

18. "Is Super-Congestion Inevitable?" Ibid. (June 1927):800–805.

19. Frederic A. Delano, "Skyscrapers," Ibid. (January 1926):1–9.

20. Morris Knowles, "Zoning—Its Progress and Application," American Society of Civil Engineers, *Transactions* (1923):1349–1364.

21. Charles H. Cheney, "Zoning in Practice," NCCP, *Proceedings* (1919):162–185.

22. Ibid.; John Ihlder, "Housing and the Regional Plan," *American City* (November 1926):636–638.

23. "Items and Ideas," Ibid. (June 1927):837–838. The bureau defined a multifamily (apartment) dwelling as any building that contained at least three housing units. Its figures applied to all cities over 25,000 people. In all likelihood similar comparisons for cities over 500,000 in population would have shown an even stronger bias toward apartment construction.

24. John Taylor Boyd, Jr., "How Intensively Must We Use the Land?" Ibid. (January 1928):107–110. Like most planners, Boyd preferred the single-family house but conceded that apartment buildings were the wave of the future. He warned his colleagues not to ignore them.

25. Dr. Ing. Walter Curt Behrendt, "Skyscrapers in Germany," *Journal of the American Institute of Architects* (September 1923):365–370.

26. George C. Nimmons, "Skyscrapers in America," Ibid., pp. 370–372; William Stanley Parker, "Skyscrapers Anywhere," Ibid., p. 372.

27. Irving S. Morrow, "On Modernism," *Journal of the American Institute of Architects* (December 1928):459–462.

28. W. H. Ham, "Factory-Made Homes," *The Survey* (February 15, 1929):656–657.

29. Harold S. Buttenheim, "Where City Planning and Housing Meet," NCCP, *Proceedings* (1929):114–121. Buttenheim was editor of *American City*.

30. Thomas Adams, "The Need of Town Planning Legislation and Procedure for Control of Land as a Factor in House-Building Development–II," *Journal of the American Institute of Architects* (March 1918):135–137.

31. Thomas Adams, "City Planning and City Building," Ibid. (June 1921):195–197; "Reserving Productive Areas Within and Around Cities," Ibid. (October 1921):316–319; and "Efficient Industry and Wholesome Housing True Aims of Zoning," *American City* (March 1921):287–289.

32. Joseph K. Hart, "Power and Culture," *Survey Graphic* (March 1, 1924):625–628. *Survey Graphic* was launched in the early 1920s by Paul Kellogg to supplement the more narrowly professional *The Survey* with articles of interest to reformers of all stripes. In special numbers it often devoted an entire issue to a single subject as it did in this "Giant Power" number.

33. Lewis Mumford, "The Next Twenty Years in City Planning," NCCP, *Proceedings* (1927):45–58; Clarence Stein, "Dinosaur Cities," *Survey Graphic* (May 1, 1925):134–138; Charles Harris Whitaker, "Cities Old and New–III," *Journal of the American Institute of Architects* (September 1926):404–407. The standard work on the RPAA is Roy Lubove, *Community Planning in the 1920s: The Contributions of the Regional Planning Association of America* (Pittsburgh: University of Pittsburgh Press, 1964).

34. Frederick L. Ackerman, "Cities of the Nth Degree," Ibid. (June 1926):289–291.

35. Mumford, "The Next Twenty Years in City Planning"; Stein, "Dinosaur Cities."

36. "Planning for an Urban Population of Thirty-Seven Millions," *American City* (June 1922):533–536.

37. Paul U. Kellogg, "The City Gate of the New World," *The Survey* (May 20, 1922):270–271.

38. "Beyond the City's Limits," *American City* (May 1923):437–438.

39. H. W. Dodds, "Economic Patterns of New York," *The Survey* (April 15, 1928):98–99.

40. "A Million Dollars' Worth of Ideas on City and Regional Planning," *American City* (July 1929):81–85.

41. Thomas Adams, "Forecast: The Regional Community of the Future," American Society of Civil Engineers, *Transactions* (1928):1146–1156.

5

From Americanization to American Mosaic

In the early years of the century social reformers had been overwhelmed by the number and variety of immigrants pouring into the cities. Some of them had perceived the newcomers as victims who needed help to cope with the intimidating new problems of urbanization and industrialization. Others had seen the immigrants in some ways as a cause of those very problems. These attitudes had been reflected in reform journals, which published a flow of material that tried to make sense of the situation, material that ranged from racist arguments for restriction to warm appreciations of immigrant cultural norms. In the passing years some of the professionals held to their nativist assumptions, but most of them came to accept the immigrants, if not always to embrace them. Their strong environmentalism convinced them that the immigrants would assimilate in time—if not in the first generation, then surely in the second. Eventually many of them broadened the very meaning of assimilation. But their position required that cool heads prevail over a long stretch of time where immigrants were concerned.

Unfortunately time was short and cool heads scarce as war fever mounted early in 1917. In April the air on Capitol Hill was still rancid with the aroma of racial nativism after the recent controversy over immigration restriction when President Wilson's request for a declaration of war plunged Congress into another bruising and divisive debate that raised disturbing questions about the loyalties of immigrants and the fruits of tolerance. In such an atmosphere reformers agonized more than ever about what to do with the millions of immigrants already living in the nation's cities. This question dominated the cultural politics of the 1920s and evoked some prickly responses from the participants in those years. During and immediately after the war the discussion revolved around the Americanization movement.

The broad aim of Americanization was to unify a culturally splintered society, but it worked in different ways to do it. Its best known manifestation was

"100 percent Americanism," an affliction that reached epidemic proportions among local politicians, Legionnaires, and chambers of commerce and was characterized by severe seizures of radical-baiting and union-bashing.

The aspirations of the new professionals who were involved in the Americanization movement were generally more modest, and their methods more moderate. Some of them, for instance, fulfilled their wartime obligations by working for government agencies whose mission, more than anything, was to unify the nation behind the war effort. A few of the new professionals even used this convenient federal platform to justify the continuation of their attempts to bring about social reform. It was in this role that Mary McDowell proposed to achieve national unity through goodwill rather than through the intimidation that was all too common at the time. Working for the Council of National Defense, McDowell and several of her colleagues, all of whom were veterans of the social justice movement, expressed their opposition to forcing Americanization upon foreigners who were not paid enough to achieve an American standard of living. These unfortunate souls had to work so hard just to survive that they rarely had either time or energy left for the night school courses that purported to teach Americanism. McDowell and her associates argued that the Americanization of industrial and living conditions must precede the Americanization of language and values among the immigrants. It was an ingenious attempt to keep the social justice impulse alive by linking it to the demands of a warfare society.[1]

Other new professionals saw no connection whatever between social justice and Americanization. John Gaus, an associate of Robert Woods at Boston's South End House, expressed this no-frills approach to the matter. Gaus was frankly appalled that there were more than two and a half million adult immigrants in the land who spoke scarcely a word of English, and he was dismayed at the lack of facilities to teach them. For this reason their "lawlessness and vice" and their "attachment to improper political organizations and local bosses" scarcely surprised him. He agreed that the neighborhood center might be of some assistance in the process of immigrant adjustment, but given the size and immediacy of the crisis, he knew that the neighborhood center by itself was hopelessly inadequate. "The problem is too vast, too complicated and too crucial," he said, "to be left to the spasmodic efforts of private agencies." Only a massive program of education carried on in a broad system of tax-funded night schools could bring the situation under control.[2] Significantly the neighborhood center as an instrument of social control was beginning to lose its attraction for many reformers at this time.

McDowell and Gaus represented different tendencies among the professionals involved in the Americanization movement. For Gaus there were no contextual considerations. The problem was massive but not subtle: millions of immigrants did not understand English and had no appreciation of American values; the solution was to teach them. He had no feel for the predicament of immigrants, and if anyone had raised the question, he would have dismissed it as irrelevant. In addition, his recommendations were edged with a hint of nativism that was not at all apparent in McDowell. On the contrary, the McDowell committee's recommendation that the children of immigrants be encouraged to preserve something of their cultural heritage contained the germ of pluralism, which was remarkable under the circumstances. Yet as different as were the perspectives of Gaus and McDowell, they agreed fully that the objective of Americanization was to unify the nation and that a massive infusion of public funds was needed for a crash program to educate immigrants in the language and institutions of the United States.

An even more basic assumption that unified these approaches to Americanization was the confident belief that individuals who had been shaped in a village culture of the Old World, and perhaps bent by the urban culture of the New, could be re-formed—Americanized—by a massive overlay of education. It was an expression of serene faith in the environmentalism that wired the policy professionals together and guided them toward a new liberalism that aimed to make happier people and better citizens by social manipulation.

Even in public health, where the medicobiological approach to disease now prevailed, environmentalism continued to play a major role because health workers insisted that social and economic variables were too important to ignore. One postwar study demonstrated that infant mortality among Jews was much lower than it was among the English and German immigrants, lower even than among native Americans. This flew in the face of accepted lore and raised questions for which there were, as yet, no certain answers. Walter Brown, who reported on this study to public health workers, admitted that the answer might be found in hereditary factors, but he preferred to emphasize the role of "habits" in this matter rather than genes, just as he did with personal hygiene, which, he said, was a matter of information, not race. As with literacy then, so also with health: the goal was Americanization and the path to it was education, especially about the relationship between the individual and the environment.[3]

This relationship was emphasized in a very different context by public health nurses. Like many of the professionals, these nurses saw themselves as altruists who gave their all to bring American standards of health to hapless immigrants. This image, which bore a distinct resemblance to the working realities of slum life, was colored and reinforced by the tales they routinely printed about themselves in their professional journal throughout the 1920s. The pattern was much the same in all of these mini-melodramas of tragedy and triumph: nurse encounters family with health problem; nurse introduces family to modern knowledge and techniques; problem is solved and family shows deep gratitude. An amputee father (German) is unable to care for his sick wife until the nurse instructs him how to feed and care for her; a tubercular mother (Greek) dies in childbirth, leaving a young daughter to manage the household under the guidance of a nurse; a young mother (Polish) keeps her babies clean and healthy because she remembers what the clinic taught her about child care when her first one was born several years earlier.[4] Most of these tales, whether of Greeks or Poles or Italians, were told in the same all-purpose dialect, which did not sound quite like anything spoken on the planet, but which did serve to establish immediately that this was a relationship among unequals, between the ignorant and the informed.

From time to time the journals of local nurses' associations held contests for these tales. Helen Gates, a Newark nurse, won a prize for her story about a public-health nurse going home at night on a crowded street car, bone tired and "tightly packed between a steaming humanity that exuded garlic on one side and whiskey on the other." Her mind wandered back over the long day, reflecting on events and people, from the helpless rheumatic in the morning to the pathetic paralytic at night. It had been a typical day of danger, frustration, and small triumphs. Now there was fatigue.[5]

There was also fulfillment—above all, fulfillment—for the real purpose of these little fantasies was to justify to the nurse her own existence. All of them projected the same image of nurses as angels of mercy bringing light where there was darkness, comfort where there was misery. In this underpaid occupation virtue was supposed to be its own reward, but altruism often has its price. In this case it was recognition, especially in the almost childlike gratitude showered on the nurses as their clients learned how to remodel their household patterns according to American standards of sanitation and nutrition.

One of the unforeseen consequences of this assertive environmentalism was the subversive influence it had on racism. There was a certain irony in this because many of the new professionals expressed a distaste for immigrant cultural patterns that could easily be mistaken for racism. In the end, however, there was no way that they could square their environmental assumptions with the belief that character was immutable through generations, that behavior was somehow "in the blood." In the past they had not often met this issue squarely, as often as not simply ignoring it. By the 1920s they were beginning to tackle it head on.

More than anything, what triggered this response was the immigration legislation of the decade, which was clearly aimed at the new immigrants from southern and eastern Europe. John Gavit, an editor of *The Survey*, discussed the subject after the restriction law of 1921 was passed. Gavit was not a pluralist but an assimilationist and was as unhappy as any racist with the huge case of "social indigestion" that the ghettoization of Russian Jews and Austro-Hungarians had caused. But he objected strongly to the racism that had so often clouded a clear understanding of the issue in the past. He disagreed sharply with the inferences drawn by the United States Immigration Commission in its famous report of 1907, which many people still consulted as "the Bible of the immigration question," but which Gavit felt to be mischievous in the extreme. It was that report which had first given official sanction to the distinction between "old" and "new" immigrants, and to the belief that new immigrants were less assimilable than old. Because of its respected source, that argument and the statistical evidence upon which it rested were a major weapon in the arsenal of racists and had played a significant role in the drive for restriction over the years. Now Gavit proceeded to dismantle the report. He demonstrated that the commission's own statistics failed to prove that different immigrant groups assimilated at significantly different rates. The commission and its partisans over the years had used this evidence to argue that certain groups were inherently less assimilable than others. Gavit dismissed this argument by demolishing the evidence that supported it.

Then he turned his attention to the renowned sociologist, E. A. Ross, who had deduced from the report that civic attitudes had "declined" as the sources of immigration had shifted away from northern and western Europe and that in all probability this decline had had racial origins. Gavit did not deny that there had been such a decline, but he attributed it to environmental factors: new immigrants had had less time in the nation to develop the proper attitudes toward civic virtue; lower wages and poorer working conditions operated against them; greater isolation in the slums shut them off from access to the appropriate ideals of political behavior in America. Gavit then produced his own set of statistics to support his contention that the civic interest of new immigrants was, if anything, even greater than that of old. Of course, that placed him in the peculiar position of insisting in one breath that the new immigrants must not be blamed for lagging behind in their political development, and in the next that they should be admired for excelling in it. But this sort of confusion did not really dilute the strength of his attack on racism in its most respectable guise. He destroyed the commission's argument with its own statistical weapon.[6] That did not prevent Congress from passing further discriminatory immigration legislation in the 1920s, but it helped to alienate the professionals even further from the thinking that justified it.

The larger part of this growing attack on racism was carried out indirectly, especially through the reports that rolled in on the assimilation of various groups of immigrants at the neighborhood level. Though often only implicitly, each of these reports was a tribute to the power of environmentalism and a denial of the relevance of heredity in this matter.

There was, for instance, evidence that Americanization was being pressed upon Italians, a group that many native Americans early in the century felt would be difficult, perhaps impossible, to absorb. A 1919 study condemned the Italians of Chicago for continuing such "antiquated" Old World practices as commercially arranged marriages and the subordination of women. These customs might at one time have been functional in Italy, but they were now cruelly out of temper with contemporary American norms. The report condemned the ethnic gettoization that preserved these Old World social relationships and concluded with an environmental solution to this environmental problem: Americanize all aspects of the Italian community.[7]

Just three years later signs that assimilation was actually taking place filled a report on the children of those Italians in Chicago. It had always been common knowledge among students of the problem that immigrant life was characterized by generational conflict. In Chicago many of the second-generation Italians fueled that conflict by fleeing " 'Little Italy' " for what they called a " 'civilized neighborhood.' " That gratuitous sarcasm was not lost on the parents and caused severe strains on family ties, but it indicated the willingness of many in the second generation to trim back on their ethnic heritage. Many of the earliest Italians in Chicago had come from the poorest regions in Italy; yet, it was their children who were now the "professional and business leaders in the colony—lawyers, dentists, real estate dealers and saloon keepers." The religious festivals, which had characterized the neighborhood until recently, were now rapidly disappearing because the "religious spell" was losing its hold on the younger generation. There was even evidence of Americanization in the muted tone of street life. Musicians who were once ridiculed by the American Musicians Union for playing " 'umpah' " music in street bands were now members of the union and no longer played in the streets. John Valentine recorded these changes cheerfully and looked forward to even greater Americanization in the future as Italians came into contact with "the better classes of native Americans" in day-to-day life. Just a simple invitation to an American birthday party, he said, ("nice girls in neat frocks, and boys with starched collars") would do more to Americanize an Italian youngster than a year of contact with social workers.[8]

If not a birthday party, then perhaps a patriotic event would do the job. That was the message in mid-decade of Robbins Gilman, a Minneapolis settlement worker. Like many social workers in earlier years, Gilman was trying to develop local leadership at the neighborhood level. He discussed the special problems of doing this in communities which were balkanized by a score of immigrant clusters that remained clannish, unsocial, and even hostile to one another, thus throwing up barriers that "retard the civic progress of the whole neighborhood." There was one mode of unification they could not resist, however, and that was their "American patriotism." He proposed to play to that patriotism by choosing a holiday and making it into a community celebration. He thought that Flag Day was the one most likely to enlist the support of local leaders and to encourage young and old in all groups to overcome their "racial differences" in the name of a neighborhood and an American identity.[9]

Like the community reformers of the Progressive era, Gilman did not consider the possibility that leadership in the slum neighborhoods might develop spontaneously among the immigrants who inhabited them. Leadership had to be taught and given direction by native Americans of honorable intentions. He told community workers that it was up to them to "find a neighborhood leader *to carry out [their] ideas*." (My italics.) And they had to do it without appearing to do it, or they would frighten away the very people they were trying to attract.

Gilman's ideas, even his words, were right out of the Progressive era, and they help to put the Americanization movement in perspective. Far from being simply a reflex of wartime intolerance, it was rooted squarely in the efforts of prewar community workers to use, and where necessary to create, neighbor-hood institutions that would teach American patterns of belief and behavior to the immigrants massing ominously in the slums. The war had amplified the fear of immigrants into something approaching a national panic and projected what had begun as an expression of localism onto the national scene. In the process "Americanization" emerged as a code word that lent an air of coher-ence and respectability to certain impulses that were less unified and in some cases less respectable than they appeared. Thus social workers could use the term to describe a fairly gradual and benign process by which immigrants learned new customs and attitudes, while 100 percenters could define it as the savage repression of all dissent. Unlike the melting-pot ideal, it assumed the existence of a more or less fixed national type and aimed in both cases for conformity to certain assumed American norms.

In the first few years after the war this cultural monism was only occasion-ally relieved by dissenters who argued that Americanization was a two-way process in which immigrants might have things to teach as well as things to learn. That was the theme of Herbert Miller's remarks to the NCSW shortly after the war when the Americanization movement was becoming superheated. Miller found the prevailing attitudes toward foreign languages in the United States absolutely ridiculous. There was no reason, he said, why the nation should not profit from the many languages spoken in the cities. Unfortunately the 100 percenters preferred to suppress them, even to the point of shaming little immigrant children from using them in public. Then, having denied the nation access to this wealth of linguistic resources, these zealots turned around and spent millions on programs in the schools to teach foreign languages to native children. Miller felt that the stupidity of this process was bound to hob-ble the Americanization programs sooner or later, and he was not at all dis-tressed at the prospect.[10]

For the public-health workers Americanization meant teaching modern ap-proaches to hygiene and nutrition to the immigrants. Since the welfare of the entire community was at stake here, there was very little room for cultural give-and-take. That is why public-health nurses were exasperated with the barriers of culture that stood in the way of their efforts to educate immigrants in health matters. Some of them, however, recognized that they were limited by cultural blinders of their own. Among them, for instance, it was axiomatic that when large families crowded small incomes, it was at the expense of hygiene and nutrition, and therefore of health. Since immigrant families were commonly larger and poorer than native families, most health workers concluded that im-migrants had too many children. A few of them, though, were able to see beyond the technical bias in their own field to the clashing systems of values that were the real issue here. They took their colleagues to task for their "pro-vincialism and ignorance" and even suggested that nurses would be wise to learn more about the history and customs of local immigrant groups in order "to perpetuate in [the immigrants] those ideals of their own which are of inherent beauty or value and which they might unfortunately exchange for lower American standards forced upon them temporarily by their economic status.''[11]

In the stifling cultural climate that settled in immediately after the war these expressions of pluralism were the exception, but by mid-decade the panic had run its course for the professionals. Immigration restriction was a fact of life by then, and while many of the professionals were unhappy with the racism embedded in the legislation, they at least felt some relief from the pressure to adapt a million strangers a year to American urban life. As the panic subsided, many of the professionals began to question the meaning of assimilation and their commitment to it. In the process the Americanizers were thrown on the defensive for the first time since the war.

By the early 1920s the movement was well under way. Ethel Bird, a Chicago social worker with impeccable ethnic credentials, attacked Americanizers for the facile distinctions they made between old and new immigrants without understanding much about either and for failing to view any of them in relation to the economic conditions that prevailed when they entered the country. Emphasizing her own Anglo-Saxon origins, she fired off a heavy salvo at Anglo-Saxon 100 percenters who believed ''that the Italian immigrant is a better prospect for citizenship when he has substituted pork and beans and brownbread for spaghetti and a salad of greens on Saturday night.'' And she still had some ammunition left for those social workers who expected immigrants to adjust to frontier values. She pointed out that these European peasants were entering an industrial nation which had vastly different personal, job, and class relationships from anything they had known in the old country. It was unrealistic to expect them to make such extensive adjustments in only one generation. Instead, she recommended vaguely a process of mutual adjustment in which native and immigrant would learn from each other.[12]

In that light the very concept of Americanization seemed evanescent, and it was precisely in that light that Bradley Buell examined it before the NCSW in 1925. Asked to evaluate Americanization in one of New York's poorest immigrant neighborhoods, Buell, an official with the Council of Immigrant Education in New York, and thus as qualified as anyone to speak on the subject, confessed that he did not have the faintest idea how to begin such a task. To be sure, he said, one might wrap certain kinds of information in neat, statistical packages—the incidence of some disease in an immigrant group, or the frequency of its use of English—but these categories only described conformity to established standards, and that was not really the same thing as Americanization, which involved one's entire way of looking at the world and behaving toward it. Nor did it help much to teach immigrants how to mouth a few patriotic shibboleths. That only led to sloganeering, which meant as much or as little as one privately wished it to mean. That was the trouble with Americanism—it meant all things to all people.

What, then, was Americanization? For 1925 Buell's answer was daring. Americanization, he said, was a process that involved the modification of one's values and attitudes, of one's total outlook. It was learned by immersion in the culture, by "the simple fact of living" in America, and was not taught in the sense that geography or English were taught. The implications of this definition were profound, for if Americanization happened simply by living in America, then it was happening to everyone all the time, though perhaps more visibly to immigrants than to natives. But that raised a disturbing question. If the dominant environment modified *all* values and attitudes, then what happened when that environment had a predominantly foreign flavor? The question was not academic by any means, since that was precisely the case in many of the big cities where immigrants and their children constituted large majorities of the population. Who established the norms of belief and behavior in those cities?

Buell raised this question specifically about New York, where natives who could trace American ancestry back to 1790 were a small minority of the population—no more than 10 percent, he thought—while Jews and Italians were almost half. In such a milieu who was the typical New Yorker, the typical American? Buell's answer was a monument to changing attitudes:

The most typical New Yorker I know is a Russian Jewess who came to this country when she was very young, who went through the famous garment workers' strike of fifteen years ago, who was a leader in the suffrage movement, not only amongst the labor group, but with the club women as well, who has lived on the East Side, West Side, up and down town, whose daughter is a member of one of the leading artists' groups in the city, and a musical and theatrical critic. . . . She is the best product of this inevitable process of adjustment and assimilation that I know.

It was an ironic reversal of the traditional position on assimilation. In New York it was now the Americans who had to be Americanized![13]

For Buell, Americanism apparently had no fixed meaning; it varied with time, place, and circumstance; it was one thing in New York and another in Kansas; its essence was change. He stood in sharp contrast to the more parochial views of prewar community workers, who believed that the environment acted selectively—never at all, it seems, on middle-class native Americans, but constantly on the poor and the foreign, to their detriment and society's also. The objective of those early reformers was to transform the foul environment of the poor into something resembling the model environment of the middle class. It took applied social intelligence, by which they meant the vigorous application of their own values, to accomplish that. Buell pursued the logic of environmentalism a crucial step further. For him the environment acted on everyone constantly, and thus shaped character constantly in an almost deterministic manner. Americanization happened with or without human will, and where human will was involved the results were as likely as not to be destructive.

Of course the logic of Buell's effort to free assimilation from the meddling of the 100 percenters quite accidentally threatened to free it from the meddling of the professionals as well. After all, the same dominating environment was at work in both cases. But Buell did not press that point, and the other public-service professionals were certainly not about to press it for him. They had enough on their hands defending environmentalism from the rampant racism of the 1920s.

That chore was not made any easier by the tendency in popular culture to associate specific ethnicity with specific crimes. Social workers had been exploring the alleged correlation between crime and immigrants for years, and were already minimizing it before the war. If anything, they concluded, immigrants committed proportionately fewer crimes than natives. The children of immigrants were another matter. Available evidence in the Progressive era indicated that they were more likely to commit crimes than either their parents or generational natives, a fact which social workers explained easily enough as a consequence of the moral no-man's-land they occupied between two cultures in tension with each other. The question was raised again in the 1920s as a direct result of the spectacular display of violent crimes related to prohibition and committed, from what one could tell in the press, primarily by South Italians and Sicilians. It forced the social workers to refine their techniques of social research and to elaborate the data that sustained their environmentalism.

How far they had come by the late 20s and how far they had still to go were demonstrated in a paper that E. H. Sutherland read to the NCSW in 1927. "Do immigrants commit more than their share of crimes?" he asked. Regretfully he admitted that no one could answer that question persuasively yet because there was still so little information available on the subject. Then, undaunted by the scarcity of data, he used what little he found to support a completely cultural explanation of criminal behavior. He confirmed the findings of earlier years that the overall crime rate among immigrants was substantially lower than that among native whites of native parents. But what about all those Sicilians committing mayhem and murder on the streets? What Sutherland found was that Italian immigrants in Massachusetts did indeed commit homicide at a rate about six times higher than for generational whites, which was on the face of it a very significant statistical difference. Did that support a racial interpretation of crime? Was there something in the genetic makeup of Italians that inclined them somehow to murder? Merely to phrase the question in those terms nowadays is to dismiss it, of course, which makes it all the more poignant that Sutherland had to address it that way in 1927. He proceeded to pick the racial argument apart by adding other variables to his analysis. Thus he found it revealing that almost all these homicides were committed by males. Furthermore he demonstrated that while the children of Italian immigrants committed more *crimes* than their parents, they committed far fewer *homicides*, fewer in fact than native white Americans of native parents. Given such enormous discrepancies between the deeds of husbands and wives, and of fathers and sons, Sutherland said, there was absolutely no way to argue that there was some discernible racial tendency for "hot-blooded" Italians to commit murder.

Eventually Sutherland's environmentalism swept him beyond the bounds of prudence dictated by his own reservations about the shortage of reliable information. Basing his observations on the slenderest of data, he concluded broadly that immigrants had a much lower crime rate than native whites; that some immigrant nationalities did "specialize" in certain types of crimes; that these were inevitably an expression of old-country cultural heritages and lasted for no more than one generation; and that both the rates and types of crimes were likely to change drastically from the first to the second generation as such American factors as mobility came into play. "Such variations as occur," he asserted, "are cultural rather than biological." [14]

In some ways this reaffirmation of environmentalism and the stirring of cultural pluralism in the 1920s were responses to the virulent nativism of the decade, though it was probably a case of the devout preaching to the devout, of professionals lecturing professionals without much immediate impact on popular racism. But their discussions did serve to clarify and set the thinking of the professionals themselves on the subject and prepared them for the international controversy that exploded from it in the 1930s.

Before that, however, their environmentalism was further clarified by their growing awareness of blacks in American society. During the Progressive era they did not pay much attention to blacks, probably because there were so few in northern cities compared to the great numbers of immigrants. Still, there were blacks caught up in the vortex of urban poverty before the war, and from time to time the new professionals did turn their attention to them. When they did, their analyses were almost indistinguishable from their discussions of immigrants.

The reformers had settled on a few themes early in the century to explain the relationship between the immigrant and American society: peasant immigrants have the capacity to become good urban Americans; some immigrants even bring the requisite adaptive qualities with them from the old country; immigrants rapidly develop organizations and institutions to serve their cultural and economic needs, and therefore promise not to be a long-term burden on the nation; bridges must be built between immigrant and native communities to relieve existing social tensions. Quite often these ideas were fed to the professionals by the more articulate immigrants themselves. [15]

Unaltered in any serious way, these themes filled a special issue that *Charities* ran in 1905 on blacks in American society. Like the immigrants, blacks were described as rural migrants to the city who were ill prepared for urban life and whose lives were thus characterized by a distressing amount of social disorganization which required social treatment.

Most of the essays in that issue were conciliatory, but conciliation was never the forte of W. E. B. Du Bois. Du Bois contributed an angry and sardonic piece on blacks in Philadelphia politics. He, too, emphasized the pattern of their migration from rural South to urban North, where they were as vulnerable as babes in Babylon. Drifting into social clubs for the good times they offered, the migrants—particularly the younger ones—soon discovered the political foundations of these clubs through the generous favors dispensed by the local boss. In this way the neophyte gradually got caught up in what Du Bois characterized as "a network of intrigue, influence and bribery" that included police, judges, criminals, prostitutes, and respected businessmen. In other words, they were drawn into the complex demi-world of machine politics. Even the "better class" of Negroes, he said, benefitted from the machine as the grateful recipients of patronage jobs. After all, Du Bois said bitterly, making a living in a racist society was not easy for any black, and it certainly took precedence over civic pride and idealism, which is why blacks responded to crooked bosses and ignored good-government reformers. It was a matter of survival. Du Bois saw a parallel between politics in Philadelphia and politics in the Reconstruction South a generation earlier. In both cases thieving whites manipulated "ignorant Negroes" in order to loot the public treasury. Learning quickly, Du Bois said, "the Negroes followed their [white] leaders and stole and looted too." The only thing that surprised him was that this should surprise anyone. The disease was not race; it was corruption, and the only cure was equality.[16] In certain ways Du Bois held the same moral position as the good-government reformers of that era, but because he was on the other side of the color barrier, he was able to grasp the functional implications of political corruption, and thus, unlike most of the "goo-goos," to blame the socially respected more than the socially despised. It was precisely the argument that a handful of settlement workers were piecing together at the time to explain the political behavior of recent immigrants.

And that was the problem too, for the plain truth was that most of the new professionals were too occupied with the "immigrant problem" in the Progressive era to pay much attention to the "Negro problem." That would come later. For the time being it was easier simply to view Afro-Americans as immigrants in blackface. Few people were aware yet that these blacks from the rural South were the vanguard of a new folk migration heading for the nation's cities. With the coming of the war, however, that became more apparent as the demand for labor rose, the supply of immigrants fell, and blacks were beckoned to fill the gap. At that point the professionals took a more serious interest in the situation.

As was so often the case, *The Survey* played a prominent role in their expanding social universe. By the time the war was over, it was already including blacks as permanent additions to the storehouse of urban problems. Early in 1919 George Haynes wrote on some of these problems. Haynes, a Fisk University professor who had advised the federal government on matters involving black laborers during the war, was genuinely pleased with recent developments in racial affairs, and almost recklessly hopeful about the future. He conceded that racism, segregation, wretched housing, and labor hostility made conditions in the North grim, but these reservations could not shake his optimism. He preferred to emphasize that tens of thousands of "peasants" from the rural

South were adjusting to factory work and moving into skilled positions; that real wages were better in the North than in the South; that housing would improve soon; that the decline of immigration would create a labor shortage; that labor leaders were promising to organize workers in the future without regard to color; that biracial conferences were sprouting everywhere to promote racial harmony. As Haynes saw it, the future was indeed promising.[17]

It didn't turn out that way, as everybody learned a few months later in the tragic summer of 1919. Until then, no city had embodied the hopes of the black labor force more than Chicago, a center of heavy industry where these recent arrivals from the South had found steady employment in spite of their lack of skills. In the meat-packing industry alone over 12,000 blacks were employed without serious problems by the end of the war. Then, at the end of July the city exploded in a frenzy of racial animosity. By the time the blood stopped flowing, more than three dozen people lay dead, more than 500 had been injured, and a few thousand had been burned out of their homes. Dead, wounded, homeless—in all cases the great majority of victims were black.

The postmortem began almost immediately. Reviewing the situation in *The Survey*, Graham Taylor remarked that nobody should have been surprised at what had happened because "the lightning that set Chicago's race antagonisms aflame did not strike out of a clear sky." The only people not aware of escalating racial tensions, he said, were those who refused to see what was before their very eyes. Taylor's friends from the Black Belt told him that the ferocious racial massacre in East St. Louis two years earlier had rung the alarm for blacks everywhere, and that many had begun to arm themselves in self-defense as a result. All the while, Chicago's black population was expanding rapidly—it doubled in the five years after 1914—and minor racial incidents were occurring with increasing frequency. Then, in late June 1919, posters appeared in the Black Belt warning ominously, " 'We Will Get You July 4.' " A wave of anxiety swept through the South Side, and more blacks than ever armed themselves. Independence Day passed without incident, but by then Chicago bristled with small arms and large hostilities. The tension was almost unbearable, and needed only a single incendiary incident to set the whole city off.[18]

Taylor's was only the first in a string of analyses that were triumphs of hindsight. The most serious attempt to understand the calamity was set in motion by Governor Frank Lowden when he appointed a biracial committee to investigate Chicago's entire racial situation in depth. Three years later the Chicago Commission on Race Relations released its report, and its conclusions suggested that there would be no rapid resolution of the American dilemma. Contrary to the wartime dream of people like George Haynes, it said that full and equal employment was not just around the corner. And contrary to a misconception shared by many, racism was not a simple reflex of economic friction. It was deeply buried in the mythic fiber of the nation. According to Bruno Lasker, who summarized the report for *The Survey*, the commission resolved the nature/nurture controversy in favor of a completely environmental explanation of any observable differences of behavior or intellect between blacks and whites. Indeed the commission helped to formulate and publicize what became the standard liberal attack on discrimination in decades to come: employers generally find Negro labor to be as efficient as white labor; depreciation of residential property in black neighborhoods is not due to the racial traits of black tenants but to the class greed of white landlords; black criminals are not genetically inclined toward crime but environmentally driven to it. Lasker placed special emphasis on the commission's observations about "group myths," pointedly quoting its discussion of the "sex myth" about blacks, including their "predilection for sex crimes" and the obsessive fears harbored by many whites for the alleged sexuality of black men. Lasker offered no explanation for these myths and fears, but he made his point effectively: white racism was too complex and deeply rooted to dissolve in wishes alone.[19]

For all the agony of 1919, at least the employment picture was still reasonably bright, but by the early 20s even that had darkened. In the recession winter of 1921 *The Survey* noted that "the latest to be employed in the industrial plants, unskilled Negroes have been among the first to be discharged." As a result, thousands of black workers in the North, released from mine and mill jobs in town and country, drifted toward the big cities, only to find that there were no jobs for them there either. And so they stood around idly because there was nothing else to do and placed a heavy new burden on local relief facilities. In Pittsburgh the labor unions, which claimed to be free of discrimination, ignored them, but the police did not, arresting hundreds of blacks as vagrants. The professionals were learning more hard truths about American racism. They learned the meaning of the aphorism "last hired, first fired." They learned that labor unions were indifferent to blacks and that police were hostile. They learned that the layers of the problem did not peel off easily. And in a Pittsburgh mission house they learned how much a part of urban America these new migrants had become. The black down-and-outers were asked if they were going to return to the South now that there were no more jobs in the North. The answer was brief and conclusive: "Like Hell we are."[20]

Public-health personnel also rediscovered blacks in the 1920s. In the past they had often employed a crude geneticism to explain differences between blacks and whites in such matters as death rates and life expectancy. Now they began to interpret observed racial differences in an environmental context. Franklin Nichols reviewed the evidence on this question and inferred from it that the health of blacks had improved wherever educational and economic conditions had been improved, thus confirming "the experience of Negro public-health experts that their people do not suffer high rates [of disease and death] because of race *per se* but from environmental conditions susceptible to correction." Since the good health of both races was affected by the poor health of either, he continued, and since differences in health were determined largely by differences in environment, it followed that the health of both races would improve as environmental fetters were removed from blacks.

Nichols was seeking to attract more black women into public-health nursing, which he set down as a prerequisite to any improvement in either the quantity or quality of health care for blacks, since public health was essentially segregated throughout the country. The training and the pay of black nurses was often inferior to that of whites, and Nichols suggested that it might be "much better for all concerned not to employ the colored nurse . . . if her training is so far below standard as to make necessary a salary difference." In fact that was one of the areas where Nichols wanted to eliminate environmental differences. Raising the educational standards and the pay would attract more and better black women into public-health nursing, and ultimately raise health standards for both races.[21]

Similar considerations worried George Shaw in mid-decade. A Philadelphia housing official, Shaw described how an already frightful housing situation had been further strained by the influx of 10,000 blacks from the rural South in the past year alone. Unaccustomed to city life on any terms, these people were now forced to live it on the worst of terms. In such circumstances, he argued, decent housing was absolutely necessary "to arrest the spread of disease and moral degeneration" not just for the good of these new Philadelphians, but for the good of the entire community. There was more than a trace of moral smugness in Shaw, but it was not, after all, substantially different from the sort that native reformers had customarily expressed toward recent immigrants. At least as important were other assumptions drawn directly from the Progressive Textbook of Urban Reform: health and morality were environmentally determined; races and classes lived in dangerous proximity in the city; consequently decent housing for those at the bottom of the social scale was not only morally correct but socially necessary.[22]

In this way the black American entered the consciousness and calculations of the new professionals. It was a cumulative process that originated in the migrations from the South before the war and expanded without undue fanfare through the early 1920s. Then in 1925 *The Survey* invited a group of black intellectuals to help broadcast the news. The result was a special issue on Harlem that announced the arrival of the "New Negro."

The emergence of black Harlem was described by the poet, novelist, songwriter and diplomat James Weldon Johnson, a renaissance man of the Harlem Renaissance. Johnson described the transformation of Harlem after the turn of the century when black tenants without sufficient housing made common cause with white landlords without sufficient tenants in this recently overbuilt section of the city. At first the response of Harlem's white residents had been apathetic, but apathy soon changed to resistance, and finally to panic and flight. The transformation was largely completed during the war when the promise of steady jobs and good pay drew thousands of blacks to Harlem from the South. What followed, as Johnson described it, was an almost trite expression of the American success myth, in which some of the most unlikely of the newcomers—the "washerwoman," the cook, the street vendor—began to invest their earnings in real estate, until blacks now owned more than $60 million worth of Harlem property. "Today," he said, "Negro Harlem is practically owned by Negroes."[23]

Johnson's pride in Harlem property owners was matched by his hopes for Harlem workers. Shrewdly he observed that black workers in Harlem differed in one significant respect from those in other northern cities. In Chicago's stockyards and Detroit's automobile factories blacks were hired by the thousands as "gang labor"—and fired the same way whenever business slackened. By contrast, he said, most black workers in New York were employed as individuals, not as units in a gang. Moreover, the increasing trend toward Negro-owned small business in Harlem was broadening the employment opportunities of black workers as individuals. One important consequence of this, Johnson felt, was that in Harlem black workers were better insulated against the shock of economic crisis than they were elsewhere in the North. Another was in the way that it transformed southern sharecroppers into northern cosmopolites. Working as a gang in a steel mill, he said, a thousand Mississippi Negroes remain just a thousand Mississippi Negroes. In the conditions of individuation that prevailed in New York, however, Mississippi Negroes "become good New Yorkers" within six months. Job security and rapid assimilation were two reasons why Johnson was confident that "there is small probability that Harlem will ever be a point of race friction between the races in New York." As it turned out, unfortunately, this analysis gave a deeper look into the mind of Johnson than into the dynamics or the future of Harlem.

More than the other contributors to this issue, it was probably Alain Locke who created for the new professionals an image of black Harlem and its inhabitants. A professor of philosophy at Howard University, Locke served as unofficial spokesman for the Harlem Renaissance in the 1920s, bringing its artists and intellectuals to the attention of the world outside Harlem. It was thus altogether appropriate that he be asked to edit this special edition of the *Survey Graphic*.

The main character in Locke's presentation was the "New Negro," and Locke was at pains to establish a separate identity for him.[24] The Old Negro, said Locke, was a product of historical forces, to be " 'kept down' " or " 'helped up' " according to sectional preferences nurtured most recently in the Civil War and Reconstruction. His southern oppressors acted to hold him down at all costs, his northern liberators to elevate him. In either case he was the white man's creation, a set of stereotypes that grew, sadly enough, from the needs of his oppressors and liberators alike. Largely as a matter of survival, blacks had played out their lives for white Americans in the roles provided by these distorting stereotypes, mammies and Samboes singing bloodless Methodist hymns. But no more. Now new social forces were emerging, drawing blacks northward into the great cities, and transforming a racial problem defined by sectional differences into an industrial problem defined by class differences. In the wake of these monumental changes the New Negro was replacing Sambo, and "race pride" was overcoming racial submission.

Yet Locke's emphasis on race pride was curiously qualified, for he conceded that this new sense of race was primarily a consequence of racism itself. It was "an attempt . . . to convert a defensive into an offensive position, a handicap into an incentive." Buried in this affirmation was the belief that racial differences were of no fundamental significance, and therefore that race pride ought not to exist. Thus race pride was an expedient imposed upon blacks by a white America that insisted upon playing the game by the rules of racism.

While whites used racism to justify shutting blacks out of American society, Locke saw race pride, under the proper conditions, as the source of moral power by which Negroes would reenter it as equals, as Americans. The choice, he said, was "between American institutions frustrated on the one hand and American ideals progressively fulfilled on the other." Reminding his audience that those ideals made no distinctions of color, he called upon blacks to take full moral advantage of the gap between a color-blind creed and a color-bound practice. In the end, he said, "we cannot be undone without America's undoing."

Although he saw hopeful signs of interracial amity among business and intellectual elites in various parts of the country, Locke had no doubt that dreams for the future centered in Harlem. The Harlem that he described was unknown to most whites at the time, which emphasizes the importance of his discussion, and, for the new professionals, of this entire issue of the journal.

Physically, said Locke, Harlem was indistinguishable from the rest of New York. Its pattern of shops, restaurants, apartments, and churches was repeated all over Manhattan. To those who commuted through it daily, as to most of the world, the only thing that set Harlem apart at all was that it was "unaccountably full of Negroes." There were other Harlems as well, little fragments of reality that were accurately enough represented to the public, yet distorted in their essence. There was the cabaret Harlem of "racy music and racier dancing" that was on "the exotic fringe of the metropolis" for the "connoisseur in diversion as well as the undiscriminating sightseer." And there was the "Harlem of monster parades and political flummery," a Harlem that was "grotesque with the distortions of journalism."

Locke introduced a different Harlem, one that was appropriate to the emergence of the New Negro. He portrayed a community that was the focus of a new folk migration, comparable in significance if not in numbers to the westward movement of the nineteenth century and to the emigration from Europe in recent decades, and similar to both in its "vision of opportunity, of social and economic freedom." Pouring in from North and South, from the West Indies, from Africa itself, drawn from city and country, from peasants and professionals, the new black migrants were a mixed lot from mixed backgrounds who discovered in Harlem the common tie of color. "So what began in terms of segregation," he said, "becomes more and more, as its elements mix and react, the laboratory of a great race-welding." In the past Negroes had shared a common condition, but not a common consciousness. Now Harlem was changing that in its bid to become the capital of a race, the "home of the Negro's 'Zionism,' " playing the same role for the New Negro that Dublin played for the new Irish and Prague for the new Czechs.

Opportunity and self-reliance, democracy and equality, Prague and Dublin—what Locke served up in these essays was a relatively bland compote of ritual American values and fashionable Wilsonian self-determination, an offering that was perfectly tailored to his audience of liberal reformers in the 1920s. Even his elitism made contact with the policy professionals at a certain level. Moreover, Locke's tone was as safe as his symbols, for he managed to assert race pride without any racist overtones and to be insistent about it without being abrasive. At a time when Marcus Garvey's racial separatism was shocking and offending many white reformers, Locke's mainstream Americanism must have been very reassuring.

In view of the continuing sporadic outbursts of racial conflict, it might also have been necessary. In Detroit the gradual expansion of the black ghetto into a previously white neighborhood led to a violent confrontation in 1927 that frightened city officials. A biracial committee was appointed to investigate the conditions of the "dark southerners in Detroit" and within a year presented a report that echoed the conclusions of the Chicago Commission a few years earlier, placing an even stronger emphasis on the primacy of environment as the determinant of behavior. Bruno Lasker related how the committee attributed higher crime rates among Negroes to the "vicious environment" in which many were forced to live, the discrimination by police and courts, and to different attitudes toward the law conditioned by historical circumstances since the days of slavery. In a similar vein the subcommittee on education traced different levels of performance in the schools to environmental factors. It conceded that a large proportion of black children were "retarded," but asserted that "the causes of retardation nearly always have an environmental basis" in such factors as working mothers, oppressive neighborhoods, or inferior schooling in the past.

Lasker's own optimism for the immediate future of race relations was at best guarded. He noted that in Detroit, as earlier in Chicago, there were no provisions made to carry out the report's recommendations. Moreover, in the event of an industrial depression Negroes, who already lived perilously close to subsistence, were likely to fight for their jobs. Thus the potential already existed for even sharper racial confrontations in the future. For Lasker the most hopeful sign was that blacks would no longer have to fight alone, since "influential individuals and groups" were now willing to join them in the quest for justice.[25]

Ralph Bunche saw different cause for hope late in the 1920s when he analyzed the role of blacks in Chicago's machine politics. Like the Progressive reformers before him, Bunche described the classic *quid pro quo* of boss politics, in which the dispossessed support a candidate in return for some sort of recognition or reward. In this case the boss was Bill Thompson, that irrepressible fox in Chicago's political hen house. Thompson, a Republican, had earlier served two terms as mayor before being defeated in 1923 by William Dever, a Democratic reform candidate. In 1927 he set out to recapture city hall from the uninspired Dever and, with the Democrats running a cruelly racist campaign, swept to a victory in which blacks provided 75 percent of the victory margin. Clearly he had benefitted from the doubling of Chicago's traditionally Republican black population since his first triumph in 1915. Bunche, himself a black, reported that "negro [sic] leaders shared generously" the political plums that were distributed locally after the election and that they were liberally rewarded as well with patronage jobs at the state level by the Republican administration in Springfield.[26]

There is a striking parallel between this essay and the report by W. E. B. Du Bois on Negro politics in Philadelphia nearly a generation earlier, but there was a striking difference also, for the Du Bois article was infused with the reform values of the era. It left no doubt that machine politics was reprehensible. Bunche, on the other hand, refused to condemn the system and even refrained from passing judgment on Thompson himself, who is not generally ranked among the more attractive politicians in an era that was not overcrowded with attractive politicians. What he did see in this election, and more broadly in northern urban politics, was the beginning of a political resurgence that would eventually lead to the enfranchisement of blacks in the South once again. It was a remarkably prescient observation.

The professionals were generally encouraged by the prospects for increasing racial harmony as the decade passed, but racism did not yield to environmentalism easily. A study of Negro public-health nurses financed by the Rosenwald Fund revealed a wide range of attitudes on the subject in 1920. Many agencies in the country expressed reservations about these nurses: they were slow in abstract thinking or reluctant to study or deficient in administrative abilities. Some of the nurses reporting, to be sure, were enthusiastic supporters of the work done by black women in the field and wished only that there were more of them. Others were less charitable and might have agreed with the Alabama official who felt that black women were uniquely qualified to work with black patients as long as they were "not overtrained until they lose the characteristics of their race" or with the disgusted health worker in Philadelphia who announced that "it was extremely unfortunate that Civil Service requirements made employment of Negro nurses possible." At the same time, Stanley Rayfield, who reported on this study, dismissed the alleged deficiencies of black nurses as the consequences of "disadvantages of environment in early years" and asserted that "community health has no bounds in race or creed and needs the wholehearted efforts of all elements in this community."[27] Obviously not all health workers agreed.

Occasionally racial stereotypes even got tangled up in data and gave an odd twist to otherwise cautious research. In a study of morbidity and mortality among black workers in Cincinnati, Floyd Allen, a public-health physician, said that the

average negro [sic] is a care-free sort of person who gives little thought to the future so long as he feels well, has plenty to eat, a place of shelter, and can indulge in the social life of his choice. It is in all likelihood this method of living, with little thought of restraint and less concern about the ill-effects, that accounts for the inception of many of the physical ills to which negroes fall heir.[28]

Actually Allen's article had nothing to do with the "inception" of health problems. Moreover, it shrewdly noted sharp *class* differences in health among blacks and strongly implied that racial differences in health were susceptible to environmental modification and eventual elimination. In such a discussion implications about the happy-go-lucky black man were gratuitous at best, but they reveal how cultural stereotyping might still short-circuit professional standards. There was also a familiar ring to the assumption that an individual who lives for the moment and indulges in sensual pleasures will pay the price with his health in the future. A generation earlier many of the professionals had projected that judgment onto the immigrants. Some of them were still doing so in the 1930s, except that the target was now more likely to be blacks.

It was to that persistent strain of racism that M. O. Bousfield addressed his remarks at the APHA meetings late in 1933. Bousfield, a physician and medical director of a Chicago life insurance company, was concerned with the difficulties that many white health workers had in communicating with black clients. Bluntly he attributed this to their ignorance of the special sensitivities of blacks, and he set about to correct some of the "common errors" that caused all the trouble. He informed them, first of all, that "Negro is a proper noun," and had to be capitalized when written. Anything less was an insult. He also gave them a few basic "don'ts" to keep in mind when they addressed a black audience: don't discuss your "former experiences with colored people"; don't boast about how unprejudiced you are; above all, don't try to warm up your audience with "the 'darky' story in dialect." No matter how innocent the intent, he said, these devices invariably trip alarms that alienate Negro audiences and had to be avoided at all costs.

At the end of his address Bousfield departed from his subject to praise "the inspired leadership of Franklin Delano Roosevelt" and to predict better days ahead under the new Democratic administration. The NRA, he noted, was already aiming for equality of wages between the races, and he fully expected that health officers would now insist that the New Deal provide equal health facilities, too.[29]

Since the end of the war in 1918 two major themes had grown out of the discussion among professionals about—and by—Afro-Americans: whatever the

Negro was, he was the product of his environment; whatever the Negro had been, he was changing into a New Negro. In Bousfield's talk these themes fused, and an old one reappeared. The new environmentalism implied racial equality; the New Negro insisted on it; now, once again, government was expected to promote it.

Unfortunately the New Negro encountered the same Old Caucasian with the same old results: poverty, misery, disease, premature death. As a consequence, the nation discovered still another Harlem in the mid-1930s. It was not the Harlem of cultural renaissance, nor the Harlem of fashionable cabarets, nor the Harlem of "political flummery," but the larger Harlem hidden behind all these public masks, a Harlem of frustration and rage that exploded early in 1935. Unlike the sporadic racial strife of the preceding two decades, the "Harlem riot" did not pit black people against white, but black people against property, against Harlem, against an entire social system. It began with an incident and a misunderstanding, then a rumor, then confusion and anger, and then all hell broke loose. It was not so much a riot as a rampage. As usual a prestigious biracial commission was appointed to hunt down the causes of this social disaster.

One thing was clear to the professionals immediately: this was not the Harlem they had encountered in *Survey Graphic* a decade earlier. That Harlem had been teeming with philosophers and poets, with property owners and independent workers, with diverse Negro subcultures fusing in a black melting pot to produce the culturally fertile and psychologically tough New Negro. There had been some muted allusions to discrimination at the time, but on the whole the Harlem of the New Negro in 1925 had been sunlight without shadows. Indeed the tone of that issue had been so resolutely upbeat that no one could have forecast from it the trouble that lay ahead.

When the trouble came, it was *Survey Graphic* once again that stepped forward to interpret Harlem for the professionals, and Alain Locke once again who was the interpreter. But this time it was a chastened Locke describing a bleak and ominous Harlem. Since the mid-1920s, he noted, conditions had gotten worse, not better; the jobs of Harlem blacks had proven to be no more depression-proof than the jobs of blacks anywhere else, which was not at all; and it had become clear that discrimination was not just the fading legacy of an unhappy sectional past, but the very heart of the problem in the North, as it had been in the South. In this way, Locke placed discrimination at the center of his discussion. Systematically he examined Harlem life in the light of evidence drawn from the report of the commission, and the conditions he found were pathetic. *Employment*: blacks were unable to find work that matched their training or abilities, could not get jobs in the very Harlem shops that depended upon their patronage, were denied entry into key unions, were even barred from some of the work relief programs of the New Deal in New York City; statistics supplied. *Housing*: blacks paid higher rents than whites for greater crowding in poorer quarters; statistics supplied. *Health*: blacks were burdened with antiquated equipment, inadequate facilities and racial understaffing in their own hospitals; statistics supplied. Locke did nothing to soften this description of a "dark Harlem of semi-starvation, mass exploitation and seething unrest."[30] With the possible exception of health workers, the professionals were long overdue to learn about it.[31]

By the late 1930s events in Germany helped to set the issue of ethnic minorities in a wider perspective. Most of the professionals had registered their disapproval of Nazism from the beginning, but they had misjudged it as a revival of Prussian militarism, a category that was conveniently at hand as a leftover from the recent world war. Besides, it all seemed so remote from the exciting social experiments that were under way in the early years of the New Deal. As a result, they did not pay much attention at all to Nazism at first. It was the dramatic anti-Semitic outburst at the end of 1938 that convinced the professionals that something quite different from Prussian militarism was at work in Germany. Shocked, they denounced the Nazi regime for its apparent complicity in the outrage. The Nazis responded by inviting the Americans to stay out of German affairs, at least until they had solved the problem of lynching in their own country. It was a painful reminder that recent efforts to pass federal anti-lynching legislation had run afoul of congressional hostility and White House indifference, and the reformers were unable to ignore it. "Every time we are moved to raise our voices in protest against cruelty and injustice in other countries," William Neilson commented sadly, "our effectiveness is diminished by the knowledge that we have not put our own house in order."[32]

But that did not silence them. On the contrary, it stirred them to carry on their discussions of minorities in American life thereafter with constant reference to Nazi beliefs and practices. Before long they concluded that racism and democracy were incompatible, arguing that since racism was basic to Nazism and Nazism held democracy in contempt, and democracy was basic to Americanism, then racism was plainly un-American. The logic of all this was not exactly unassailable, but the argument was effective nevertheless because it juggled symbols that took precedence over logic for most Americans.

This conviction that democracy and racism were mutually exclusive played a major role in the growing latitudinarianism of the professionals. In a special number of *Survey Graphic* early in 1939 they worked out their position in considerable detail. William Neilson set the tone in his overview of the minority situation in the United States. He surveyed America's record with its many ethnic, religious, and ideological groups and gave it a mixed review. The treatment of French-Canadians was improving, he said, but the situation with Mexican migrant labor was deteriorating and might blow up at any time. He was solicitous of the civil liberties of Jehovah's Witnesses in their struggle against local authorities who were trying to compel their children to salute the flag in school, but he was not willing to extend those rights to domestic fascists, whom he was prepared to suppress with the armed might of the state if necessary, because their beliefs implied the use of violence against American institutions.

On the whole Neilson concluded that things were improving for the nation's minorities, and he was optimistic about the future. His one major reservation involved the status of blacks and Jews in America. He saw no cause to rejoice over the limited gains made by blacks since Reconstruction while many parts of the country still systematically denied them equality of opportunity, equality before the law, and the right to vote—the fundamental moral, legal, and political rights of all Americans. Moreover, now that the meaning of anti-Semitism had been laid bare by developments in Germany, Neilson was unwilling to remain silent before the "Nazi falsehoods" of that "mouthpiece of Nazi government," Father Charles Coughlin. To stand by passively just because Jews had made impressive strides in politics, the professions, and the arts in recent years was to lend credence to Coughlin's lies, and thereby to jeopardize the freedom of all Americans. "We are all in some respects members of minorities, racial or religious, economic or cultural," he said, "and once the democratic principle is abandoned no one's liberty is assured." [33]

By universalizing the concept of "minority" in this way, Neilson's argument represented a significant shift in the manner of perceiving ethnic groups in American society. Ordinarily in the past even the most generous assimilationists had viewed minorities in terms of a we/they society. *We* are the custodians of American norms; *they* will assimilate those norms and become perfectly respectable Americans like us in time. As Bradley Buell had done in the mid-1920s, Neilson erased the distinction between "we" and "they"; as a result his nation of minorities pointed toward a pluralistic society that was reasonably casual about who had to conform to what, and therefore had enough room in it to accommodate the quirks and customs and fancies of all sorts of groups— except those he chose to characterize as domestic fascists.

Other contributors to this issue made a detailed exploration of the territory sketched in by Neilson. Lewis Gannett hammered away repeatedly at the parallel between Jews in Germany and blacks in America. "The Negro in the South," he said, "is as the Jew in Germany, today." And again, but without sectional limitations this time, "Like the Jew in Hitler's Germany, [the American Negro] is a second class citizen." Until America lived up to its democratic obligation to include Negroes as full-fledged members of society, Goebbels was perfectly justified in condemning his American critics for their hypocrisy. [34] Gannett then documented his charge of hypocrisy by discussing the educational, economic, political, and social status of blacks in the United States. What made his discussion especially noteworthy was that he set it in a comparative framework. He did not simply say that black children in Alabama received a poor education, which everyone already knew, and which after all was only a judgment open to argument, but that the one-third of Alabama's school children who were black were educated with only one-eighth of the state's educational funds. That moved the discussion from the level of misfortune, which was perhaps the province of the pulpit, to the level of inequality, which was decidedly the domain of the bench. Gannett dealt in similar terms with voting and jury duty in the South and with housing all over the country. Throughout this angry essay his standard was "democracy," by which he apparently meant equality of opportunity. The bitter reality was that he had to emphasize his point with reference to a different minority in a different nation.

Not that there was cause for rejoicing about the condition of Jews in America. Alvin Johnson, the director of New York's New School for Social Research, made that point in his analysis of the rapid spread of anti-Semitism in the United States in the past few years. Johnson viewed anti-Semitism as an anomaly in the liberal democratic state, and, worse, as a threat to the very survival of democracy in the hands of conservative businessmen who might wish to manipulate the Jewish question for sinister political purposes, as they had in Germany. Johnson identified several strains of anti-Semitism, ranging from "instinctive anti-alienism," which was not really anti-*Semitism* at all, through the farmer's hatred of middlemen and the businessman's fear of competition, to the "parlor anti-Semitism" of wealthy men who tried to express virility in front of their approving women by mouthing blood-curdling sentiments, and the demented anti-Semitism of those people who could not make sense of the world except in terms of vast conspiracies. These ideas were spread by more than 800 organizations, from the one-man show run on a shoestring by some fanatic to the nationwide network financed, in all probability, by Nazi Germany. In spite of this recent upsurge of anti-Semitism, Johnson was optimistic, in part because the roots of democracy were deep in America, and in even larger part because the historic conditions on which anti-Semitism fed were now disappearing. He pointed out hopefully that third-generation Jews were finally dropping the Yiddish language, that they were leaving their residential enclaves, and that they were breaking away from their "unhealthy concentration in commercial pursuits." Instead, he said, one found them nowadays increasingly in the working class. There were even some encouraging signs that they were moving to the soil.[35]

There were many themes running through Johnson's brief essay, not all of which were handled smoothly. Not the least of them was his own ambivalence—his strong conviction that anti-Semitism was un-American and perhaps a capitalist plot, and at the same time his aversion to what might be called the symptoms of Jewishness, its "clannishness," the use of Yiddish, the excessive pursuit of commercial enterprise. He was also inconsistent about the meaning and future of anti-Semitism. He was hopeful for the future because the conditions that stimulated anti-Semitism were fading; yet his whole essay was about the shocking *increase* in anti-Semitism precisely when a second and even a third generation of Jews were abandoning some of the visible symbols of their Jewishness. At the same time, he described a few completely irrational expressions of anti-Semitism that seemed to exist independently of time and historical circumstance, and therefore to cast a shadow over the future of this problem. Johnson also expressed the timeless American reverence for the farmer and mixed it uneasily with the very timely infatuation with the working class, just when Jews were preparing not to enter the working class but to leave it, and not for the soil either. In contrast to Neilson, Johnson expressed an abiding commitment to assimilationism and a faith in the power of the environment to bring it about. That was the bedrock of his assumptions.

For the next year or so, until "preparedness" began to dominate their allusions to Germany, the professionals found Nazism a useful point of reference in their mounting attack on racism. The assimilationists among them liked to point out how anyone could become an American; the pluralists, on the other hand, preferred to admire the American mosaic, with its "tradition of tolerance toward minority groups which is the very foundation of our democracy."[36] Assimilationists and pluralists alike found it convenient to bolster their positions by contrasting them with the refusal of the Nazis either to accept Jews as Germans or to respect them as an internal minority. Any tendency toward excessive pride by the professionals was normally balanced by an equal tendency toward self-criticism. When they spoke of the "tradition of tolerance" in America they knew they were speaking of an ideal and that there was an uncomfortable gap between ideal and reality. Perhaps for that reason they were all the more eager to bring Germany into the discussion. It enabled them to say that over there things were getting worse, over here, better. Somehow it seemed to narrow that gap between ideal and reality.

By the early years of the century the United States had become unmistakably urban, and its cities undeniably "foreign." That is why the cultural history of those years was tense with movements trying to define some standard of Americanism to fix on the nation. Although these movements varied considerably in style and content, they did share a common tendency to find their inspiration in the past. Looking back, nativists saw a largely Anglo-Saxon population, found the nation's greatness in the qualities of that population, and acted to shut down immigration that did not conform to that image. Advocates of "temperance" believed that new immigrants did most of the drinking in the nation and that drink was undoing all the old values of production; they acted to memorialize those values in laws that anathematized alcohol and stigmatized the people who consumed it. It was in a similar spirit of trying to preserve a fading America that many of the early professionals looked fondly back to images of family and village in preindustrial society and tried to recreate them in the urban neighborhood.

The war intensified all of these movements. For the new professionals it meant broadening the context of their thinking from the neighborhood to the nation and thus attracted many of them to the Americanization movement. But nationalizing their efforts only pried them loose from their commitment to the village values of the past without offering anything more concrete in its place than an ill-defined notion of Americanism. They wanted the immigrants to conform to that, but they were not really clear about just what "that" was.

By the mid-1920s a new breed of public-service professional, usually younger than the pioneers in the policy fields and drawn increasingly from various ethnic minorities, began to advance the idea of cultural pluralism as an alternative. There was nothing new in honoring immigrant cultures, of course. Many of the professionals had been paying homage to them for years. But homage did not necessarily imply pluralism because it did not insist that these cultures be preserved and fashioned into a pattern for the nation. The settlement workers who encouraged immigrants to display their quaint native costumes and folk dances on scheduled ethnic days never really doubted that the descendants of those immigrants would one day soon conform to American standards. With few exceptions they were profoundly committed to assimilationist ideals.

Between the wars many of the professionals rejected that model. For them the ideal was not one dominant culture that would absorb all the others or one that would emerge from the homogenization of many, but a culture of cultures, a mosaic. Some of the professionals were attracted to this ideal in the 1920s. Others were frightened to it in the late 1930s when they saw how easily monoculturalism was fused with racism in Germany and how destructive an alloy it produced. Thus by 1940 pluralism was competing on more or less even terms with assimilationism for acceptance by the professionals as the model for America's future.

The emergence of pluralism signified a dramatic change in the way that many professionals addressed the problem of minorities in American society. The assimilationists had put a premium on movement toward an American ideal. In the past their discussions had been framed in terms of how rapidly the new immigrants were moving in that direction. Implicitly they placed most of the burden on the immigrants themselves. The pluralists claimed to respect all minorities on their own terms. Their analyses tended to concentrate on the limits of American tolerance rather than on the rate of immigrant assimilation, and thus to lay most of the burden on American society rather than on the immigrants. This shift added to the increasing emphasis on discrimination in American society and helped open that process, too, to the diagnosis and treatment of the policy professionals.

The growing understanding of Nazism helped the professionals put environmentalism and racism in the proper relationship to each other. The biological assumptions of Nazi racial thinking meant that no amount of education or indoctrination could ever make a Jew, or a Slav, or a Gypsy into a German. The new professionals proceeded from environmental assumptions about the adaptability of individual character and believed that with time and the proper conditioning anyone could become an American—whatever that was. Racism was inherently *exclusive*; environmentalism was inherently *inclusive*.

Among the new professionals between the wars, then, racism collapsed under the weight of environmentalist beliefs. At the turn of the century intellectual systems for ranking races had been respectable modes of academic thinking. They claimed the support of science and offered legitimized ways for social critics to weigh alternative solutions to the problem of minority groups in

American society. And racism had its share of adherents in the burgeoning public-service professions at the time. By the end of the 1930s the role and meaning of minorities in American society was scarcely better understood than it had been a generation earlier, but racism was now under attack as a mode of analysis. It had lost whatever credibility it ever had as science, and its consequences in Germany were forcing the professionals to address its consequences in the United States. As much as anyone, they made racism an unacceptable category to use in public discussions of minority problems.

That left environmentalism unchallenged in their eyes as a social creed for policy decisions. On those terms environmentalism offers an explanation and a solution for every social problem; it tells us what is wrong and what to do about it. But it does not, by itself, tell us *how* to do it. That comes from other sources.

NOTES

1. "Making the Foreign Born One of Us," *The Survey* (May 25, 1918):213–215.

2. John Merriman Gaus, "A Municipal Program for Educating Immigrants in Citizenship," *National Municipal Review* (May 1918):237–244.

3. Walter H. Brown, "Health Problems of the Foreign Born," *AJPH* (February 1919):103–106. See also George T. Palmer and G. Arthur Blakeslee, "Infant Mortality in Detroit," Ibid. (May 1921):502–507; and William H. Davis, "The Relation of the Foreign Population to the Mortality Rates for Boston," Ibid. (January 1924):9–21.

4. Margaret Mary Hutchinson, "Life," *The Public Health Nurse* (February 1923):93–95; Dorothy Deming, "A Greek Tragedy," Ibid. (April 1928):170–172; Ruth H. King, " 'Clean An' Regular,' " Ibid. (September 1929):477–478.

5. Helen Gates, "Nurse-in-Gray," *Public Health Nursing* (July 1931):315–317.

6. John Palmer Gavit, "Americans by Choice," *The Survey* (February 25, 1922):815–821.

7. "Chicago's Italians," Ibid. (April 19, 1919):115.

8. John Valentine, "Of the Second Generation," Ibid. (March 18, 1922):956–957.

9. Robbins Gilman, "Leadership and Strategy in Community Organization," NCSW, *Proceedings* (1925):385–390.

10. Herbert Adolphus Miller, "Treatment of Immigrant Heritages," Ibid. (1919):730–735.

11. Michael M. Davis, Jr., and Bessie Ammerman Haasis, "The Visiting Nurse and the Immigrant," *The Public Health Nurse* (October 1920):823–834.

12. Ethel Bird, "Social Attitudes Conditioning Immigrant Maladjustments," NCSW, *Proceedings* (1923):303–309.

13. Bradley Buell, "Results from the Standpoint of Americanization," Ibid. (1925):369–375; and "The Immigrant in the Community," Ibid., pp. 616–626.

14. E. H. Sutherland, "Is There Undue Crime Among Immigrants?" Ibid. (1927):572–579.

15. This was particularly evident in articles written for *Charities* during much of 1904 by representatives of many different ethnic groups.

16. W. E. B. Du Bois, "The Black Vote of Philadelphia," *Charities* (October 7,

1905):31–35. See also Fannie Barrier Williams, "Social Bonds in the 'Black Belt' of Chicago," Ibid., pp. 40–44.

17. George Edmund Haynes, "Negroes Move North," *The Survey* (January 4, 1919):455–461.

18. Graham Taylor, "Chicago in the Nation's Race Strife," Ibid. (August 9, 1919):695–697.

19. Bruno Lasker, "The Unmaking of a Myth," Ibid. (October 1, 1922):46–49.

20. "A New Negro Migration," Ibid. (February 26, 1921):752.

21. Franklin O. Nichols, "Opportunities and Problems of Public Health Nursing Among Negroes," *The Public Health Nurse* (March 1924):121–123.

22. George H. Shaw, "Housing Problems in Philadelphia," *AJPH* (May 1924):401–403.

23. James Weldon Johnson, "The Making of Harlem," *Survey Graphic* (March 1, 1925):635–640.

24. This discussion of Locke is drawn from two essays that he wrote for this issue of *Survey Graphic*. See Alain Locke, "Harlem," Ibid., pp. 629–630, and "Enter the New Negro," Ibid., pp. 631–634.

25. Bruno Lasker, "The Negro in Detroit," *The Survey* (April 15, 1927):72–73, 123.

26. Ralph Johnson Bunche, "The Negro in Chicago Politics," Ibid. (May 1928):261–264.

27. Stanley Rayfield, "A Study of Negro Public Health Nursing," *The Public Health Nurse* (October 1930):525–535.

28. Floyd P. Allen, "Physical Impairment Among One Thousand Negro Workers," *AJPH* (June 1932):579–586.

29. M. O. Bousfield, "Reaching the Negro Community," Ibid. (March 1934):209–215. Bousfield obviously knew his audience. A few years later the president of the APHA eased into his presidential address with a sexually oriented darky story. See Arthur T. McCormack, "Public Health the Basic Factor of Social Security," Ibid. (November 1937):1079–1088.

30. Alain Locke, "Harlem: Dark Weather-Vane," *Survey Graphic* (August 1936):457–462, 493–495.

31. James H. Hubert, "Urbanization and the Negro," NCSW, *Proceedings* (1933):418–425.

32. William Allan Neilson, " 'Minorities' in Our Midst," *Survey Graphic* (February 1939):101–103.

33. Ibid.

34. Lewis Gannett, "We're Another," Ibid., pp. 109–112.

35. Alvin Johnson, "The Rising Tide of Anti-Semitism," Ibid., pp. 113–116.

36. "The Mosaic of America Today," *Public Health Nursing* (November 1940):649.

6

Planning and Control

Government had played an important role in the plans of the new professionals from the beginning. Their concern for health, welfare, morality, and efficiency was already reflected in a sprawl of local and state laws that regulated housing, sanitation, and working conditions early in the Progressive era. In the super-heated climate of the 1910s the reformers turned to Washington, where their activities helped bring in the first federal legislation for social welfare. Throughout those years they generally had to scratch and claw for every concession from government at any level. Then, during the war the federal government found the professionals useful, and the professionals in turn were delighted to contribute their time and expertise now that their purpose was the government's purpose. By the end of the war they could look back with some satisfaction over a quarter century of activity in which they had established their reputations and taken the first strides toward their goals in a steadily expanding political arena. They had every reason to look ahead to a postwar era of "reconstruction" in which local, state, and federal governments would play a central role.

As things had worked out over the years, their attitudes toward reform and government were closely linked. They emerged from the war with a strong feeling for both, and when their passion for reconstruction cooled in the early 1920s their commitment to government—especially to the federal government—wavered. By then reconstruction was beginning to seem fanciful to many of them.

The whole process was reflected in the city planning movement. By the end of the war planners were agreed that federal action for social reconstruction was the order of the day. Elmer Jensen, one of many architects gravitating toward the planning movement at the time, expressed his satisfaction with the progress of reform in recent years. He praised the wartime use of experts in the nation's service, suggesting that this had set the precedent for a future in which trained intelligence would be employed as common practice by government acting in the public interest. With that in mind he predicted that the federal government would continue to expand its public welfare activities after the war, using planners and architects to design decent housing and rebuild the cities along more sensible lines.[1]

Alongside the early views of Frederick Ackerman, Jensen's expectations were modest. Ackerman ridiculed the way that cities were planning without coordination and without real purpose, as if each stood isolated in an economic and moral vacuum. Boston planned for Boston, New York for New York, Philadelphia for Philadelphia, when it was now possible to formulate a plan for the entire Atlantic Coast, indeed for the entire nation. This plea for integrated "nation planning" looked far beyond the physical layouts of rivers and harbors and the relationship of city and countryside to a realm of social and moral perfection which he felt to be within reach. Still flush with the fever of wartime activism early in 1919, he proclaimed that America's "national purpose" in peacetime as in war was to achieve a level of democracy "which assigns to the individual the highest value and yet demands that for the good of all he victoriously subordinate himself."[2] In broad strokes Ackerman portrayed a future shaped by federally directed national planning, humanized by democratic values, and socialized by community rights. It was the high-water mark for one variant of Progressive thought.

To men like Jensen and Ackerman the war had finally proved the need for planning. For public-health workers it was a different story. Health professionals had not had to wait for the war to confirm the value of their calling. They had grown accustomed to success in health affairs since the 1890s, when they experienced the first in their remarkable string of victories over communicable diseases. Thereafter their reports time after time told of reduced rates of illness and death, of more vibrant health and greater longevity. The unbroken curve of professional success left them completely unprepared for the shock they felt in 1917 and 1918 when hundreds of thousands of young men were found to be physically or medically unfit for military service and for their complete helplessness before the murderous flu epidemic at the end of the war. These experiences convinced them that the federal government must get more involved in health affairs through a vast expansion of activities in research and education, and by establishing a federal department of health with cabinet status.[3] On that as a minimum almost all of them could agree. Some of them had even larger plans for the federal government.

That was particularly true of the shrinking minority in the profession who persisted in placing health in a social context. Their stronghold in the APHA was the Sociological Section, which had been founded in the Progressive era before the medicobiological outlook had become so dominant among public-health workers. When Ira Wile addressed it as chairman in 1920, he spoke to the widening gap between private medicine and public health, and he made his own position pointedly clear. "Social medicine," he said, is antithetic to individual medicine in its basal concepts. It aims to function through the social group for the benefit of the social group. It recognizes health as a right rather than as a privilege. It refuses to acknowledge the propriety of a stratification of the population in so far as health is concerned, and aims to afford equal opportunities for all groups of the population, regardless of color, creed or social and economic distinction. Socializing medicine, in a word, is democratizing medicine.

This involved what Wile called "a transference of viewpoint from the individual to the mass," and ultimately "a reinterpretation of existent problems in the light of social causation, social pathology, social diagnosis, and social treatment."

More than simply curing disease or preventing it, what Wile had in mind here was "creating health" through organized efforts on a nationwide basis to raise living standards. Thereafter, "creating health" became a rallying cry in the public-health movement, and helped infuse the profession once again with a social outlook by the 1930s. Prudently, Wile explained that he had no wish to do away with private practice. It would survive, he said, but it was obviously not equipped for the mission he had outlined. Although he offered no concrete program here for creating health, Wile was clearly thinking in terms that included extensive activities by the federal government. He supported the idea of housing subsidies and demanded that departments of health throw their weight behind all measures that might increase family income and establish minimum living standards.[4]

Thus for Wile, as for most of the public-service professionals, the war itself did not snuff out the impulse for social reform. If anything, it confirmed their belief in the march of progress, it encouraged them to carry their commitment to social welfare into the early postwar era, and it persuaded them that the federal government was where they should work to carry out their most ambitious projects.

In the next several years this consensus broke down. Many of the policy workers began to feel that there was something unprofessional about social passion; embarrassed, they abandoned reform. Others gave up on government entirely and put their faith instead in private agencies and institutions. Still others continued to call for government activism, but concentrated primarily on the state and municipal levels. Only a relative handful continued to look to Washington for inspiration or the fulfillment of social ideals until late in the 1920s. These changes were apparent within a few years of the armistice.

Among the first to express their doubts were the planners, many of whom had been enthusiastic participants in federal housing programs during the war. Clarence Stein did not even wait for the war to end to reject a federal solution to the housing problem. He did not object to federal activism in wartime, when men of broad vision and large abilities ran things cheerfully and effectively, he said, but he had absolutely no faith in the federal government to do anything constructive after the war, when a pork-barrel mentality would dominate Congress and small men would run the federal bureaucracies. When he proposed using unemployed ex-soldiers in public works projects after the war to build schools and low-cost housing and to develop harbors, it was on the condition that it all be done through the state governments and that it be done quickly before the "interests" had a chance to come together and defeat these programs.[5] Stein's reservations about a federal solution were rooted in his contempt for federal politicians and bureaucrats, not in free-market fears about government welfare programs.

Frederick Ackerman, who had had such high hopes for "nation building" in 1918, was having some serious second thoughts two years later; by then his social analysis had shifted palpably leftward, and his hopes for a solution within the system had dimmed appreciably. It was pointless, he said, to expect the excesses of capitalism to be curbed by a government that was run by capitalists for capitalists. He elaborated upon this point a few years later when he attacked housing subsidies as a fraud because they served primarily to subsidize property owners, producers of building materials, builders themselves, and lending institutions.[6] For very different reasons, then, Stein and Ackerman both soured quickly on government planning.

By the early 1920s many other professionals were muting their calls for federal assistance or abandoning the idea altogether, though rarely for the same reasons as Ackerman. There were even public-health workers who looked exclusively to the private sector for a more effective distribution of health care. Ernst Meyer, a health expert with the Rockefeller Foundation, estimated that there were 34 million cases of illness annually that were denied medical treatment. This neglect did not affect the rich, who could afford to pay for care, he said, or the poor, who received it free in clinics. It struck at the middle classes, and the reason was that the medical profession had priced itself out of their reach because its traditional approach through individual physicians was grossly inefficient. Meyer's solution was to reduce costs by rationalizing and collectivizing medical services in private, fee-supported medical centers or clinics. These centers would provide comprehensive health services on a community basis, with the best physicians and specialists using the most modern equipment.[7] In a way, Meyer's plan was the medical analog to the idea of the neighborhood center which had attracted so many social workers in the Progressive era. The idea of private community health centers won a great deal of support among public-health workers in the 1920s.

Still, most of the professionals in public health saw those centers as adjuncts to government programs, not as replacements for them. As often as not they pressed for an expansion of government activities, and they did not hesitate to recommend some nakedly oppressive procedures in the name of public health. But they almost always trimmed their suggestions to the dimensions of municipal government in those years. Early in the decade, for instance, Hardy Clark described the crushing work load piled onto health officers in recent years, and outlined a plan for the administrative reorganization of municipal government that would shift some of the burden from health to welfare departments. At the center of his plan he placed a "welfare agent" whom he endowed with vast discretionary powers to deal with the ignorance, bad habits, and general disorder in child rearing that made a menace of so many households. This agent would control everything from the prenatal care of the unborn to the complete home environment of the growing child, including "instruction in hygiene, social diseases, [and] prevention of tuberculosis."

The real novelty in Clark's plan was his proposal that welfare nurses be empowered to administer a battery of tests, which they would use to grade each family on such things as the quality of home atmosphere (such as sunlight, cleanliness of bed clothing, playmates of children), the "remedial physical condition of children" (skin diseases, neglected teeth, overweight), and the "social or character qualities of children" (sense of responsibility, use of time, "foolish remarks"). Each "test" had ten "questions" worth anywhere from 0 ("very bad") to 10 ("perfect") points. Clark implied that there was some objective scale for grading the tests, but obviously in such matters perfection was strictly in the eyes of the beholder. As a consequence so was corrective action, which was no small matter as it turned out, since Clark was not just working out some hypothetical model. He was advocating the widespread use of the system already practiced in Long Beach, California, where he was a public-health physician, and where children who received an unacceptably low grade on the "test" were sent to a municipal correctional center for character training—repeatedly if necessary.[8]

Professional health officials had never hesitated to support governmental action that might limit personal liberty, as long as public health was the intended beneficiary, but they were reluctant to concede the same right to those whose interests might prove detrimental to the health movement. That was the way they responded to the fundamentalist effort in the 1920s to ban the teaching of evolution in the schools, which they attacked ferociously because it aimed to translate by legislation the opinion of one interest group into a code of conduct to which everyone had to conform, thus curbing basic freedoms.[9] There is no record, however, that they expressed similar concern for the repressive implications of Hardy Clark's Long Beach plan. This squabble over when to justify government repression (its supporters *never* call it that) has become one of the abiding differences between traditionalists and modernists in the twentieth century and a recurrent test of the limits of freedom.

Social workers were probably more faithful to the federal government than other professionals in the decade, but only marginally so. It was that faith that sustained John Fitch when he bitterly attacked U.S. Steel for its unrelenting opposition to the eight-hour day in the aftermath of the corporation's smashing victory in the postwar steel strike. Fitch pointed out that steel workers, forced to work an eighty-four-hour week, were left with no home life, no social life, no recreation. What shaped their lives was constant, unrelieved, numbing fa-

tigue. The consequences of this situation, he said, were so destructive to society that they gave the public cause to work for change. But how? With the
workers unable to win concessions and the corporation unwilling to grant them,
a negotiated solution in the private sector seemed out of the question. In Fitch's
view the only solution was for the federal government to legislate the eight-
hour day across the industry.[10]

At the same time, other leaders in the field simply ignored the federal government, even when they discussed the same broad social topics that had had
reformers thundering for federal legislation before the war.[11] As much as anything else, this probably reflected their appraisal of the men who ran Washington at the time. If many of them gave up on Washington for a while, it was
because they felt that Washington had given up on them.

By the later years of the decade the professionals had difficulty holding their
silence, and their accumulated grievances began to spill over in suggestions for
greater federal action. As early as 1926, Richard Bolt outlined a system of
federal-state cooperation in public health that foreshadowed developments in
the 1930s. A pediatrician, Bolt was fed up with sloganeering about personal
liberty and states' rights when it came to questions of health. "Socially and
economically," he said, "the whole country is so interdependent that the welfare of one state may condition the welfare of all." In such a situation it was
foolish to rely upon the states alone. Instead he proposed a compromise in
which the federal government would subsidize the states for public health, and
the states would administer the funds in order to fend off the bureaucratic controls of a federal government that had no feel at all for local problems. He
pointed approvingly to the Sheppard-Towner Act of 1921, which allocated federal funds for the states to use in promoting maternity care and infant hygiene
and welfare. Opposed only by some private doctors and religious cultists, he
said, the measure had been especially effective in the poorer states (which
never would have appropriated the funds on their own) and had the unanimous
support of public-health officials all over the country. What Bolt wanted was
the extension of this principle to other areas of public health.[12]

When John Lapp voiced similar concerns a year later in his presidential address to the NCSW, it was like a call to arms. Lapp was disgusted with the
prevailing mood of "excessive individualism" in the country, with the appalling revival of Social Darwinism, and in general with the "philosophy of the
jungle" that appeared at the moment to dominate American society. He appealed for a return to the spirit of social justice, and he minced no words in
spelling out that "government is the only agency that can effectually protect
human beings in their essential integrity. Legislation is the means by which
conditions favorable to justice may be created."[13]

Sentiments such as these gathered support well before the stock-market crash
in 1929, especially as professionals pondered the anomaly of increasing technological unemployment in the midst of dazzling prosperity. The way they saw
out of that situation was to make a major commitment to public works. Paul

Kellogg spoke elegiacally of "the people who drop through the fissures of our prosperity." To save them America needed some equivalent of the English and German systems of unemployment insurance. What Kellogg proposed, however, was nothing like that. Instead of unemployment compensation he blocked out a long-term system of public works to relieve endemic unemployment and, if necessary, to check the downward spiral of depression. He predicted that "this problem of security (would) be the great social cause of the next ten years." [14] For the summer of 1929 that was not a bad forecast.

The social implications of economic instability were a major topic at these predepression meetings of the NCSW. While Kellogg took on technological unemployment, Dora Worcester was tackling the subject of living standards for the working poor. In some ways this was an even more sensitive matter, since it raised questions about the persistence of poverty among those people who practiced the virtue of hard work. Worcester condemned the Hoover commission report on economic trends as a cover-up that used gross statistics on consumption to hide the misery that prevailed at the lower end of the social system. She accepted the estimates of $2,000 per year as a subsistence income, observing that this would not provide for lettuce in the diet or a radio in the parlor, and then pointed out that the average full-time wage for a factory worker was less than $1,300. In the face of this information, she said, no one could deny that millions of Americans lived at a level below subsistence not because they were lazy or improvident but because of "the prevailing wage scale in American industry." [15]

Periodically in times of relative prosperity Americans who live in comfort discover with surprise and indignation that there are many other Americans who don't. It is part of the "progress-and-poverty" mentality. This rhythmic rediscovery of poverty is often a powerful stimulus to social reform. It played a major role in the social-justice movement of the Progressive era and was more than tangential to the reformism of Lyndon Johnson's Great Society in the 1960s. Unheard above the din of clacking ticker-tapes, the reformers were rediscovering it in 1929 before the crash and were beginning to work out analyses of the problem, and solutions to it, that supplemented past wisdom and became the stock-in-trade of liberals for many years to come.

This rediscovery of poverty in the late 1920s enabled the professionals to take the first impact of the depression almost in stride. When the stock market collapsed in 1929, scarcely any among them thought that a depression lay ahead, and certainly not a Great Depression. They were already aware of growing technological unemployment and the first year of the depression seemed to be little more than an extension of it. Anyhow, President Hoover had promised not to let the situation get out of hand, so they were not terribly alarmed. Even before the crash many of them had begun to consider the possibility of stabilizing business by plunging into public work programs. William Parker, an architect, suggested that government money spent on such projects at the beginning of a recession would encourage private capital to reinvest, thus maintaining production and employment and preventing a downturn from sliding into a depression.[16] That predepression suggestion dovetailed nicely with Hoover's pledge, immediately after the crash, to "speed up the construction activities of the Government" if necessary. Architects felt reassured, and they looked forward eagerly to 1930 when lower building costs would act as an incentive to the construction industry.[17]

By the following spring professionals were still hopeful, if no longer exactly buoyant. Social workers were growing concerned with what they called the "unemployment situation." The Family Welfare Association of America sent out a questionnaire to its members and discovered that relief expenditures in January were double what they had been just one year earlier. Nevertheless, well over half the welfare agencies expected conditions to improve in the next few months while only one-quarter were pessimistic about the near future.[18] Even the gloomy stories filtering out of such industrial areas as Detroit did not stampede the professionals.[19] Throughout 1930 they were wary of the faltering economy, but they remained unconvinced that it was anything more than a passing squall.

That all changed in 1931. By the time the depression was ending its second year, the tone of their reports was darkening. The trend was apparent in the impact of a "rent riot" in Chicago's Black Belt that ended when the police killed three people at the demonstration. The news shocked Chicagoans because the black community there was usually rather quiescent, traditionally conservative in politics and orthodox in religion to all outward appearances. But there are limits to quiescence, and those limits were violated by prolonged official indifference to rising unemployment and deteriorating housing conditions in Chicago's Black Belt. Local radicals helped direct the rising unrest into neighborhood demonstrations against eviction, until one of the demonstrations erupted into violence. To white politicians who promised breadlines blacks were now responding, "You tried that last winter, brother; what we want out here is jobs."[20] To the reformers the unrest was understandable but unsettling.

The prevailing response to this economic deterioration was to advocate relief of one sort or another. The preference of the reformers was for work relief, and their journals were studded in the very early 30s with tales of work relief in various cities. In Detroit, Frank Murphy rode to power as mayor on a platform dominated by the promise of relief in that stricken city, and once in power he began to emphasize the need for massive *federal* aid. In Indianapolis, work relief was giving the taxpayer something for his money and sustaining the morale of the poor, because they were earning public funds with honest work. In Cincinnati employers were persuaded to share responsibility with public officials by retaining the entire work force at reduced hours while local and state governments took up the slack with programs of public works.[21] Such activities, which were widespread early in the depression, preserved the illusion that a temporary emergency could be handled by private and public initiatives at the state and local levels.

From the outset, however, there were those who insisted that for an emergency of this size no solution was possible without federal intervention. At first these admonitions were limited primarily to the reformers who were already inclined toward federal solutions before the crash, but by 1932 almost all the professionals came around to that position. Flogging Congress for its inactivity as early as 1930, *American City* demanded an immediate emergency appropriation of $1 billion for public works to stimulate the economy and make a positive contribution to the nation in the form of better bridges, highways, and flood control.[22]

Still, people in positions of authority were slower to come around to this position. In the past the response to economic crisis had always been retrenchment, and that was the course that was followed in most parts of the country in the early 30s. In 1931 half the health agencies that responded to an APHA questionnaire said that they suffered minor budget cuts. A year later more than two-thirds of these agencies were cut by an average of 11 percent. Salaries suffered, and in some cases entire health departments were eliminated.[23] Thus by 1932 cutbacks were seriously eroding the professional activities of the reformers.

They were also eroding their spirits. In the first year or two of the depression the professionals acted as observers commenting on the casualties of hard times. Then suddenly they were the casualties. One social worker described how it felt. At the outset, he said, there had been the months of feeling sorry for the growing ranks of the unemployed, observing them—shabby-genteel apple salesmen on streetcorners, beaten men in breadlines, stunned men on park benches—and wondering what it felt like to be in such a pitiful state. He learned soon enough when he found himself out of a job. At first he didn't mind because now at least he had the time to do things he had been putting off for months—an article to write, some books to read, concerts to hear, foreign neighborhoods to explore, friends to visit. But it did not work out that way because idleness is not the same as leisure. Life began to lose its tang for him. First he was listless; then anxiety set in. "You lived from mail to mail, fearing to leave the house." Maybe the next mail would bring a job. For a time optimism fought off fear, but eventually fear won out. After that even eating and sleeping were difficult. For the first time in his life he thought of himself as a failure. The only thing that relieved him from the growing panic were the occasions when he was able to do volunteer work. It did not pay him anything, but at least he was able to regain his self-respect, knowing that he could still do something positive, that he could still help others. He drew a lesson from that. He learned that only useful work could keep up one's morale—not relief, nor merely "made work," but "real work, work with a purpose, work that builds up self-respect and a sense of worthwhileness that will serve as a bulwark against the destructive flood of the feeling of inferiority."[24] That became a basic principle of social welfare in the 1930s.

For architects the outlook was just as bleak. Even in the best of times most of them did not have to beat off clients. By the end of 1931, as they approached the worst of times, their morale was sinking rapidly. All about them they observed cities in disrepair. Here they were, uniquely equipped to design utopias from this rubble, and instead many of them had to beg for jobs on federal building projects. The government was employing over two hundred private architects temporarily on such projects late in 1931, but the funds were due to run out, and those jobs would then revert to architects permanently employed by the Treasury Department. The AIA therefore supported a bill in Congress to renew the funds for these projects, rationalizing its position in ideological terms (The use of *private* architects on public projects stunts the growth of bureaucracy and promotes the republican ideal of private initiative), when all it really wanted were more jobs for hungry architects. But the bill was defeated and architects were forced to join the breadlines in growing numbers.[25] In his presidential address to the AIA, Robert Kohn made no effort to gloss over the crisis. The raw truth was that architects were desperate for jobs and often desperate for food, he said. In New York City alone there were 1,700 unemployed architects and draftsmen early in 1932. Many had had to take jobs as office help or repairmen. Others were not so fortunate.[26]

By 1932, then, the public service professions were drying up for lack of funds, and the professionals themselves were in a state of anxiety and despair from the unemployment that was spreading through their ranks. In short their condition was not much different from that of anyone else in the country. As a matter of principle and professional commitment they had been demanding for decades that government help those who were not able to help themselves. In the early 1930s they added self-interest to principle when they found themselves without jobs and began to use their professional associations as pressure groups to try to get them. It is not surprising that they responded to the New Deal with unparallelled enthusiasm.

Even before the election of 1932 many of the policy professionals believed that action would be taken soon, if only because they were convinced that action had to be taken soon. That feeling permeated the NCSW meetings at Philadelphia in 1932. A few years earlier many professionals had taken at face value President Hoover's pledge to act against further economic deterioration, but the President's currency was being heavily discounted at these meetings. His Secretary of the Interior, Ray Lyman Wilbur, addressed the conference and assured the audience that there was nothing to worry about, that children were really thriving in the present emergency because adversity was pulling families closer together again. The social workers listened in disbelief and then hooted derisively at Wilbur for the rest of the week. One participant observed maliciously that at least Wilbur advanced the cause of democracy by stimulating some very free speech at the convention. The sense of betrayal by the Hoover administration was expressed by the city manager of Cincinnati, who fumed that Hoover had promised in 1928 to abolish poverty but since then had " 'succeeded only in abolishing security.' " Amid the outrage there was a general sense at the conference that federal relief was inevitable, that federal unemployment insurance was not far down the road, that federally subsidized housing as a part of a public works program was at least a possibility, and that a Republican administration was not likely to provide any of these things.[27]

Even in the months between election and inauguration, when the nation was careening, rudderless, toward total collapse, the professionals buzzed excitedly at the prospect of social regeneration. They took heart from a New Dealer like Rexford Tugwell, who said that the road to prosperity lay through increased purchasing power, and that the way to increase it was to implement a public works program of great magnitude. To meet the worst aspects of the crisis, he advocated an immediate program of direct relief for the indigent, but the center of his scheme was a recommendation to start at once on a $5 billion public works program, with special emphasis on slum clearance.[28] Of course Tugwell did not have carte blanche from Roosevelt, as the professionals—and Tugwell—found out soon enough. But they knew he was part of the new president's "brains trust," and that alone was enough to raise their hopes about prospects for the immediate future.

Katherine Tucker, a leader in the public-health nursing movement, expressed the confidence and some of the lingering uncertainty that the professionals felt in 1933. "We face the fact that we are entering upon a new era, a new order," she said, "chaotic at the moment in so many aspects of life but full of untold possibilities." She did not know exactly what lay ahead—who did?—but she knew that it would demand some "fundamental readjustments." She predicted that government planning would replace anarchic groping and that programs now would be national in scope because problems were now national in scope.[29]

The professionals were not disappointed. Indeed by the following summer they were almost ecstatic. In February Tugwell's $5 billion proposal might have seemed wildly excessive. Yet in the National Industrial Recovery Act (N.I.R.A.) alone $3 billion were designated for public works, quite apart from emergency relief. And that was only the beginning. By early summer reality was outstripping fantasy. Gertrude Springer described it all when she contrasted the changing attitudes of social workers at their last three conventions. She spoke of "fears that stalked the meeting two years ago [1931] when social work shrank from the unpredictable." In 1932 there had been a "do-or-die spirit" in the face of national confusion. At the recently concluded meetings in Detroit the transformation was astonishing. No longer content with their role of "social stretcher-bearer," they left those meetings proudly as professionals "with a sense of partnership in a changing order."[30]

The government's approach to the new order was an inchoate mixture of work relief and outright dole whose only real purpose was to keep millions of people going from one day to the next. But most of the professionals felt that the New Deal carried a larger promise, that it must be more than just a patchwork of measures improvised on the spot to meet the worst consequences of privation. For all the misgivings that many of them had about the N.I.R.A.

and the Agricultural Adjustment Act (A.A.A.), they perceived in those measures, and in the statements of such figures as Tugwell, something like their
own commitment to the rational control of blind social forces through planning.
They believed that if the government could produce systems and agencies to
plan the economy, it could also devise schemes for social welfare, and perhaps
that it might eventually integrate all these social and economic programs into
one enormous national plan. They were sounding once again as some of them
had sounded at the end of the war. As early as 1933 some of them spoke out
for the systematic national planning of social policy. By the late 1930s almost
all of them were committed to it.

Even before Roosevelt's inauguration there were important professionals who
expressed their belief that planning must guide social policy in the future. Robert Kohn spoke to that issue a month before Roosevelt entered the White House.
Kohn, a recent president of the AIA, wanted to be sure that architects were in
the vanguard of this movement. He defined planning as the fusion of science
and vision, and was confident that architects would learn to apply it to society
easily, since they already practiced it with respect to the family in its immediate
physical surroundings. Kohn predicted that a decade of public works lay ahead
in which America's cities would be rebuilt, and he wanted to be certain that
such an undertaking would be carefully integrated with a program of "long-
term nation wide planning."[31] The need for architects in such a vast scheme
was clear to Kohn. Apparently it was clear to the Democrats as well, for a few
months later, when Kohn addressed the NCCP, he was Director of Housing in
the new federal Public Works Administration.

After the New Deal swept into Washington, most of the policy professionals
rushed to the support of national planning with enormous enthusiasm. A month
after the inauguration social workers jumped in with both feet. The occasion
was a conference on National Economic Objectives called in April 1933 by the
AASW to outline a national plan for social and economic policy. The position
paper that issued from this conference was not an official statement by the
association, but the committee that issued it read like a Who's Who in social
work and certainly represented the thinking of the social work establishment at
the dawn of the New Deal. It was a milestone.

As general principles the committee asserted that society had an obligation
"to provide a minimum standard of living for all" and that legislation for "a
comprehensive plan [to] govern social and economic organization" would be
necessary to achieve this standard. Anything less, they warned, was likely to
lead to the use of "force and violence" by both the right and the left.

Their specific proposals flowed from these principles. Committee members
opposed any form of the dole because it was demeaning to the individual and
proposed instead that the government meet the immediate crisis with a crash
program of meaningful work relief. For the future they wanted a permanent
program of public works directed toward resource development, institutional
construction (such as schools), slum clearance, and public housing. In the area

of social insurance they demanded a system of unemployment compensation, a program of universal contributory insurance for old age pensions, and, more vaguely defined, some sort of comprehensive national system of medical care. Finally, for any industry where the position of labor was weak they recommended government intervention to abolish child labor and regulate wages, hours, and working conditions.[32]

Some of these proposals—wages, hours, and child labor, for instance—required no special funding beyond the costs of administration. The social insurance programs would be financed by contributions from employers and workers and would also require very little money from the government. Relief and public works, however, were major programs that would draw heavily from tax revenues. Since they were aimed at social programs, the committee felt that they should be supported by social taxation, which was both more equitable and more efficient. Specifically it urged the use of graduated income and inheritance taxes and a tax on the "unearned increment" of property to pay for social programs.

In all this there was very little that was really new. "Outdoor relief," public works, and "progressive" modes of taxation all reached back into the nineteenth century. Social insurance was a staple of the prewar social justice movement, and the idea that individual misery had social causes was the bedrock assumption of public professionalism. That social inaction might trigger social revolt was a deeply rooted fear at the turn of the century; that it might lead to fascism was a much more recent concern, of course. Managed wages and hours was a recent idea, but it did not originate with the public-service professionals.

It was not in its parts that this scheme was striking, but in its entirety. The platform of the Progressive party in 1912 had incorporated many of its proposals but had advanced them individually. The committee saw them as parts of an integrated program for a fully planned society coordinated and managed on a national scale by the federal government. For a plan that did not anticipate any fundamental reordering of social or property relations, its scope was truly breathtaking.

It was precisely this unwillingness to disturb fundamental social relations that some social workers attacked vigorously. The most persistent voice in this faction belonged to the remarkable Mary van Kleeck, a radical who served as director of Industrial Relations for the Russell Sage Foundation. Van Kleeck was invited to the conference, but she dissented sharply from the majority in a paper that clearly marked out the boundary between the new liberalism and the new radicalism.

Traditionally, she said, social workers served the rich by helping to distribute part of their surplus wealth to the poor in order to mute the rumblings of social discontent. Now the entire system was crumbling, and she wondered whether social workers were really prepared to face the full implications of this situation. So far they seemed content to support the administration and the economists who advocated national planning. But national planning, as they discussed it, meant nothing more than planning for a company, or at most for an industry on a national basis. The inescapable fact was that the economy was thoroughly interrelated, and no effort to plan it issue by issue, company by company, or industry by industry could possibly succeed. The entire economy had to be planned as an integrated whole, just as it was in the Soviet Union. There stood the model that social workers had to confront, she said, and in doing so they were going to have to decide whether their social objectives could ever be realized within the prevailing economic system.[33]

A year later the lines were drawn even more dramatically. By then the AASW had virtually endorsed the New Deal by congratulating Congress and the president for the programs established in the areas of economic planning, relief, conservation, and public works. When the NCSW met in May, William Hodson, its president, also cast his lot with the Democratic administration. Realistically, he said, social workers had only two choices. One was to modify the existing order by planning to serve the general welfare. The other was to abandon the existing order and replace it with something entirely new. Social workers who were tempted to choose the second alternative must be warned that in America "Fascism and not Communism would be the probable result of breakdown in democratic government." Put that way, of course, social workers did not have two choices, they had no choice. They could only join Hodson and build upon established institutions.[34]

But Mary van Kleeck would have none of it, and she swept the convention along with her. At a conference addressed by such notables as Tugwell, Hopkins, and Aubrey Williams from the Roosevelt administration, and by such famous names in the profession as Hodson, Lubin, Breckenridge, Rubinow, and Lindeman, it was van Kleeck who created a sensation and emerged the dominant figure. In three different papers she vented her feelings about New Deal social and economic planning. She argued that the National Recovery Administration (NRA) was being used by big business as a weapon against any meaningful labor organization (less radical figures than she were also taking that position at the time), and that in the impending class war social workers should cast their lot with the working class, even though the issue might not be resolved short of revolution.[35] Then she really rocked the conference with a presentation on the meaning of government. At a time when few social workers had more than a faint understanding of Marx and most of them believed that government was a neutral force standing above conflicting interests and responsive to democratic majorities, van Kleeck informed them that it was in fact an instrument of the dominant economic class, and that behind all the furious activity in Washington there sat a government which yielded only what was painfully pried out of it. The New Deal was a fraud! Social workers must therefore refuse to work for its phony government programs and should align themselves instead with their clients, the workers, in a quest for a truly socialized, planned economy.[36]

The effect was electrifying and set the tone of the entire conference. Gertrude Springer described these meetings each year for *The Survey* and each year made an effort to capture their special character. This year she stood in awe of the "van Kleeck sensation," the more so because of the mild, uncharismatic nature of the woman. She described how 1,500 people had packed themselves into a five-hundred-seat hall and how they had answered van Kleeck's "cool, beautifully reasoned and dispassionately argued case" against the New Deal with the wildest ovation she had ever heard at the conference. She was certain that this was the most radical conference ever. "As someone pointed out," she said, "there have always been radical sideshows, but this year the radicals had the big tent and the conservatives were in the sideshows." And yet she could not help but wonder whether the radicalism of the young converts would survive the trip home, "when the mass emotion engendered at the Conference meets the stark realism of local communities and quite possibly finds personal security endangered."[37]

Perhaps it was the stark realism of local pressures that did it, perhaps not, but when the NCSW met a year later in Montreal, the radicalism was decidedly muted. The force of the previous year's near hysteria was spent now, Springer noted, and the dominant tone this year was cool analysis. Social workers had come to Montreal to sharpen the tools of their trade, not to build a new world. They were still willing to lift their gaze to the heavens, "but their feet remained firmly on the realistic foreground of their own experience."[38] Clearly, the moderates were back in control.

The issue of planning continued to attract social workers for the remainder of the decade, but the sharp line separating liberals from radicals was obscured, particularly after the Popular Front tactic took hold in 1936. After that the left minority made a shaky truce with the New Deal for the next few years, and in domestic matters was more concerned with organizing workers—including social workers—than with organizing planning. The liberal majority, on the other hand, never lost its interest in planning, but in the second half of the decade seemed content to work for it, as van Kleeck had charged, on an issue-by-issue basis and to postpone comprehensive national planning until some future date.[39]

Public health officials also began to advocate planning on a national scale in the 1930s. Their focus was primarily on health insurance, which had first been put forth late in the Progressive era by the American Association of Labor Legislation. At that time it had run afoul of opposition from private physicians who managed to defeat it in several state legislatures.[40] In the 1920s the issue lay dormant until it was revived by the Committee on the Costs of Medical Care, which was founded in 1927 as a private organization of about fifty members, most of whom were physicians, some in public health, some in private practice. In the next several years the committee issued more than two dozen research reports on the economics of health needs in the United States, and then wound up its affairs in 1932 with a report that echoed through the 1930s and after. The key section in the report recommended the implementation of a broad program of medical coverage. In the beginning it was to be financed through a system of voluntary private insurance, but if that did not work for some reason, the committee had no objection to the use of taxation, or some combination of taxation and contributory insurance, to pay for the program. The American Medical Association (AMA) was so upset by this report that its journal denounced the proposal as "socialism and communism, inciting to revolution."[41]

Thus even before the Roosevelt administration came to Washington, the battle lines were being drawn on this issue and the combatants identified. On the one side, public health personnel fought for some form of collectivized health care; on the other, the AMA spearheaded the forces fighting against it.

When the Social Security Act of 1935 made some federal funds available for public health, the APHA glowed with excitement. The president of the association saw an opportunity to put a national health plan into effect, with federal, state, and local governments working together to administer it.[42] Indeed, the first step toward formulating such a plan was already being taken. With the enthusiastic support of Harry Hopkins and his Works Projects Administration (WPA), the U.S. Public Health Service was beginning to gather data for a National Health Inventory. The objective was to make a systematic inquiry into the nation's health and medical facilities, into the extent of disability from all causes, into the occupational distribution of sickness and death, and into the reporting and treatment of communicable diseases by public health agencies. At its peak the project was expected to employ 6,000 public workers. Without the financial and human resources of the WPA such an undertaking would not have gotten off the ground, and without such a survey a national health plan was simply not possible.[43]

The promise of national planning was also attracting city planners in the early 1930s. Actually city planning had been outgrowing its name for several years. Regional planning had beguiled many of the professionals in the 1920s, and by the time the Democrats stormed into Washington in 1933, the planning movement was becoming a loose association of professionals that included parks, forest, and resource planners as well as the still dominant core of city and regional planners. Whatever their specific interests, almost all of them agreed on the need for national planning to make the nation function more efficiently, or indeed for it to function at all.

Of course any hope for national planning to succeed had to rely upon massive federal intervention into areas where the federal government traditionally feared to tread. That could have been embarrassing for the planners, because in the 1920s most of them had ignored the federal government, and some had been absolutely derisive about it. As it turned out, however, they swung around completely without even blushing and supported federal planning in the 1930s. Indeed some of the most scornful from the 1920s were soon hard at work for New Deal agencies. This growing alliance between city planners and federal officials was already apparent at the NCCP in 1933, where at least seven papers were presented by eager federal bureaucrats on a broad range of topics that included slum clearance, regional planning along the Tennessee River, and national planning.[44] From those meetings onward the fortunes of city planners were tied squarely to the federal government.

What the planners meant by national planning was a comprehensive but flexible plan for the entire nation that the federal government would formulate and coordinate from the proposals submitted by state and local planning boards across the country. A few people had toyed with this idea in the 1920s and had been dismissed as cranks or worse. By 1933 the cranks were staffing federal agencies. In such imposing measures as the N.I.R.A. and the A.A.A. the new administration was already demonstrating its willingness to encourage planning on a national basis, and while that was not quite the same thing as national planning, it was only a step short of it.

Moreover, the government had already established an agency which, with the proper leadership, could take charge of national planning. This was the National Planning Board, which had been set up in 1933 as an agency of the Public Works Administration (PWA). Chaired by Frederic Delano and staffed by such people as Charles Eliot and Charles Merriam, the board appeared to be primed for large-scale planning. But as an agency of the PWA it was ultimately responsible to Harold Ickes, who was quite capable of dallying for months over the potential for corruption in planning a single housing unit and was thus temperamentally unsuited to turning the board loose on anything like planning an entire nation.

From the outset there was tension between Ickes and the planners, and among the planners themselves, over just what the board was supposed to do. As a result it did not do much of anything in its first year or two. It recorded information on public works, it encouraged the organization of state planning boards, and it made occasional recommendations, but it did not work seriously on formulating a national plan. It went through a number of incarnations in the 1930s— the National Planning Board, the National Resources Board, the National Resources Committee—gradually broadening its proposals, yet always falling far short of the dream the professionals had of a comprehensive national plan.

Part of the problem was that there was very little support for a national plan outside the administration and a great deal of confusion about what the idea really implied. With much fanfare the Soviet Union was pushing ahead with its first five-year plan at the time, and to many Americans the idea of comprehensive planning smacked of bolshevism. Charles Eliot tried to calm those fears by arguing that the idea of planning was as old as the Constitution, which, in a stunning application of planner's license, he characterized as the nation's first plan. He then traced the blood lines of the idea through Hamilton, Gallatin, and Clay right down to Hoover. More conservative about the substance of planning than many of his colleagues—he preferred physical to social or economic planning—he still never for a moment questioned the principle.[45]

Frederic Delano had more faith in social planning than Eliot. He was positive that it could be made to work as part of a national plan if only it could be presented to the public as the kind of transcendent cause, like a war, in which people could fulfill themselves with great effort and sacrifice. On those terms he called for the federal government to "do something substantial for the underprivileged" by providing a national plan that would be "Physically, Socially, Economically and Spiritually adequate to the American people." [46] Delano's rhetoric and his outlook were redolent of the fading charity ethos, and reflected a sense of *noblesse oblige* that was rare among New Deal officials. But it was a charity outlook now linked to the idea of national planning in Washington, and it is quite improbable that anyone would have made that linkage a half dozen years earlier.

In 1939 the National Resources Committee was rechristened once again, this time as the National Resources Planning Board, and was made a part of the Executive Office of the president. Delano remained as chairman, but Charles Merriam, a member from the beginning, became increasingly influential, and as a result the board became increasingly liberal, moving, for instance, into the delicate area of race relations for the first time. By the early 1940s it was beginning to put together a postwar agenda for liberalism, raising the hopes of its friends and the hostility of its foes. After the 1942 elections, however, the conservative coalition was firmly in control of Congress and implacable in its determination to trim back New Deal social programs. One of the victims was the National Resources Planning Board, which Congress killed in 1943. It never did draw up a national plan.

It had all seemed so promising to the professionals in the 1930s when the federal government first invited them to help reform society. Everyone agreed that reform had to be grounded firmly in planning, and everyone knew that planning was based upon some sort of relationship between present knowledge and future goals. It was that area of "present knowledge" that brought the professionals into the picture, because their professionalism was built upon their special grasp of the knowledge necessary for planning, upon their expertise.

They seemed scarcely aware at the time that this "knowledge" might be elusive or conjectural, that it might consist not only of facts, but of inferences drawn from those facts, and of projections made from those inferences, that it might be laced with value judgments, and that it might mislead them altogether. The way they measured the growth and distribution of population and the projections they made from these observations illustrate the point painfully.

The facts were that the flow of immigration had been closed down to a trickle in the 1920s and that birthrates were declining even more dramatically than deathrates among certain elements of the population. Since it was demonstrable that these facts—especially those involving birth and death rates—had been occurring for several decades, the professionals inferred that they were looking at long-term trends which would continue indefinitely into the future. Thus in the early 1930s informed estimates suggested that population would crest at around 150 million in 1950, and would thereafter enter into a long period of gradual decline. In the spirit of the times the professionals wished to plan accordingly.

Planners, for instance, predicted that urban and suburban growth would both come to a halt presently; that the resultant lessening of pressure on land would lower land prices, which would lower assessed valuations, which thus might well lower tax revenues; that the population of children would decline, as a result of which schools and playgrounds, currently badly overcrowded, would become adequate without any expansion in the future; and that a much higher percentage of the population would be over forty-five years of age before long, which would lead to disproportionately high chronic unemployment in that age category. City planning in the future, they concluded, would have to take these factors into consideration.[47]

These population trends also affected the thinking of public health figures. Frederick Osborn pointed out that current birthrates were not quite enough to replace the population. By itself that might not be alarming information, he noted, but in a larger context it was a very disturbing factor. First of all, the only reason birthrates were anywhere near replacement was because of the extremely high rates in many southern rural areas among the "isolated and ignorant" elements of the population. Second, left alone, the trend toward declining birthrates would no doubt continue until, in twenty years (1960), the rate of reproduction would be 20 percent below the level of replacement. In a highly competitive world this would bring drastic measures down upon the country. Osborn wanted immediate action to forestall the likelihood of draconian solutions in the future, and his recommendations were in perfect harmony with the times. We are already affecting birthrates, he said, by disseminating birth control information among the poor and ignorant. What we need to do now, he continued, was to encourage the "competent and responsible parents" to "contribute their share, or more than their share," by having larger families. And so he proposed that the government engage in a program of community subsidies to the more "competent" families so that they would be able to absorb the costs of additional children in stride.[48] By various means, then, the government was to discourage births among the poor and encourage them among the middle and upper classes.

It is not that the professionals had their facts wrong. On the contrary, they were quite accurate as far as they went. To many of them the knowledge of population trends demonstrated that a science of society was at hand and justified the tremendous faith they had placed in the federal government by the late 1930s. The trouble was that this knowledge was far more complicated than they dreamed. It was honeycombed with hidden value judgments and included some sheer guesswork about the future that the professionals were pleased to call "projections." It was this knowledge that served as the basis for many of their planning recommendations, and considering the amount of research that had gone into it, there was really nothing unreasonable about it. But it turned out to be spectacularly wrong.

NOTES

1. Elmer C. Jensen, "The Architect in Civil Life," AIA, *Proceedings* (1918):62–63.

2. Frederick Ackerman, "Nation Planning," *National Municipal Review* (January 1919):15–25. See also Ackerman, "American Reconstruction Problems—Nation Planning," *Journal of the American Institute of Architects* (November 1918):506–509.

3. Rupert Blue, "Are We Physically Fit?" *AJPH* (September 1919):641–645; Lee K. Frankel, "The Future of the American Public Health Association," Ibid. (February 1919):87–93; George M. Price, "After-War Public Health Problems," *The Survey* (December 21, 1918):369–374.

4. Ira S. Wile, "Meaning and Purpose of Socializing Medicine," *AJPH* (December 1920):969–972. Wile, "Sociological Aspects of Housing," Ibid. (April 1920):327–331.

5. Clarence S. Stein, "Housing and Reconstruction," *Journal of the American Institute of Architects* (October 1918):469–472.

6. Frederick Ackerman, "Where Goes the City Planning Movement? V. Drifting," Ibid. (October 1920):351–354; Frederick L. Ackerman, "Subsidized Housing," Ibid. (May 1923):219–220.

7. Ernst Christopher Meyer, "Community Medicine and Public Health," *AJPH* (June 1920):485–495.

8. G. Hardy Clark, "Municipal Administration of Health and Welfare Departments," Ibid. (May 1921):401–407.

9. Livingston Farrand, "Social Work and Health Programs," NCSW, *Proceedings* (1923):17–18; "Religion, Pseudo-Religion, Science and Public Health," *AJPH* (December 1925):1090–1092; "Evolution and Progress," Ibid. (July 1926):824–825.

10. John A. Fitch, "The Long Day," *The Survey* (March 5, 1921):783–798.

11. See for instance Robert W. Kelso, "Changing Fundamentals of Social Work," NCSW, *Proceedings* (1922):6–13; and William J. Norton, "What Is Social Work?" Ibid. (1925):3–14. Each of these was a presidential address to the NCSW.

12. Richard Arthur Bolt, "Federal Subsidies to the States with Special Reference to Health," Ibid. (1926):215–222.

13. John A. Lapp, "Justice First," Ibid. (1927):3–13.

14. Paul U. Kellogg, "Unemployment and Progress," Ibid. (1929):80–102.

15. Daisy Lee Worthington Worcester, "The Standard of Living," Ibid. pp. 337–353.

16. William Stanley Parker, "The Road to Plenty," *The Octagon* (February 1929):5–6.

17. C. Herrick Hammond, "The Prospect for the Building Industry," Ibid. (November 1929):3–5; see also "The Outlook for 1930," Ibid. (December 1929):3.

18. "Great Increase in Relief Expenditures and in Unemployment Reported by Charity Societies," *American City* (April 1930):114.

19. Helen Hall, "When Detroit's Out of Gear," *The Survey* (April 1, 1930):9–14, 51–54.

20. Frank L. Hayes, "Chicago's Rent Riot," Ibid. (September 15, 1931):548–549. See also Ewan Clague, "Philadelphia Studies Its Breadlines," Ibid. (November 15, 1931):196–197.

21. William P. Lovett, "Detroit Feeds Its Hungry," *National Municipal Review* (July 1931):402–404; William H. Book, "How Indianapolis Combines Poor Relief With Pub-

lic Work,'' Ibid. (September 1931):513–515; C. O. Sherrill, ''The 'Cincinnati Plan of Stabilized Employment' at Work in an Unemployment Emergency,'' *American City* (April 1930):113–114.

22. ''Unemployment Relief and Items for Mayors and City Managers,'' Ibid. (November 1930):5; ''To Relieve Distress and Hasten Good Times,'' Ibid. (December 1930):85. See also Gertrude Springer, ''The Fighting Spirit in Hard Times,'' *The Survey* (June 15, 1932):260–269.

23. Louis I. Dublin, ''The Health of the People in a Year of Depression,'' *AJPH* (November 1932):1123–1135.

24. ''How It Feels,'' *The Survey* (February 15, 1932):529–530.

25. Louis La Beaume, ''What of Architecture?'' *The Octagon* (November 1931):3–4; La Beaume, ''Federal Employment of Private Architects,'' Ibid. (December 1931):3–4; Frank C. Baldwin, ''Government Competition with Private Business,'' Ibid. (September 1932):4–5.

26. Robert D. Kohn, ''The President's Address to the 65th Convention,'' Ibid. (May 1932):4–6; ''Unemployment Relief in New York,'' Ibid. (February 1932):29.

27. Gertrude Springer, ''The Fighting Spirit in Hard Times,'' *The Survey* (June 15, 1932):260–269.

28. ''Five Billions for Public Works and Housing?'' *American City* (February 1933):43.

29. Katherine Tucker, ''A New Year,'' *Public Health Nursing* (January 1933):3.

30. Gertrude Springer, ''Partners in a New Social Order,'' *The Survey* (July 1933):243–250.

31. Robert D. Kohn, ''The Future Is to the Planners,'' *The Octagon* (February 1933):3–4.

32. Linton B. Swift et al., ''National Economic Objectives for Social Work,'' *The Compass* (May 1933):10–19.

33. Mary van Kleeck, ''A Planned Economy,'' Ibid., pp. 20–24.

34. William Hodson, ''The Social Worker in the New Deal,'' NCSW, *Proceedings* (1934):3–12.

35. Mary van Kleeck, ''The Effect of the N.R.A. on Labor,'' Ibid., pp. 428–437; and ''The Common Goals of Labor and Social Work,'' Ibid., pp. 284–304.

36. Mary van Kleeck, ''Our Illusions Regarding Government,'' Ibid., pp. 473–486.

37. Gertrude Springer, ''Rising to a New Challenge,'' *The Survey* (June 1934):179–180. On the ideological factionalism of social workers in the 1930s see Jacob Fisher, *The Response of Social Work to the Depression* (Boston: G. K. Hall, 1980).

38. Gertrude Springer and Helen Cody Baker, ''Social Workers View Their World,'' *The Survey* (July 1935):195–207.

39. See for instance Alfred K. Stern, ''Housing: A Ten-Year Program,'' *Survey Graphic* (January 1936):23–26.

40. Ronald L. Numbers, *Almost Persuaded: American Physicians and Compulsory Health Insurance, 1912–1920* (Baltimore: Johns Hopkins University Press, 1978).

41. I. S. Falk, ''Planning a National Health Program,'' NCSW, *Proceedings* (1939):111–118. Falk had served on the committee as associate director in charge of research.

42. E. L. Bishop, ''Public Health at the Cross-roads,'' *AJPH* (November 1935):1175–1180.

43. Josephine Roche, ''Economic Health and Public Health Objectives,'' Ibid., pp. 1181–1185.

44. See the entire issue of NCCP, *Proceedings* (1933).

45. Charles W. Eliot, 2d, "National Planning," *City Planning* (July 1934):103–111. On the National Planning Board see Marion Clawson, *New Deal Planning: The National Resources Planning Board* (Baltimore: Johns Hopkins University Press, 1981).

46. Frederic A. Delano, "On National Planning," *The Octagon* (October 1934):3.

47. Frederick F. Stephan, "Population Trends and City Planning," *American City* (April 1934):39–41. See also Harland Bartholomew, "Technical Problems in Slum Clearance: The City Planner's Viewpoint," NCCP, *Proceedings* (1933):121–130.

48. Frederick Osborn, "Population Trends and Public Health Problems," *AJPH* (November 1940):1331–1336.

7

Public Welfare and Professionalism

Although the public-service professionals had been pressing for welfare legislation since early in the century, they did not have anything very substantial to show for it before the New Deal. In the 1920s, when they chose to cultivate their professionalism, many of them proclaimed that reform was passé altogether. The journal of the American Association of Social Workers (AASW) had very little to say in the 1920s about the social causes of poverty, but it overflowed with articles on such things as "A Measurement of Professional Training," "Training Schools and the American Association" and "Will Future Members Have Technical Training?" By the end of the decade the association felt confident enough to tighten its requirements for membership and thereby presumably for qualification as a professional social worker. Then in 1930 it proudly informed its members that they would be classified as social workers for the first time in the forthcoming census, and thus "graduated into the professional class" in the esteem of the federal government.[1]

This smug professionalism was shocking for a group of people who claimed to dedicate themselves to the problems of others. But it did at least allow social workers to put some psychological distance between themselves and the degrading Flexner report of 1915. Otherwise, when they weren't honing their professionalism, most of them in the 1920s claimed to be more interested in doing social work than in redoing America.

In the 1930s everything changed. The New Deal came down on the professionals like a flash flood and swept them away with it. With the federal government opening new avenues to the future every month, it seemed that anything was possible. In this heady atmosphere the AASW rediscovered reform and the belief that doing social work *was* redoing America. Public-health experts acted as if they would finally be able to lead the American people to eternal health, if not eternal life. Planners were eager to redesign the entire nation and rebuild it from the city centers outward. Fervor was in style again.

The policy experts expressed opinions about everything that was happening in those few dense years, but the professional implications of their born-again reformism are perhaps most clearly visible in their responses to social insurance and public housing, two of the most far-reaching social reforms of the era.

At the AASW conference on National Economic Objectives in April 1933, when the direction the New Deal would take was still uncertain, social welfare leaders had produced a number of position papers which in some ways anticipated the federal social insurance policies of the next few years. But the Social Security Act that Congress finally passed in 1935 was an omnibus measure full of compromises that left the reformers with mixed feelings. Its major provisions established a system of old age pensions and offered incentives for the states to pass their own unemployment compensation laws. In addition, the act contributed a substantial amount of money to public-health programs and offered economic assistance to dependent or disabled people who were not already covered by some other federal program.

While the professionals were enthusiastic about these measures, many of them were disappointed with the manner in which they were to be organized and funded. They were unhappy, for instance, that the act turned over the unemployment compensation program to the states, which is a measure of how their views had changed since the conference on social and economic objectives two years earlier when they were resigned to having the states handle this program. The states had had a dismal time trying to cope with unemployment in the early days of the depression, and social workers had no confidence that incentives would coax a better performance out of them now.

They were more generous in their praise for the system of old age pensions, but they were by no means uncritical of it. Some of them felt that too many groups were excluded from the program, others that the maximum monthly annuity was absurdly low, and almost all of them that the method of funding the pensions was all wrong. On this last point, they were nearly unanimous in asserting that the federal government should finance at least a portion of the program out of general tax revenues. Linked to the growing demand for a more steeply graduated income tax, this implied some redistribution of income through the pension system. Congress had rejected that approach, however, and had settled instead for a system of compulsory payments to be shared by employer and employee, thus limiting the government's role merely to administering the system.

A few of these welfare workers were completely contemptuous of the act and demanded that the system be scrapped in favor of one in which the federal government would play a dominant role in both the finances and administration. Still, most of them were willing to take what they had, and felt that the Social Security Act, for all its flaws, was at least a reasonable beginning because it had established the principle of social responsibility for economic security. "What is important," said Isaac Rubinow, "is that we forcefully resist any effort to retrace such real steps as have been taken or abandon positions already won.'' Repeal in the name of ideological purity would be unforgivable. The real challenge, he concluded, was to build upon the principle established in the act.[2] The AASW concurred in this middle-of-the-road position. Aware of the limitations of the act, but appalled by the position on social welfare taken by the Republican candidate, Alf Landon, in the 1936 presidential campaign, it said that it was a question ''of part of a loaf or none at all.''[3] Obviously it was willing to settle for part.

At that, half a loaf proved to be almost more than social workers could digest. They realized immediately that the act would have a profound impact on American society, but only afterward did they begin to understand that it would have a profound impact on the practice of social work as well. Only a few years earlier the casework approach had narrowed the outlook of many of them to the individualized treatment they could provide to client and family. Now various government programs employed thousands of social workers to assist millions of people, and the numbers were soaring by the day. Ewan Clague, a social worker employed by the Social Security Board, predicted that the need for public welfare programs would continue into the distant future because of the special problems of an aging population (once again, a projection of population trends) and increasing technological unemployment. Clague believed that the extension of such programs as unemployment compensation to an entire class of wage earners would lead to a serious modification of the social work ethos. In the future, he said, practitioners would have to pay more attention to the ''mass character'' of ''individual maladjustment,'' and to alter their training accordingly. The tendency to carry on social work through government agencies would continue to expand on those terms.[4]

Almost immediately two positions developed on this question. The more moderate group, which included Clague and many of the most visible figures in the field, foresaw little or no need for the government to employ social workers in the administration of the old age pension program because that plan applied universally and equally to all groups that qualified. There was no means test or time limit on annuities, and therefore no need to decide on an individual basis who qualified for the program or when payments should be terminated. With other programs in the Social Security Act, such as unemployment compensation or aid to dependent mothers, tens of thousands of individual decisions had to be made monthly. Was an unemployed worker really trying to find a job? What was the precise financial condition of a widowed mother of young children? The expertise of the social worker would come into play in answering questions such as these.[5] Other welfare workers wanted more. For them the Social Security Act only scratched the surface of necessity. Florence Sytz of the Tulane University School of Social Work took issue with the moderates on the future of social workers in social insurance. She accused these timid professionals of limiting themselves by thinking only in terms of casework, whereas social work had always been committed just as much to social vision and must now expand in that direction.[6]

Individual adjustment versus social reform! It was the same argument that had occupied social workers since the emergence of casework two decades earlier, only now it was set to the up-tempo rhythms of the New Deal. Sytz attacked the moderates who invoked professional standards to limit the reform impulse in social work. If social workers were not competent to handle such questions, she said, then it was up to them to broaden their training until they were. The Social Security Board itself recognized this when it suggested that the administration of unemployment compensation in the future be handled by a class of experts specially trained in such subjects as the history and economics of unemployment. The program did not need any more clerical workers, she said; it needed broadly trained reformers.

For all of their sharp differences, both the moderates and the militants recognized that the New Deal was forcing major changes onto the field of social work and that the meaning of professionalism in the field would have to adapt to these changes. Most of them agreed that the process would be most effectively coordinated and directed in the thriving schools of social work. They realized that the phenomenal growth of welfare agencies in the New Deal had established reciprocal relationships between government needs and schools of social work. With that in mind they began to plan for professional schools to include training for public welfare work in government, and they fully expected this trend to expand in the years to come as the Social Security program took root in American society.[7]

In fact that was a reasonable assessment of what was already taking place in the colleges and universities. Schools of social work had begun to adjust to federal welfare initiatives even before social work educators had had much chance to share ideas and shape a national strategy on the matter. A 1936 survey conducted by the AASW revealed two significant trends. First of all, schools of social work everywhere were bursting at the seams. And why not? At a time when unemployment was still a demoralizing factor in national life, government jobs were opening up from coast to coast for people with training in social work. Thus in Seattle the School of Social Work at the University of Washington was filled to capacity; in Madison the University of Wisconsin had had to turn away qualified applicants in the recent school year; enrollment for graduate courses in social work at Ohio State University was "especially heavy"; Smith College and Simmons College both reported the largest enrollment for social work in their history.

Second, schools of social work were indeed adjusting their curricula to the new liberal imperative of government assistance in social welfare. At a time when many universities were forced to cut faculty, the Pennsylvania School of Social Work had just hired four instructors to expand its offerings in public social work by adding such novel courses as Economic Backgrounds of Security and Relief, Personnel Policies in Public Administration, and Social Case Work in Public Relief Agencies. At Smith College the School of Social Work was placing some of its students in government agencies for "supervised practice," and directing others into two new courses in Society, Government, and Labor Policies. At Bryn Mawr, at Tulane, at the University of Cincinnati, and at Indiana University courses were offered in Unemployment Insurance, in Problems in Public Welfare, in Social Legislation, in Taxation and Social Work. The Atlanta School of Social Work was giving courses that emphasized the "vastly increased government welfare functions and also . . . new legislation affecting social welfare." St. Louis University, more ambitious than most at the time, was planning to launch an entire curriculum in public welfare with a full-time director.[8] With universities hiring new faculty to teach new courses to train new students for new jobs in government, that reciprocal relationship bonded schools to government in a complex fashion that had both economic and professional implications.

In 1938 the AASW finally published a formal statement of its position on government assistance and social insurance programs. Framed in very general terms, the statement did not really say anything new but served instead to put an official seal on positions that most social workers had been supporting since the inception of the New Deal, and in some cases since early in the Progressive era. The association called for "direct, positive action on the part of federal, state and local governments" to relieve distress for the duration of the economic emergency and to expand the insurance programs founded in the Social Security Act. Specifically it demanded a better system of unemployment compensation, by which it meant larger benefit payments for a longer time. It also wished to bring more groups into what had begun as a very limited system of old age insurance. And it called upon the government to advance social insurance into the area of health care.[9] This final request was a plea for what became the great lost cause of the public-service professionals in the 1930s.

By the time the Committee on the Costs of Medical Care issued its landmark report in 1932, most health workers were already committed to some form of publicly funded health insurance. They closed ranks behind this reform in the early years of the New Deal and, not surprisingly, were bitterly hostile toward the AMA for opposing the inclusion of health insurance in the Social Security Act. In fact, all that prevented this issue from breaking out into another wild melee between public and private practitioners of medicine was the belief of most observers that health insurance had little chance at that time to get through Congress and the unwillingness of reformers therefore to endanger the whole program by letting it stand or fall on the question of medical care.

The issue of health care festered for the next few years and then came to a head once again at the National Health Conference, which met in the summer of 1938 at the suggestion of President Roosevelt. The organizers of this conference cast a wide net for delegates and managed to bring in representatives from industry, agriculture, labor, dentistry, women's organizations, and the American Legion. That created a facade of broad representation for the conference, but the fact is that nearly one-third of the delegates were physicians, most of whom were warm friends of the public-health movement. Indeed, for all practical purposes the conference was controlled by public-health people from the outset and reflected their viewpoint at the conclusion. The conference committee was chaired by Josephine Roche, recently the assistant secretary of the Treasury in charge of the U.S. Public Health Service, while the technical committee that provided much of the information to the delegates was staffed entirely with people from the fields of welfare and public health.

The technical data that guided the conference were drawn from the national health survey undertaken three years earlier in conjunction with the WPA. They informed the professionals that 18 million people lived in counties without anything that could pass even vaguely as a hospital; that illness, chronic disability, and death increased and medical care decreased in direct proportion to the degree of poverty; that altogether about 40 million people in the nation received inadequate medical care; and that the great majority of working people were able to absorb ordinary medical costs, but had no way of coping financially with medical disaster.[10]

The conference made a number of recommendations which indicate the directions in which public-health professionals wanted to proceed. It called for a general extension of public-health, maternal, and child-care services; it called for a vast expansion of hospital facilities; it asked for a special program of medical care for the "medically needy" poor; it asked for compensation in all cases of medical disability not covered by some other governmental program; and it proposed a general program of medical insurance financed either through compulsory contributions or federal taxes, or some combination of the two.

The recommendations provoked a sharp debate at the conference. Paul Kellogg, a veteran of these wars, acknowledged that many citizens had honest and principled reservations about the prospect of millions of people leaning on the federal government for medical assistance, but in a crisis, he said, he "would rather have more people lean on the broad shoulders of Uncle Sam for this purpose than on the narrow and cadaverous shoulders of the Elizabethan poor laws." S. S. Goldwater, New York City's commissioner of hospitals, replied that he had grave doubts about where this sort of thinking was leading the nation. In matters of health his guiding principle was that "self help is preferable to outside aid." He was willing to consider public assistance on a local basis in cases of extreme emergency, but federal health care of any kind was anathema to him because the "effective and economical administration of medical aid for the masses [was] well nigh impossible." The contestants in this debate could not have been more polarized.

For its part, the AMA preferred not to enter the fray just yet. Its spokesmen did express a desire to join with public-health personnel soon in a campaign "for the betterment of health care," and its president, Irvin Abell, did inform the conference that the association was currently conducting "a painstaking study" of the needs and methods of medical care in every county in the country. But until that study was finished, the AMA was obviously not prepared to comment on the recommendations of the conference. Public health leaders responded predictably to word of the AMA study. Hugh Cabot commented venomously that he could hardly wait to see what information private physicians would contribute on the health of people who were too poor ever to see them. Clearly Cabot and his colleagues expected that nothing good would come from the AMA health survey and that the association would dig in its heels above all on the issue of health insurance.[11]

They were not disappointed. The controversy broke out again at the annual meetings of the APHA convention, where the AMA made its report in language that was rubbery enough to stretch from Boston to San Diego, and broad enough to contain a major debate over most of the proposals made at the National Health Conference.[12] What it came down to, however, was this: the AMA differed sharply from the APHA on most issues, but the differences on those matters were negotiable, and compromise solutions were at least theoretically possible. On the issue of universal health insurance, however, there was no possibility at all for compromise because the conflict involved a matter of principle, not of degree. In the end, the AMA rejected compulsory health insurance on the grounds that it would cost too much, would be bureaucratic and undemocratic, and would inevitably fall victim to political manipulation. And that was that.

Perhaps the public-service professionals should have sensed a shift in the tides of politics in 1939 when Robert Wagner introduced a health bill into the Senate that did not include medical insurance or disability compensation. For all practical purposes the Wagner bill gutted the National Health Program, which surprised and disappointed the professionals, since Wagner, more than anyone in the Senate, had carried the fight for social welfare through the 1930s. They criticized the bill, and they carped at Wagner's loss of nerve, but they remained invincible in their faith that health insurance was just around the corner.

This misplaced confidence was related in some ways to their self-image, especially to the way they perceived their own professionalism. They saw themselves as scientists and altruists in an age of science and compassion, and they did not hesitate to make these points by invidious comparisons with private physicians. In his presidential address to the APHA in 1939, Edward Godfrey condemned the AMA and private practitioners in general for their insistence on limiting medical service to a "fee-for-service" basis only. He characterized this practice as an atavistic survival from the days "when medicine was more largely pastoral" and dismissed it as "utterly inconsistent with the scientific and technical advances of the past quarter century." The carefully cultivated image of the family doctor with a fatherly concern for the health and welfare of his patients did not impress Godfrey. "The 'personal relationship' argument has been overplayed," he said. Nowadays, "the kindly physician 'with a heart of gold' who 'grannied' the children but practiced the medicine of his student days, is no substitute for the doctor who uses the knowledge and instruments of modern science." He was convinced that private physicians did not do anything as well as public health clinics. Apparently they did not even granny their patients better, because he spoke proudly of the "satisfactory personal relationships [that] have been maintained between physician and patient in many government medical services." [13] The APHA wanted good health for "three-thirds" of the people. In his eyes it was clear that the AMA did not. As soon as the American people realized that, health insurance would become a fact of life.

Reminiscing about the fifty years of the Massachusetts Public Health Association, C.-E. A. Winslow explored these themes. He described the years when public health was "made precise and effective by the new science of bacteriology," and he recited the entire litany of victories over communicable diseases in the twenty years that followed. He discussed the current era with its emphasis on the "physiological organism" and then turned to the future, forecasting an era of "Constructive Medicine" in which public health practices would bring "vigor and efficiency and joy in living" to everyone through broad programs in mental health, nutrition, housing, recreation, and economic security. Yesterday, he said, public health had been an "engineering science"; today it was a "medical science"; he was eager for tomorrow when it would be a "social science" participating in a "constructive remoulding of the social environment." [14]

Science, altruism, social control, and the search for community were all themes inherited from the Progressive era. By the end of the 1930s the ideologists of public health were fusing them in such a way that they became the very essence of their professional commitment.

This revitalized social sense was bolstered by that part of the Social Security Act which authorized federal grants to the states for health work. These grants were only a minor part of the act and went virtually unnoticed by the general public in the din that was raised over old age pensions and unemployment compensation. But their significance was not lost to public-health authorities, on whom the money and recognition fell like manna on hungry wayfarers. In 1936 Thomas Parran acknowledged the impact the act was already having on the field. Parran, who was surgeon general of the United States as well as president of the APHA that year, sensed that the association was "invested with a new life, a new interest in the contemporary scene, and a new zest for the task" that lay ahead. With public health now taking on a new layer of social significance, he urged his colleagues to proceed wisely in reshaping the field for the future. [15]

They needed little encouragement. Awash in federal funds for the first time, they found themselves faced with the novel problem of "finding the human resources to match the dollars." [16] Undaunted, they plunged ahead and expanded public health programs dramatically in the next few years. In 1935, before the Social Security Act was passed, not one state had had a program to combat pneumonia. By 1940 thirty-four states had such programs, and federal funds carried almost two-thirds of the cost. In Pennsylvania alone there were 175 health stations doing laboratory analyses and dispensing the new sulfa drugs without charge in the struggle against pneumonia. Programs in industrial hygiene, dental hygiene, and cancer control were springing up everywhere. Between 1935 and 1940 the number of counties with full-time health programs in the United States more than doubled. Health workers were apprised of these professional advances regularly and were fully aware that the Social Security Act made them possible.[17]

There was an important side effect to all of this as well, for as the number and size of health programs grew, the number of people working in them soared. In the first year of the act alone the expansion of public-health services was responsible for the employment of more than 3,000 people, including 500 physicians and 1,000 nurses. Added to the 6,000 nurses ("themselves destitute") already working in community health projects financed by federal emergency funds, the work generated by the act made some welcome inroads into the ranks of unemployed health professionals.[18] And they were acutely aware of that also.

The Social Security Act contributed to the professionalization of public health even more directly by paying the tuition costs for doctors, nurses, and sanitarians, many of whom had had no education at all specifically in public health, to advance their training in the field. In its first five years this program assisted more than 4,000 trainees to broaden their education in public health. Encouraged by these signs of increasing professionalism, health officers very early worked out a uniform set of minimum qualifications for employees in public health. The standards they established were not binding, but their very existence put some pressure on state and local officials to hire competent personnel instead of well-connected but ill-prepared political hacks.[19] Then in 1939 the Social Security Act was amended so that state employees who dealt in any way with Social Security funds *had* to be hired on the basis of merit alone. The specific method of selection was left to local officials, but now at last they were compelled to pay attention to professional credentials first and only after that to political considerations.[20]

The professionals had been agitating for a generation to have public health removed from politics with only a few local successes. Now in one stroke the federal government appeared to do it over the entire nation. With Washington funding health programs and forcing higher professional standards, it is no wonder that public-health workers were fervent in their commitment to the New Deal.

For years they had fought vested interests and doubting Thomases over their assumptions that health was a matter of public concern, that ill health was a cause of poverty and dependency, and that good health was a prerequisite to human progress. These assumptions were critical because they put a moral gloss on public health, made it a social issue, and justified government activism in the field. With the nation drawing toward war in 1941, Abel Wolman, a recent president of the APHA, praised the Social Security Act for chiseling these propositions into stone, thus apparently ending the dispute forever. He concurred with the surgeon general's judgment that public health was now "a people's cause" that had revolutionary implications as profound as those of the Renaissance and French Revolution.[21] Thanks to the Social Security Act, public-health personnel all over the nation were working diligently to carry out the social implications of that revolution.

In the years between the wars the broad issues that animated the new professionals were not much different from those that had engaged them in the Progressive era. Such matters as poverty, health and welfare, social order and efficiency, the place of ethnic minorities, and the role of government in public life continued to hold their attention. What changed in some cases were their ideas about the content and weight of those issues. Thus before World War I, as Robert Wiebe has pointed out, the child was the center of interest for welfare reformers and often influenced their attitudes toward such related matters as health, education, penal reform, and maximum hours for working mothers.[22] After the war the symbolic and unifying power of this issue lost its force, and nothing replaced it. Social reform, such as it was in the 1920s, did not really have a center. The issue that emerged to serve this purpose in the following decade was public housing, which connected with all the new professionals and drew them together in common cause. By the time the Housing Act of 1937 was passed, they had made it a panacea for what ailed the nation and the center of a broad program of social reconstruction for the future. In the end the New Deal's performance in this field never matched its promise, but for many years the possibilities in public housing excited the policy experts as nothing else did.

For a brief period at the end of World War I some of the professionals agitated for a large-scale program of housing construction that would continue the work begun during the war and remove urban development from the soiled hands of real estate operators and building speculators.[23] But the question became academic when these policy workers lost confidence in public subsidies after 1920. Without a practical means there could be no end, only a vision; and without either effective means or ends there could be no movement, only a discussion. And so the professionals continued to discuss housing in academic terms throughout the 1920s.

John Ihlder was a case in point. Ihlder was one of the founders of city planning in the United States, and remained on the scene to become a strong supporter of New Deal housing programs in the 1930s. In 1922 he addressed the NCSW, reviewing the past and present of housing reform in the nation and dwelling particularly on current zoning practices. It was a surprisingly limp paper, which warned professionals in guarded tones against the efforts of speculators to trim building codes and practices. Then Ihlder paid a curious compliment to zoning for providing a "very effective flank attack at a time when frontal attacks were practically impossible." Even more cryptically, he observed that conditions now were finally changing, "and it is possible that frontal attacks will soon again become possible.''[24] What frontal attacks? That was not even a euphemism; it was an evasion. If he was alluding to anything, it was to public subsidies; yet, discussing the housing situation with an audience of social workers in 1922, apparently he found it more comfortable to smother the subject than to confront it.

Usually the solution offered to the housing shortage for the poor was some variation of the trickle-down approach. Lawson Purdy was one of the planners who supported this method. Purdy admitted that there was a problem with housing just then but not a crisis. Therefore the best way to handle the housing needs of the very poor was to encourage private industry to build for the very wealthy. When the rich moved into their new dwellings, others a cut below them socially would move into their old dwellings, and so on down to the very poor, who would move up into units vacated by those just above them socially. Local government would then demolish the poorest quarters that were left vacant at the botton of the heap. That way, according to a New York architect who had studied the problem, low-income families could be ''housed in good second-hand homes, just as they now ride in good second-hand automobiles.''[25] Just how long all this would take was not clear, but ''good second-hand homes'' for the poor were obviously not just around the corner.

The only significant exception to the trickle-down method was embodied in a New York State law passed in 1926 primarily to meet the needs of Manhattan, where the housing shortage was unbearable. Basically the bill provided a major tax break to any limited dividend corporation that would build low-income housing for the poor.[26] It was an indirect subsidy that was a far cry from the measures of the 1930s and later, but in the 1920s it stood like a monument to governmental activism. The trouble was that very little venture capital at the time was flowing toward such projects. The 6 to 7 percent return allowed by the law was not very attractive compared to the returns promised, for instance, by speculation in the stock market. And so the bill caused a flurry of excitement among the professionals when it was passed, and eventually it did encourage the construction of some low-cost housing, but in the end it fell far short of expectations.

At the end of the decade, even before the stock market collapsed, the professionals revived the discussion of outright subsidies. Edith Elmer Wood raised the topic somewhat timidly when she addressed the National Housing Conference in 1929. Wood concentrated on the middle third of the population, recommending that they receive government loans to assist them into decent housing. That would open up their newly vacated quarters for occupancy by the lower third. The rich could take care of themselves. What saved this from being just another form of trickle-down housing was her insistence that if the vacated quarters of the middle class should prove in any way to be inadequate for the poor, the government should step in and subsidize low-income housing. Subsidies had been effective in Europe, she said, and there was no reason why they should not work well in America as well.[27]

After the onset of the depression *American City* took the lead in demanding housing subsidies, which it saw as a major outlet for much-needed public-works expenditures. By 1932 many of the professionals agreed. Robert Kohn was only one of the many prominent architects calling for an extension of public works into housing projects for the poor at that time.[28] But perhaps the best insight into changing attitudes was provided by John Ihlder, the city planner who had been so reticent in discussing the housing problem a few years earlier. In 1922 he had hoped vaguely for frontal assaults from unnamed sources for unspecified purposes. In 1932 he minced no words. The slums had to be demolished so that federal funds could finance the construction of low-income housing. Ihlder felt that there was a problem of human degradation at the lower end of the social scale which the nation could no longer tolerate. Anticipating one source of dissent from this judgment, he asserted that society had to provide decent housing even for the "shiftless," if only to protect their children and safeguard community tranquility.[29] Ihlder had finally clarified what he had meant ten years earlier by "frontal assaults."

The idea of federal subsidies for low-cost housing thus gained momentum as the depression deepened in the early 1930s. The professionals, who had generally shunned the subject in the 1920s, were prepared to endorse it by the time Franklin Roosevelt entered the White House in 1933, and they were overjoyed in June when Congress authorized the construction of subsidized low-cost housing through the Public Works Administration.

From the beginning, however, the government and the professionals were at odds with each other over the purpose of this venture. The objective of the government was to stimulate the construction industry and put people back to work as part of its effort to revive the economy. The two-year limit originally imposed on the program was enough by itself to discourage the development of any long-range social vision in public housing.

To the professionals public housing was an opportunity for social reconstruction. William Biddle, a professor of social work, discussed the possibilities at the NCSW in 1933. Biddle looked forward to a day when the government would become more aware of the increasing amount of leisure time available to most people and would plan housing projects with better facilities for "creative and participatory recreation," including space for arts and crafts, theater, clubs, classes, and music, as well as nursery schools, playgrounds, and athletic equipment. The Housing Authority could then work with local educational and cultural groups to devise programs to use these facilities. Eventually the housing projects would become planned communities providing the physical and spiritual basis "for a rich, satisfying life for tenants" and for a "more self-reliant citizenry."[30] This was nothing less than the old neighborhood ideal in modern dress, now vastly more ambitious with its prospects for federal subsidies and great new tracts of government housing.

That same summer an assortment of 500 housing experts, city planners, and architects met in Cleveland to discuss the implications of the government's breakthrough in slum clearance. The primary theme at this conference was the need to build vast tracts of low-cost housing. Anything less—putting a new building or even a whole block of decent housing in a larger slum district—was doomed to fail because of the corrosive power of a blighted district. Only an entire neighborhood, "large enough to create and preserve its own atmosphere," could stand up to slum rot. There was a unity of purpose at this conference that led its participants to believe that they were on the verge of solving what had been one of America's truly intractable problems over the decades.[31]

Loula Lasker, who reported on this conference for *Survey Graphic*, also shed light on one of the apparent paradoxes of the 1930s, the unbounded optimism of intellectuals and professionals in the face of unprecedented human misery in America. Her specific point of reference was the Tokyo earthquake, which had destroyed the city in 1923 and given planners a chance to rebuild it according to the fundamentals of their own calling. The result, she observed, was a beautiful modern city that was a tribute to city planning. Her point was that there was opportunity in catastrophe. Applied to the New Deal, this meant that the professionals now had an unprecedented opportunity to erase the errors of the past and work for a humane society according to the principles of their expertise and the generosity of their values. In that context the depression was almost providential.

The ideal of public housing as the key to social redemption ultimately rested on the first principle of social policy professionalism. As sociologist Edwin Burdell reminded city planners at their annual conference in 1933,

The recognition of the influence of environment on human behavior is at the bottom of the movement for slum elimination. New housing is provided in the expectation that the improved physical environment will result in improved standards of conduct, more stable and happier family life, and . . . less vice, crime and disease. . . . A rehousing program that does not have as its basis this aim of fundamental social rehabilitation is nothing more than a brick and mortar proposition.

Burdell illustrated his point with a discussion of the impoverished southern whites and blacks who inhabited the slums of Columbus, Ohio, a class made "shiftless and irresponsible," he said, by generations of poverty and despair in their native region, not by any innate racial qualities or irremedial character defects. With decent housing, some tutelage, and the chance for a job they could all be salvaged.[32]

The Regional Planning Association of America (RPAA) contributed to the discussion of housing in the summer of 1933. The RPAA wanted the government to shape its housing policies with the neighborhood unit in mind and to plan in such a way as to avoid class segregation of any sort. Because it offered the prospect of mixed social classes in the same housing developments, this proposal was audacious for the time, but the RPAA saw no problem with it, since housing standards, it said, were the same for all classes, the only significant differences being in the amount of space and the mechanical accessories demanded by the well-to-do. Finally, while the RPAA recognized the need for architectural and technological innovation as a long-range goal, it stressed that, for the first year at least, the goal must simply be to make decent new housing available to the poor. *"For immediate results,"* it concluded, "social experiment must precede mechanical experiment."[33] (Italics in original.) In this way the RPAA, which had spun utopian dreams in the 1920s, was drawn closer to the mainstream in the 1930s, by the lure of government funds for low-income housing.

As it happened, there was no need to choose between social and mechanical innovations in the first year, or in the second either, since no new housing was built under PWA authority in that period. William Haber took this into consideration when he discussed the urban future with city planners in 1935. First of all, he assured them that the future *was* urban, since the heralded "back-to-the-farm" movement of 1931 and 1932 had recently reverted to the customary country-to-city flow of modern times. The challenge, he said, was to make cities livable by devising a program to raze the slums and rebuild urban areas around decent housing for everyone. Then Haber tackled the problem that was central to the whole housing movement. Ordinarily, he said, the distribution of incomes prevented the poor from renting even the most spartan accommodations in new housing units. Only when rentals were pegged below cost could the poor be adequately housed. That much was understood by planners and housing experts and was what justified government subsidies in the first place. The trouble was that the discussion of public housing to that point had been stalled by Harold Ickes's insistence that public works projects be self-liquidating, which was plainly not possible if units were rented below cost. There were only two possible solutions to this problem, said Haber. The first was for the government to square rentals with income by a policy of permanent subsidies to keep rentals artificially low. In that case the projects would not be self-liquidating but would be paid off instead out of general tax revenues, which would mean that higher-income groups would assume some responsibility for the welfare of the poor through an indirect redistribution of income. The second was for the government to take drastic steps to raise the income of the poor, which would mean national economic planning, and probably some *direct* redistribution of income.[34]

By 1935, then, a consensus was growing among the professionals that public housing should be at the heart of a program to rebuild the cities at the neighborhood level on an egalitarian basis. The emphasis varied from one professional to the next, but the elements remained fairly constant.

Ordinarily a certain vagueness characterized the proposals to put public housing at the center of urban reconstruction, but the professionals were quite clear about how they expected it to improve the nation's health. They cited evidence from English studies, which demonstrated that children in public housing were taller and heavier than their counterparts in city slums, and that the longer they lived in decent housing, the greater the disparity became. Such data confirmed the commitment of professionals on this matter, and supported the surgeon general's demand for a broad program of slum clearance and low-income housing as preconditions for the reduction of mortality and illness rates in the nation.[35]

It was not that public-health workers were only first discovering the effect of housing on health. In the past, however, their housing policies, like all housing policies, had been essentially negative. Their aim was to prevent disease, and they had thus limited themselves to such activities as closing polluted wells and condemning unsanitary buildings. Their methods reflected the regulatory impulse of the Progressive era, but in the breathless atmosphere of the New Deal, this regulatory approach seemed hopelessly dated and inadequate.

Even before the depression health officials had moved beyond merely preventing disease to "creating health," and the housing movement of the 1930s fit this approach to health perfectly. That was the message of C.-E. A. Winslow early in 1937 when he announced that conditions were finally ripe for the government to produce the sort of low-cost housing that was essential to foster the physical and mental well-being of the poor. He implored Congress to set the wheels in motion by passing Senator Wagner's housing bill, and he declared that the APHA had already begun to prepare for a vast new housing program by creating a Committee on the Hygiene of Housing.[36] Including planners, architects, builders, engineers, physicians, home economists, and sociologists, this committee was a classic application of the public-service outlook to a new breeze in the social climate.

Congress finally passed the Wagner-Steagall Housing Act later that year. The act established the United States Housing Authority to supervise the new program; it divided authority between the cities and Washington in such a way that local officials would do most of the planning for public housing and the federal government would do most of the spending on it, and it appropriated $500 million to launch the program. The implications of the bill were profound. Until then public housing had been a temporary program of limited scope. But Congress placed the Wagner-Steagall Act under the general-welfare clause of the Constitution, which gave public housing an air of permanence and social merit that had been missing before and led the professionals to give it a larger role than ever in their scheme of things.

Some of them even found great significance in the lesser provisions of the bill. For instance, the limitations it imposed on construction costs might easily have soured architects, who were notoriously more concerned with keeping up high standards than with bringing down high costs. But Walter McCornack, a pillar of the architectural establishment, saw these limitations as a challenge for architects to reexamine antiquated methods in the light of modern technology. After all, he said, the purpose of the bill was not to bail out builders, or landowners, or construction workers but to provide decent living conditions for

the poor. Could architects build better units for less money as automobile manufacturers had done? He thought they could and felt that the new housing bill
gave them an opportunity at last to move constructively into public life.[37]

This was not just hollow boasting, since techniques to lower the unit costs
of housing already existed. One of these was implicit in the design concept of
architectural modernism and involved nothing more complicated than the elimination of certain traditional architectural decorations. Elaborate cornices and
other frills were costly to build and costly to maintain. Public housing, either
as "individual cells in a multicellular structure" or as detached units, would
be cheaper without them and, according to the new functional esthetic, more
attractive.[38]

There were also possibilities for impressive savings in prefabrication. This
technique had been developed in the 1920s, but, along with other modes of
construction, had been abandoned in the early years of the depression. Then,
thanks to the new housing act, a tract of fifty prefabricated houses was put up
in Fort Wayne, Indiana, late in the decade under the direction of the U.S.
Housing Authority. The matter was suddenly off the drawing board.

The professionals observed the Fort Wayne project, they discussed it, and
they were almost unanimous in condemning it. For one thing, the houses had
a tacky quality about them that raised doubts about their durability. How long
would it be before they were just another slum? For another, they were jerry-
built with no effort to make a real community of them, which violated the
fundamental principles of the professionals. To make matters worse, some architects began to have second thoughts about prefabrication altogether. Not
only did it imply a dreary standardization that assaulted their esthetic ideals,
but it carried with it the possibility of rendering them obsolete.[39] Technological
innovation was one thing; technological unemployment was quite another. That
was one saving that even the most public spirited among them were not eager
to pass on to the government.

John Essig, an official with the Fort Wayne Housing Authority, was furious
at this rejection by the professionals. He accused them of living in a wonder-
land of abstract theory that was completely out of touch with reality. The reality, he said, was that fifty families were now housed far better and more cheaply
than they had been before the units went up. One of these families had been
living in a tent, and others had been without decent sanitation or heating of any
kind. Did the planners prefer that they live like that again? He admitted that
these "portable" houses were far from ideal, but he welcomed them nevertheless as a way for a few people to get out of the slums for the time being.[40] His
point of reference was what had been; the professionals' point of reference was
what could be. They were no longer interested in simple expedients, or in
devising methods for trimming a few dollars per room from the cost of public
housing. In the end, it was not the specific provisions of the Wagner-Steagall
Act, but its promise of long-term commitment that cemented their allegiance
to public housing and placed it more than ever in the forefront of their social

vision. They had come a long way in the few years since 1933, when many of them seemed willing to accept any sort of housing the government would build.

For that reason the argument that tied good health to good housing received even more attention in the late 1930s than it had before the Housing Act was passed. This argument was part of the growing awareness of the social framework of health, and the prophet of this new awareness was Yale University's renowned professor of public health, C.-E. A. Winslow. As chairman of the APHA's new Committee on the Hygiene of Housing, Winslow worked tirelessly after 1937 to preach housing to health officials and health to housing officials, always making sure to emphasize the intimate relationship between the two. His theme was the need for public health to move beyond engineering and medicine into social science, so that it might deal with the entire social and economic environment.

That was finally possible because the Wagner-Steagall Act made public housing primarily a municipal affair. This localism virtually guaranteed that the needs of health workers, which varied from one city to another, would be at the center of all future projects for slum clearance and housing construction and would encourage the application of the new social approach to public health.[41] In this way the housing commitments of the New Deal and the educational efforts of Winslow and others were working to expand the consciousness and the activities of public health workers in the nation's cities.

Like the other professionals Winslow believed that the purpose of public housing was to improve health and to reduce crime, delinquency, and human degradation. And like the other professionals he viewed it as part of a grander scheme, for he too had a vision of society unified by a revival of the old communitarian spirit in the new housing projects. Winslow made this a focal point in his writings before the war. He emphasized that public housing must not become simply a collection of individual dwelling units. To preserve democracy, he said, it must fit into projects planned to re-create the "neighborhood spirit" and endow the residents "with a sense of belonging to a well ordered and self-respecting community."[42]

The neighborhood ideal had run an erratic course with the new professionals since the turn of the century, but never did it seem closer to reality than in the late 1930s, when Harland Bartholomew laid down the planner's dictum that no housing be built without a city plan and then implied that no city plan was worth much if it did not conceive of housing in a neighborhood context. "Our city plans," he said, "will be of limited value if their ultimate effect does not produce good neighborhoods."[43] He would have been hard pressed to find a city planner who disagreed.

The professionals realized that housing could only be effectively integrated into neighborhoods after some hard-nosed research and planning with local imperatives in mind. Carl Feiss was an architect and planner who spoke out for the neighborhood ideal in housing, but he refused to generalize beyond that because cities varied so widely in their physical and social characteristics. He counseled against proceeding at all until a thorough survey was completed of the neighborhood in question.[44] Discussing some of the complexities involved, Feiss touched upon an issue that was beginning to trouble the professionals and others in the nation. He observed that many cities had neighborhoods that were ethnically homogeneous, and that in the South racial divisions were so sharp that they affected zoning and were often written into city plans, however covertly. Though Feiss was scarcely a racist, he insisted that these neighborhoods had a certain ethnic integrity that housing authorities would at least have to consider in accepting tenants for housing projects.[45]

In fact, the ethnic question in public housing was a matter of controversy almost from the beginning. May Lumsden expressed the cosmopolitan ideal when she described the opening in New York of one of the nation's first housing projects, where tenants were selected by a complex point system (the competition was fierce) that completely ignored ethnicity. Lumsden was proud to announce that the project now housed Jews, Italians, Russians, and Poles living together amicably as Americans.[46]

Others were not so pleased with this turn of events. Carl Feiss noted that there were exceptions to the enthusiasm felt by most young architects for the new housing programs. He had been talking recently with a well-known New York architect, and the man had told him disgustedly that he would have gone into his father's brokerage business if he had thought that " 'architecture would ever come to the all-time low point of building shacks for dagoes and wops.' "[47]

If "dagoes and wops" did not send that architect into the brokerage business, perhaps Robert Weaver sent him packing a year later. Weaver, one of the relatively few young black bureaucrats with the New Deal, surveyed the racial situation in public housing and presented it as a mixture of hope and frustration. Acknowledging the primacy of localism in this matter, he said that the handling of racial affairs in public housing would be about as democratic as the communities in which the projects were built. Since Weaver's discussion had already touched upon the racism that constantly simmered near the surface of American life and occasionally boiled over in some of the housing projects, he could not let the matter rest there without yielding to despair. His solution was to call for "intelligent planning and socially conscious management carried out by local authorities" who faced up to racial issues squarely. If that were done, he felt that public housing would "make a definite contribution to the national ideal of equality of opportunity regardless of race, creed, color, or religious affiliations."[48] Weaver's wish that racial harmony might promote American values in neighborhood public housing projects summarized the state of public-welfare idealism at the time and anticipated the direction it would take in the years that followed.

There was another implication in Weaver's paper that was not so immediately apparent. In his unobtrusive wish that effective planning and management lead the way to racial harmony he was quietly entering a plea for the principles of expertise and social control that had been an integral part of the new professionalism all along and a sensitive issue in the public housing movement of the 1930s.

Traditionally in the United States housing had been regulated almost exclusively in the marketplace. Only in recent years had a few limited concessions been made to public regulation in certain areas relating to health and safety, and in zoning. When the federal government entered the field of low-income housing through the PWA in 1933, the rules changed completely and permanently. Thereafter, decisions that had been made in the marketplace would be made for public housing by government bureaucrats influenced to some extent by public-service professionals. Indeed, many of the young bureaucrats in the 1930s had themselves been trained originally as health and social workers, or as architects and planners. And they had so many questions to answer. Just what was decent housing anyhow, and who defined it? What was the acceptable ratio of persons to living space? With the government subsidizing rentals, what proportion should the tenant be required to pay? What criteria should be employed in selecting—and rejecting—tenants? In a clash of values, which ones took precedence in public housing decisions? For instance, where racism was a dominant factor in local cultural patterns, would localism prevail over egalitarianism? Were bathtubs and refrigerators necessities or luxuries? How much long-term "guidance" should be given tenants to assure proper maintenance of the units, and at what point did this guidance impinge upon the liberty of the individual? Every one of these questions implied an answer that drew upon specific values as well as expertise and implied some degree of social engineering. As a result, every one carried a heavy potential charge of controversy.

The question of unit design illustrates this point. It revealed cracks in the facade of public housing from the very beginning. Winslow and Twichell addressed the problem from the perspective of health experts in a lengthy report they made for the Committee on the Hygiene of Housing in 1938. Reflecting the concerns of the "new" public health, the report spoke to the presumed psychological needs of prospective tenants, as well as to their physiological needs. It contained recommendations for the proper temperature of units, for ventilation ("The odors given off from the body have been proved to exert a definitely harmful influence upon appetite and therefore upon health"), artificial lighting, noise insulation, and play space for children. Even more contentious were the criteria set up for "fundamental psychological needs," including space for "adequate privacy," "opportunities for normal family life," facilities to prevent "undue physical and mental fatigue," and provisions for "esthetic satisfaction in the home and its surroundings." These and other requirements were all rooted as much in subjective judgments as in objective research. If implemented, they would affect everything in the housing units from building materials to apartment layouts, configuration of buildings, human relations and, of course, costs.[49]

Health officers were not the only ones with a stake in public housing. Architects were also deeply involved, and many of them were having problems accepting some of the restraints built into the Wagner-Steagall Act. According to the act, housing authorities were required to provide "decent, safe and sanitary" housing at the lowest possible cost. It was that proviso about low cost that was giving architects all the trouble. A. C. Shire, the technical director of the U.S. Housing Authority, discussed their plight in a hilarious critique of their inept performance in designing public housing. As Shire saw it, the problem was not that architects refused to comply with federal restraints, but that they did not know how. They had been trained to elitist standards but hired for lower-class needs. Unfortunately they seemed to be unable to invent their way out of this dilemma, unable to think beneath the lofty ideals that clouded their minds. They wanted public housing to look like Georgian mansions, he observed sardonically, and went into shock when they learned that tenants hung their laundry out to dry and put their garbage out on the street for collection— in plain sight! Since their education had obviously not prepared architects to design low-cost housing, Shire suggested that the simplest solution was to revise architectural education in the future.[50]

Then to complicate matters even further, Elisabeth Coit, a New York architect, disclosed that the tenants had their own ideas about design, and that what *they* wanted was not necessarily what any of the experts wanted. Architects, for instance, were inclined to design units with large living rooms and small kitchens, because their technical training and often their personal backgrounds idealized homes with those proportions. Low-income tenants, many of whom still followed immigrant patterns of behavior around the house, complained about this allocation of space because they tended to carry on much of the family's social life in the kitchen. They were willing to sacrifice space in the living room for a large kitchen. They had other preferences as well. They preferred kitchen sinks to flush toilets, and they preferred bathtubs to showers, which reminded them of public bathhouses.[51] But the architect might shave his costs a bit by designing his unit for a shower, which took up slightly less space than a tub. Whose wishes were to prevail here? Like the Syrian couple and their public-health nurse clashing over a christening party years earlier, this was not a question of who was right and who was wrong; it was a problem of cultural patterns in conflict. The difference was that this time the government stood by as a final arbiter if all else failed.

That could be avoided of course if professionals could influence the values and behavior of the tenants. Edwin Burdell, a sociologist at MIT, showed how this might be done by employing social workers in housing projects to "educate" the tenants. After all, he said, "normal people" in our culture "prefer cleanliness to dirt, quiet to noise . . . activity to idleness." But by itself moving people from filthy slums into bright new housing would change little. What they needed was someone to demonstrate the principles of good housing management to them. Social miracles came only from social intelligence, and that meant trained personnel running educational programs in the projects. Burdell noted that Americans had the wisdom to depend upon science and technology in industry. Why then, he wondered, did they not "require at least the same scientific approach to the social reconstruction of [their] blighted areas?"[52]

In fact, there was already a certain amount of social manipulation taking place in the projects, often in the name of "education." In New York the Housing Authority worked out a system of assigning points for a variety of factors, including the tidiness, number and age of children, and the "financial responsibility" of applicants to one of the nation's first PWA housing projects. The authority then had only to tabulate scores in order to establish a rank order of preference for the applicants. In this way the management of the project could make its selections with "mathematical impartiality," protected from the pressures of wily politicians and the pleas of "sad-eyed mothers." In the process, of course, this exercise established criteria that tended to skew the occupants toward middle-class standards and did so in the guise of icy objectivity. The tenants were chosen from the poor (though by no means the poorest), which meant that they came disproportionately from immigrant backgrounds. No doubt many of them were not assimilated to native middle-class norms. That accounted for the management's hopes to "achieve improvement" in the "taste and social behavior" of the applicants, not by "prodding" but by example.

The case of "Mrs. M." illustrates what some of the housing managers had in mind. Mrs. M. was an Italian woman whose fervent old-country patriotism had induced her to deck out her living room in red, white, and green light bulbs. When the project manager saw this spectacular display, she "expressed surprise" to Mrs. M., whereupon Mrs. M. assured the manager that she would replace the colored bulbs with white ones.[53] The manager's "surprise" doubtless involved a degree of psychological intimidation and was perceived, as it was meant to be perceived, as a cue to change bulbs. In this way Mrs. M. was educated in good taste. The pressure applied at the Michigan Boulevard Garden Apartments in Chicago was even less subtle. Michigan Boulevard was a public housing project recently opened for black families. The social director of this project routinely investigated the backgrounds of applicants and reported her evaluation "of the family's probable ability to adjust to the new environment." The social director was also obligated "to visit the tenants whenever there [were] instances of maladjustments, overcrowding or repeated complaints."[54] Every effort was made to impart an air of middle-class respectability to the project.

In a sense the government's public housing program gave the professionals a laboratory in which to apply and test their theories. At first many of them thought that training in social work would be sufficient to assure effective project management, but they soon realized that there was a business side to management that was not met by training in social work. As a result, in 1936 the National Association of Housing Officials proclaimed that housing management was a new profession in America and sponsored the nation's first course in public housing management.[55] In the next few years such courses became fairly commonplace in training managers, whose duties generally included collecting rents, checking up on tenant incomes, caring for grounds and buildings, and dispensing homemaking and social advice to people who had never lived in modern housing before. By 1940 some of the professionals were recommending that national standards of professional competence in housing management be established in broad courses of study and training at major universities. The need clearly existed, said Hugh Carter, and congressional control of the purse strings certainly provided a basis for enforcing such standards.[56]

As it had in the past, professionalism was about to spawn a new profession. As it would in the future, government was about to set the terms.

NOTES

1. "Say 'Social Worker' to the Census Man," *The Compass* (February 1930):1.

2. I. M. Rubinow, "Social Security—1936 Model," *The Survey* (February 1936):35–37. For accounts of the origins of Social Security see Roy Lubove, *The Struggle for Social Security, 1900–1935* (Cambridge: Harvard University Press, 1965); Daniel Nelson, *Unemployment Insurance: The American Experience, 1915–1935* (Madison: University of Wisconsin Press, 1969); Daniel S. Hirshfield, *The Lost Reform: The Campaign for Compulsory Health Insurance in the United States from 1932–1943* (Cambridge: Harvard University Press, 1970).

3. "Social Security—More or Less?" *The Compass* (October 1936):2.

4. Ewan Clague, "Social Work and Social Security," *The Survey* (January 1937):5–6.

5. Joanna Colcord, "Social Work and the Social Insurances," *The Compass* (August 1937):8–9; Arlien Johnson, "Social Work and the Social Insurances—Will Present Opportunity to Apply Old Skills to New Tasks," Ibid. (December 1937):6–9.

6. Florence Sytz, "Maintenance Is Not Enough!" Ibid. (November 1937):10–12.

7. Leah Feder, "Changing Emphasis in Professional Education," NCSW, *Proceedings* (1938):208–221; Robert W. Kelso, "Tomorrow's Social Work Training," *The Survey* (September 1936):259–262.

8. "Professional School Developments for 1936–37," *The Compass* (November 1936):7–11.

9. "An Outline of the Position of the American Association of Social Workers in Respect to Governmental Employment, Social Insurance and Assistance Programs," Ibid. (May 1938):22–24.

10. Reginald M. Atwater, "National Health Conference—A Review," *AJPH* (October 1938):1103–1113, and Arthur J. Altmeyer, "The National Health Conference and the Future of Public Health," Ibid. (January 1939)1–10.

11. I have constructed this debate from "Conference Gleanings," in Atwater, "National Health Conference—A Review," pp. 1110–1113.

12. Irvin Abell, "Attitude of the American Medical Association Toward the National Health Program," Ibid. (January 1939):11–15.

13. Edward S. Godfrey, Jr., "Health for Three-Thirds of the Nation," *AJPH* (December 1939):1283–1291.

14. C.-E. A. Winslow, "A Half-Century of the Massachusetts Public Health Association," Ibid. (April 1940):325–335.

15. Thomas Parran, "Reporting Progress," Ibid. (November 1936):1071–1076.

16. "What Shall We Think of Social Security?" Ibid. (October 1935):1140–1141.

17. E. R. Coffey, "Public Health Expands Its Facilities Under Title VI, Federal Social Security Act," Ibid. (April 1941):297–304.

18. Parran, "Reporting Progress."

19. C. E. Waller, "Progress Under the Operation of Title VI of the Social Security Act," *AJPH* (November 1938):1298–1304; Mayhew Derryberry, "Educational Qualifications of Staff Members in Health Departments," Ibid. (June 1940):645–651.

20. Harry B. Mitchell, "The Merit System and Public Health," Ibid. (November 1940):1343–1347. See also Dorothy Deming, "Setting up New Minimum Qualifications for Public Health Nurses," Ibid. (February 1941):158–161.

21. Abel Wolman, "For Whom the Bell Tolls," Ibid. (December 1941):1243–1247.

22. Robert Wiebe, *The Search for Order* (New York: Hill and Wang, 1967), p. 169.

23. Elmer C. Jensen, "The Architect in Civil Life," AIA, *Proceedings* (1918):62–63. See also Frederick L. Ackerman, "The Government, The Architect and The Artisan in Relation to Government Housing," Ibid., pp. 86–89; Lawrence Veiller, "Slumless America," *National Municipal Review* (August 1920):493–498; and Ira S. Wile, "Sociological Aspects of Housing," *AJPH* (April 1920):327–331.

24. John Ihlder, "The Housing Situation," NCSW, *Proceedings* (1922):278–281.

25. Lawson Purdy, "The Housing of the Very Poor," *American City* (July 1928):128–129; John Taylor Boyd, Jr., "Establishing Low-Cost Housing as a Basic American Industry," Ibid. (November 1928):149–152.

26. "Slum Clearance Policy Adopted by New York State," Ibid. (June 1926):620–622.

27. "Is Government Aid Necessary in the Financing of Low-Cost Housing?" Ibid. (March 1929):99–100.

28. Robert D. Kohn, "The President's Address to the 65th Convention," *The Octagon* (May 1932):4–6.

29. John Ihlder, "A Constructive Housing Program from the Community Point of View," NCCP, *Proceedings* (1932):33–37.

30. William W. Biddle, "Social Aspects of Large-Scale Housing," NCSW, *Proceedings* (1933):426–433.

31. Loula Lasker, "The Chance to Rebuild the U.S.A.," *Survey Graphic* (August 1933):420–421, 431.

32. Edwin S. Burdell, "The Social Problem Involved in Securing the Benefits of Slum Elimination," NCCP, *Proceedings* (1933):131–142.

33. "A Housing Policy for the Government," *The Octagon* (June 1933):6–7. See also Eugene H. Klaber et al., "A National Housing and Rehabilitation Policy," Ibid. (July 1933):8–10.

34. William Haber, "Social and Economic Factors in City Planning," NCCP, *Proceedings* (1935):232–239.

35. May Lumsden, "Health and the New Housing," NCSW, *Proceedings* (1936), 562–568. Speaking to the same issue, Haven Emerson disagreed. It was not so much the quality of housing *per se* that affected health, he argued, as the way in which housing was used and people fed. The real culprits were overcrowding and poor nutrition, and neither slum clearance nor new housing directly addressed those problems. See Haven Emerson, "Health Benefits To Be Expected From Better Housing," Ibid., 569–578.

36. C.-E. A. Winslow, "Housing as a Public Health Problem," *AJPH* (January 1937):56–61. See also R. L. Reiss, "British and American Housing," *Social Service Review* (June 1937):195–215.

37. Walter R. McCornack, "The Beginning of a Great Building Program," *The Octagon* (August 1937):3–5.

38. A. C. Shire, "Constructive Criticism of Architects," Ibid. (September 1939):3–6; Carl Feiss, "To Teach Housing is Also to Teach Architecture," Ibid., pp. 14–16.

39. Loula Lasker, "Fort Wayne's Fifty Houses,"*Survey Graphic* (May 1939):324–325; George H. Gray, "An Evaluation of the Fort Wayne Housing Project," *The Octagon* (May 1939):6–8; "City Planning—Housing—Small Houses—Prefabricated Houses," Ibid. (August 1936):4–9.

40. John Essig, "Evaluating Various Evaluations of the Fort Wayne Housing Project," Ibid. (July 1939):13–14.

41. C.-E. A. Winslow, "Housing and Health," *Public Health Nursing* (July 1940):434–439; C.-E. A. Winslow, "Opportunities and Responsibilities of the Health Officer in Connection With Federal Housing Acts," *AJPH* (November 1938):1269–1276.

42. C.-E. A. Winslow, "Housing and Health," *Public Health Nursing* (July 1940):434–439.

43. Harland Bartholomew, "The Location of Housing Projects and the City Plan," *Planner's Journal* 4, no. 3 (1938):57.

44. Carl Feiss, "The Location of Housing Projects and the City Plan," Ibid., pp. 59–61.

45. Ibid.

46. May Lumsden, "First Families," *Survey Graphic* (February 1936):103–105.

47. Feiss, "To Teach Housing Is Also to Teach Architecture."

48. Robert C. Weaver, "Racial Minorities and Public Housing," NCSW, *Proceedings* (1940):289–296.

49. C.-E. A. Winslow and Allan A. Twichell, "Healthful Housing," *AJPH* (March 1938):354–372.

50. A. C. Shire, "Constructive Criticism of Architects," *The Octagon* (September 1939):3–6.

51. Elisabeth Coit, "Notes on Design and Construction of the Dwelling Unit for the Lower-Income Family," Ibid. (October 1941):10–30.

52. Edwin S. Burdell, "Rehabilitation of the Blighted District—A Cooperative Enterprise: The Share of the Sociologist," NCCP, *Proceedings* (1935):278–286.

53. May Lumsden, "First Families," *Survey Graphic* (February 1936):103–105.

54. Beatrice Greenfield Rosahn, "Social Management of Housing," *The Survey* (February 1936):38–40.

55. Ibid.

56. Hugh Carter, "How Shall We Manage Housing?" *Social Service Review* (December 1940):723–729.

8

Conclusions

By the late nineteenth century many middle- and upper-class Americans looked upon the consequences of urbanization with growing concern. In their eyes the cities were esthetically repulsive, commercially spastic, culturally balkanized, morally depraved, medically lethal, socially oppressive, and politically explosive. They believed that the poor were alienated from their work, from their communities, and from each other, that they lived in unspeakable privation, and that all the traditional institutions of social cohesion and melioration were in complete disarray. The family? Forced to adjust to an impersonal and exploitative economic system, the family was breaking apart. The church? In an increasingly secular society the church was losing its authority to shape values and morals. Charity? Private charity and other voluntary modes of local social assistance seemed hopelessly inadequate to relieve the burdens of poverty and economic insecurity in the new industrial order. Unwilling to sit by idly while their world came apart, these concerned citizens began to commit themselves to varieties of social action which led in time to the development of the modern social policy professions.

In the beginning this process was quite spontaneous, the result of specific individuals, generally unknown to one another, acting with very little precedent and no clear idea of where they were heading. Soon others like them took note and repeated these actions, then repeated them again until they began to fall into a pattern of related responses to related conditions. In the next generation these early, fumbling efforts were polished to a professional finish. Instead of individuals like Jane Addams, Charles Chapin, and Daniel Burnham, it was associations like the AASW, the APHA, and the ACPI that supervised the development of public service by the 1920s.

The labors of the early new professionals often engaged conflicting motives, and to the modern viewer appear at times to have pulled in opposite directions. For instance, they were sincerely touched by the plight of the poor, and were moved to help them by softening the conditions of the workplace. At the same time, many of them feared the wrath of the wretched or recoiled from the cultural norms of the foreign, and wanted to improve them by altering their behavior. To these reformers, changing the way the poor thought and behaved, ate and dressed, related to one another and to society in general, was just another way of helping them.

To many historians in recent years, however, neither the motives nor the reforms of the new professionals have appeared to be so innocent and benign. They feel that the reformers were more interested in dominating the poor than in helping them. For that reason these historians have found it useful to emphasize "social control" instead of what earlier historians referred to as "social justice." Either they imply that social justice was merely an artful camouflage for social control, or that these concepts are incompatible altogether, that the repressive nature of social control is necessarily hostile to the liberative qualities of true social justice.[1]

In some ways this revisionism has led to a healthy reassessment of the problem. Certainly historians were far too credulous in their reading of the reformers in the past and too reverential in writing about them. It was necessary to remind us that they were not saints after all, that their altruism was complex and at times suffocating, and that their reforms were often resented and resisted by the very people whom they wanted to help. There is no doubt that their efforts fell short of some platonic ideal of social liberation. Indeed there is no doubt that social control was one of their aims.

But to condemn them as repressive because they wished to impose controls is to miss the point. All societies impose controls, and controls are by nature repressive, are *intended* to be repressive. The early professionals would have been bewildered by the entire discussion. As a matter of fact they invented the phrase "social control," and most of them saw no conflict between welfare and control. They saw these as complementary methods in a seamless quest to reintegrate a fragmented society. That is what the whole discussion of community rights and the police power was all about—the repression of certain liberties by imposing controls in the name of public welfare. In a different way it is also what the model of the neighborhood center was all about. To be sure, the reformers could be insufferably arrogant in their assumption that a fractious nation should be realigned to suit *their* values, but they generally managed at least to respect the difference between repression and oppression.

Early in the century the purpose of the controls they wished to impose—the goal of repression—was primarily to restore a sense of community to urban life. Their point of reference was an image in the past, a memory of towns where voluntary associations had helped families and individuals through hard times, where the intimate knowledge that people had of one another had laced the community together and given it meaning. At the same time the willingness of most of these reformers to deal with urban realities more or less on urban terms prevented them from drifting off into hallucinations about an idealized past. They were quite aware that village culture was dying, but they wanted to salvage from it that feeling for the wholeness of life and the relatedness of people that defined for them the idea of community.

As a consequence, they set about trying to reconcile familiar cultural patterns with unfamiliar economic and demographic developments, in order to give community a modern meaning in an urban context. They were pioneers in discovering ways to protect individuals and families from the worst effects of economic insecurity in industrial society. At the same time, they worked on creating an institution where people could establish human relationships once again. Their very image of community involved an attempt to adapt traditional values to modern conditions. It was not defined by occupation or avocation; it was not a loose association, or a social system, or a psychological affinity group. It was a *place* and it had geographical boundaries around it, as it had had in the past. In the Progressive era that place was the city neighborhood, which the professionals felt was small enough to foster a sense of human scale, yet urban enough to reflect the realities of the modern world. In the neighborhood center they conceived of an institution that would supplement, and if necessary supplant, the family and the church as agencies of socialization. They were convinced that it would serve as the nucleus of the community and help to unify the lives of its inhabitants.[2]

At the same time they realized that the neighborhood could not be fitted out to cope with poverty and disease. Perhaps the village had taken care of its own in simpler times, but the class segregation of the modern city made that impossible. How could a neighborhood care for its own when the cost of care was rising and everybody in the neighborhood was already poor? For that purpose the reformers looked first to municipal by-laws for the authority to regulate health and housing conditions, then to state governments for the authority to regulate working conditions, and finally to state and federal governments for a measure of protection against economic insecurity. By around 1910 they were beginning to reach a loose consensus among themselves about the kinds of controls they wanted and the kind of society they envisioned. They looked inward for informal local controls to shape the cultural tone of the community, and they looked outward to governmental controls for protection against economic disaster. And they saw it all happening in the context of a federated nation of neighborhoods.

The changes they proposed were not really fundamental, but they were novel and relatively complicated. Because they were the only people with any real expertise in these matters, they offered to supervise the process of reconstruction themselves. In fact, at times they almost insisted on it. They saw themselves as a kind of priesthood defined by their monopoly of the knowledge and expertise required to steer society in the general direction of perfection and in the specific direction of ends which they assumed were more or less universally desirable.

The professionals were aware that the controls they recommended would

pinch a bit. Builders would have to conform to prescribed standards, and landlords would have to maintain them. Immigrants would have to abandon practices that threatened community health and would be encouraged to abandon
others, such as certain dietary customs, that jeopardized their own well-being
and eventually worked against what the professionals saw as the community
good. And naturally taxpayers would pay a bit more to employ the small cadre
of people needed to administer these controls. All that, the reformers believed,
was a small price to pay for a humane social order that brought alienated individuals together again in an integrated community.

That consensus broke down in the 1920s when the professionals lost the
sense of crisis that had brought them together in the first place. Why this should
have happened is still not altogether clear. Why did Porter Lee define social
work as social reform before the war and then almost contemptuously dismiss
reform in the 1920s? What made John Ihlder muffle his reform intent in the
1920s and trumpet it in the 1930s? Historians have explained the loss of social
zeal in the 20s variously as an expression of soured idealism after the war or
as an escape from the generally oppressive political and cultural climate of the
decade or as a consequence of the partial successes scored by reformers before
the war or simply as an effect of spent energy.

No doubt each of these factors played a role, but the retreat started even
before the war when health workers began to focus on individual pathology,
when social workers discovered casework, and when many city planners began
to scale their ambitions down to the limitations of zoning. In each case increasing specialization within the profession offered an alternative to social engage-
ment, and in each case the alternative suggested a need to concentrate on the
individual, or at most on a sliver of the social environment. Moreover, these
developments were thoroughly congenial to the changing economic ethos of the
1920s, when a revitalized success ethic emphasized the primacy of personal
qualities once again, rather than social or environmental considerations. It is
not unlikely, then, that the decline of reform sentiment in the 1920s resulted
as much from elements intrinsic to professionalism as from those extrinsic to
it.

In addition, an obsession with professionalism itself seems to have been a
factor. In the Progressive era, when professionalism was still a novelty of uncertain value, the reformers were not yet tyrannized by its precepts. Later, in
the 1930s, they felt secure enough in their professional status to pay attention
to other matters. The pivotal years in this transformation were the 1920s, when
the reformers spent an inordinate amount of time and energy agonizing over
their credibility. They had learned from physicians and lawyers in recent years,
and apparently from the public as well, that professionalism was the key to
respectability, and so they labored to establish their credentials as professionals. They behaved as if they had to convince themselves before they could
convince the public, and perhaps they were right. As a result they worked on
the trappings of professionalism with such dedication that many of them lost

sight of what they had set out to do in the first place. They raised their standards, they purged their deeds of feeling, they coated their endeavors with a crust of hard-boiled realism, and in their exaggerated concern with form many of them forgot about substance.

Even where their thinking continued to fix on social change and reform, it no longer focussed necessarily on the neighborhood. Communitarian localism did survive into the 1920s, but it seemed a weary idea by then and lost ground to rival visions. A few of the professionals explored a new kind of communitarianism that was built around function rather than location. Indeed it is surprising that the professionals, who worked so hard in the 1920s to improve their occupational image, did not find functional communitarianism more attractive than they did.

Others preferred to lose themselves in the charming lunacy of visions that bore roughly the same relation to reality as the Emerald City of Oz. These urban fantasists anchored their thinking in technology and dreamed spectacular dreams of cities that had great populations in them, but were somehow devoid of people. Complementing these visionaries in some ways were the regional dreamers who welcomed technology as a means of balancing city and country living, but generally refused to consider the urban side of the question seriously, and thus left their regions without any genuine metropolitan core.

Still others took the city for what it was—a huge plexus of problems that could not be avoided—and tried to improve it. Some of them made an honest effort to set the city in its regional context. Others, especially the zoners, had difficulty seeing the city whole at all, and were content to work on its parts. Regionalists and zoners shared a no-nonsense approach to the city that came down directly from the "city-useful" planners of the prewar years and concentrated as much upon making the city work from day to day as they did upon building a monument to the future.

At the same time the professionals showed an increasing awareness of the implications of manipulative social control. Many of them were concerned primarily to do a better job of it by making manipulation itself more sophisticated, more professional. Others were troubled by the way this placed an almost insurmountable social distance between the professionals and their clients. The first group tried to reshape democracy so that the new professional elitism could function as part of the system. The second group worried that democracy and professionalism were intrinsically incompatible and contemplated ways to relieve the tension between them without seriously modifying either.

The 1920s were years of debate over meanings and alternatives. Everything was still new and indeterminate for these public-service professionals. They considered different ways to soften the impact of modernization, and they pondered the relationship between some of these alternatives and the older values of democracy and communitarianism. They flew off in different directions, they made a few startling detours, they agreed on very little. But they asked some hard questions, and they uncovered some hard realities.

Under the enormous pressure of economic crisis and the shower of dollars that poured from Washington after 1932, the professionals drew together once again around many of the same basic themes that had unified them in the Progressive era. Social welfare and a strong federal government were prominent among these themes, of course, as politicians, journalists, and historians have reminded us for decades. But the impact of the New Deal on professionalism itself, and questions relating to professional perspectives on ethnicity, social control, and localism have received less attention, though they played a significant part in the thinking of public-service personnel in the 1930s and were related in important ways to the more familiar themes of welfare and government.

From its very outset the New Deal changed the direction in which influence flowed between government and professionals. Except perhaps for a few judicial decisions which had encouraged certain policy options and limited others, this influence had passed primarily *from* the professionals *to* government in the past, especially as policy experts contributed in one way or another to the shaping of social legislation in the states. The New Deal altered that pattern. First of all, federal programs required federal agencies to administer them in Washington and elsewhere in the nation, and that meant the creation of thousands of jobs at a time when work of any kind was scarce. Second, the existence of vast new federal programs in health, welfare, and housing, and the ballyhoo that accompanied them, made the new professionalism publicly respectable to a degree that it never had been before. Third, government programs made it almost mandatory for schools of social policy to rethink and revise their curricula in order to prepare students for the social policy jobs opening up in the federal bureaucracy. Finally, federal programs fostered higher standards in public-service work by subsidizing fieldworkers to upgrade their education, and by compelling local governments to favor professional over political considerations in their hiring policies. The result of all this was that social-policy professionalism moved from the periphery to the center of American society and attracted thousands of people who would otherwise have found different—or no—outlets for their energy and talent.

The impact of the New Deal, and of the 1930s in general, on the way the professionals thought about ethnicity was another matter. This problem had almost overwhelmed reformers at the turn of the century. The vast majority of them had responded with one form or another of cultural monism. Even those who, like Jane Addams, worked heroically to convey a sense of the immigrants' dignity to native Americans did not doubt that the melting pot would prevail in the end. After the United States entered the Great War, many of the reformers worried that the recent immigrants were not responding with sufficient ardor to the call of battle. In a sense they perceived the persistence of immigrant cultural norms as a threat to national security, and in the fever of the moment turned impatiently to the Americanization movement. If the newcomers did not assimilate willingly, then perhaps coercion was in order. But coercion was not really the style of the professionals. In this case it was only a transient impulse, by no means universal among them. As time passed, it yielded to softer attitudes, either to a more benign assimilationism or, especially after the mid-1930s, to cultural pluralism. With the exception of color bars, federal programs acknowledged class, not culture. One had to demonstrate need, but presumably not religion or national origin. Thus housing officials pointed proudly to the ethnic integration of (white) federal housing by the end of the decade, as if these projects expressed something fundamentally American. In addition, the professionals discovered to their horror from the Nazi example just how short the distance was from cultural unity to cultural tyranny. Together these factors encouraged the reevaluation of ethnicity in American life, and contributed to the growing cosmopolitanism of the professionals.

In the earlier years, when parochial attitudes toward ethnicity prevailed, the reformers aimed to bring the immigrants *into* the community they were trying to create. By the end of the 1930s, when cosmopolitan attitudes were spreading, more and more of them contemplated opening the community *out* to "minority" groups. At all times their objective was to unify urban life and restore a sense of wholeness to it.

That same powerful drive toward communitarianism helps to explain the revival of localism as a major element in the thinking of the professionals during the New Deal. From the point of view of the lawmakers, especially of the Roosevelt administration, concessions to local leaders were often the compromises necessary to get any legislation at all through Congress. Thus the New Dealers often deferred to local interests in the rural South and urban North because much of their support came from those sources of power. They were not too zealous in supervising the distribution of parity payments in the cotton South, for instance, or in monitoring the hiring policies for WPA projects in many northern cities. But that was not localism as much as it was naked political realism.

With the professionals localism was once again a way of addressing the world. Among social workers, housing experts, and city planners it was a legacy from the neighborhood ideal of the Progressive era, now revitalized by the welter of programs being patched together in Washington. Even public-health workers, who had worked so diligently years earlier to persuade the uninformed that bacteria recognized no boundaries of geography or ethnicity, now swung wholeheartedly behind the localism implicit in their revived social approach to public health.

Thus after the Social Security Act was passed in 1935, public-health programs expanded rapidly in the cities under the guidance of experts with an acute sensitivity to local issues. In 1936 two prominent health officials cited New York City, "with its enormous heterogeneous population . . . its hosts of localized areas of custom, environment, understanding and thought" as an argument for localism in the application of public-health programs. Neither in

New York nor anywhere else, they said, could the health officer proceed without an "intimate knowledge" of the specific community he served.[3]

Health workers responded in similar fashion to the Housing Act of 1937. Because the Wagner-Steagall Act was far more decentralized than earlier New Deal housing policies, it was made to order for this revived localism, a fact which did not escape the attention of C.-E.A. Winslow. Winslow felt that health officers would occupy a central position in new housing programs because they knew more of the local lore of a city—its "racial groups," their customs, their psychology—than anyone. This knowledge would make them indispensable in planning and locating specific housing projects and would be a valuable check against the tendency for local politicians to pack these projects with the party faithful.[4] A housing program centralized in Washington could never be that sensitive to local needs.

The trouble was that the *money* was centralized in Washington, and the people who handled it there—the legislators who appropriated it and the bureaucrats pouring into the city to administer the programs—had other things on their minds than the needs of the faceless poor in neighborhoods they had never seen. This friction between localized needs and centralized financing reflected the basic dilemma of the new policy professionals. From the preindustrial values of nineteenth-century America, which many of them had absorbed as children, they learned what society ought to be. From the modern values of science and technology they learned how to make it that way. The problem was that the technological values that shaped their means often clashed with the personal values that informed their ends. That was not yet apparent to most of them in the Progressive era because federal participation in their schemes remained only a forlorn wish in those years. In the 1930s, however, the conflicting needs and wants of professionals at the local level and bureaucrats at the national level (who were themselves often recruited from the ranks of the professionals) created a tension that would bedevil welfare policies in the years to come.

Even at high noon of the New Deal some of the professionals were beginning to cool off at the prospect of distant bureaucracies trampling on local or even personal priorities. Howard Smith expressed his disillusion with the United States Housing Authority (USHA) scarcely more than a year after it had been created. This was not the automatic protest of some mossback who opposed New Deal welfare policies as a matter of conditioned reflex. An architect, Smith was completely sympathetic with the aim of public housing and had embraced the program enthusiastically at first, especially when he learned that it was to be primarily a matter of local responsibility. Something had gone wrong, however, and Smith soon discovered that architectural plans drawn up at the local level according to local needs (as the local architect perceived those needs) were being rejected in Washington. As a result, he said, the USHA was becoming an "initiating" agency, actually dictating the design of housing projects from Washington in many cases. This process was creating bureaucratic tensions and delays that he felt would never "be tolerated in the sound profitable private practice to which competent architects [were] accustomed."[5]

Of course the bureaucrats at the USHA in Washington might have replied that the rules governing the private practice of architecture did not apply to the design of enormous housing projects for subsidized, low-income tenants. For that there were no rules yet. The architects and the administrators were writing them as they went along, and it was becoming apparent that the principles guiding architects at the local level were often on a different wavelength from those guiding bureaucrats at the federal level. Without some sort of institutional framework to protect them, local interests were the probable losers in any such conflict as that. Certainly those interests might look very frivolous from Washington and consequently very costly. But then, from the urban neighborhood Washington's demands might appear to be arbitrary and insensitive to human needs.

Grace Coyle discussed this problem in her presidential address to the NCSW in 1940. That she even thought in these terms was a measure of the tremendous changes wrought in American society by the depression and the political response to it. There were millions of people, she noted—millions!—now dependent upon the federal government for one form or another of public welfare, often for the very food necessary to keep them going from one day to the next. It was a numbing thought. Coyle admitted that it would be impossible to return these functions to local government, but she feared that the continued centralization of social welfare in Washington would doom democracy in the long run. Her solution was to call vaguely for "some new kind of community organization" to defend local interests against the hostile forays of remote, centralized government. The alternative was to permit "the evils of bureaucracy" to swamp the legitimate needs of the people and bring on the worst disaster of all, "a cynical disillusion with the workings of our democracy."[6] Still, "some new kind" of organization did not point the way to a solution at all. It only added Coyle's voice to the growing number of professionals who were beginning to perceive that there was a problem.

As the New Deal wound down, then, some of the policy professionals began to sense in it a dilemma that really mirrored the paradox in their own thinking. How was it possible to create a feeling of community in industrial society without vast subsidies from the central government? Yet how was it possible to have centralized subsidies without the centralized controls that would almost certainly destroy any last vestige of community feeling? It is a dilemma that many of them are still trying to resolve.

NOTES

1. Books that take this attitude toward social control early in the century include Christopher Lasch, *The New Radicalism in America, 1889–1963* (New York: Alfred A.

Knopf, 1965) and *Haven in a Heartless World* (New York: Basic Books, 1977); James Weinstein, *The Corporate Ideal in the Liberal State* (Boston: Beacon Press, 1968); and M. Christine Boyer, *Dreaming the Rational City: The Myth of American City Planning* (Cambridge: MIT Press, 1983). Gerald Grob rejects this line of thinking in "Reflections on the History of Social Policy in America," *Reviews in American History* (September 1979):293–306. The argument is summarized by the essays in Walter I. Trattner, ed., *Social Welfare or Social Control? Some Historical Reflections on "Regulating the Poor"* (Knoxville: University of Tennessee Press, 1983).

2. For a discussion of the neighborhood center movement, and in general of communitarian thinking among certain Progressive reformers, see Jean B. Quandt, *From the Small Town to the Great Community: The Social Thought of Progressive Intellectuals* (New Brunswick, N.J.: Rutgers University Press, 1970). The theoretical and historiographical implications of "community" in the nineteenth century are discussed in Thomas Bender, *Community and Social Change in America* (New Brunswick, N.J.: Rutgers University Press, 1978).

3. John L. Rice and Margaret Barnard, "District Health Administrations in Large Cities," *AJPH* (April 1936):321–326.

4. C.-E. A. Winslow, "Opportunities and Responsibilities of the Health Officer in Connection With the Federal Housing Acts," Ibid. (November 1938):1269–1276.

5. Howard Dwight Smith, "The Architects and the USHA," *The Octagon* (October 1939):36–38.

6. Grace Coyle, "Social Work at the Turn of the Decade," NCSW, *Proceedings* (1940):3–26.

Bibliographical Essay

Because I am uncomfortable with generalizations based upon the writings of a few "representative" figures studied in depth, I decided to ground this study in as wide a survey of the new professionals as was feasible. This meant that I had to sift through the ideas of three distinct groups, along with a few collateral organizations and transient individuals, over a period of forty years. The problem was that these literate, articulate, and often combative people left more material behind them than I could handle in a lifetime. All this is to say that historians, like the people they write about, must make choices that will affect the outcome of their efforts, and one of their central choices involves the sources they will use. In this case I chose to pass over the letters, diaries, memoirs, and books of "leading" professionals, and to concentrate instead on sources that were likely to include not only the most prominent figures in each field, but a large number of second-echelon personnel as well. For this purpose I felt that the best sources were the papers presented at major annual conferences, the "establishment" journals in each profession, and the material published in a few of the journals that tried to connect the new professionals with each other and to bring their ideas to a wider audience of concerned nonprofessionals. That at least limited me to a few tens of thousands of essays, papers, articles, and editorials.

For the formative years of social work and social welfare the basic source is the annual volume of *Proceedings* (1900–1916) published by the National Conference of Charities and Corrections (NCCC). Each year this volume printed the papers read at the most recent conference of social and charity workers. In 1917 the designation of these meetings was changed to the National Conference of Social Work (NCSW), and the *Proceedings* were published under that name for the remainder of the period under consideration (1917–1941). In 1922 the recently formed American Association of Social Workers began to publish its official journal, *The Compass* (1922–1941). Five years later the School of Social Service Administration of the University of Chicago began to publish the *Social Service Review* (1927–1941). These sources are basic for social work in those years, and they yield a generous amount of information on the other public-service professions as well.

For city planning in the early years of the century the basic source is the *Proceedings*

(1910–1934) that were published annually by the National Conference on City Planning. These volumes included not only the papers read at the meetings, but some of the often-spikey discussions that followed. Beginning in 1935 the *Proceedings* were published as part of the *American Planning and Civic Annual* (1935–1941). Also very useful is *City Planning* (1925–1934). First published in 1925, this journal was succeeded by the *Planner's Journal* (1935–1941) a decade later. The growing interest of architects in city and regional planning can be followed in the *Proceedings of the Annual Convention* (1902–1931) of the American Institute of Architects (AIA) in the *Journal* (1918–1928) of the American Institute of Architects, and beginning in 1929, in *The Octagon* (1929–1941), which succeeded the *Journal*.

For developments in public health I used the *American Journal of Public Hygiene* (*AJPH*, 1902–1941), which became the *American Journal of Public Health* in 1911, and *Public Health Nursing* (1910–1941). In addition, the NCCC/NCSW commonly held sessions—sometimes several—on public health and published them in its annual *Proceedings*.

Although I did not include civil engineers among the new policy professionals, their comments on the issues and people of reform were often useful. They can be followed in the *Proceedings* (1900–1934) of the American Society of Municipal Improvement (American Society of Municipal Engineers after 1931), and in the *Transactions* (1901–1939) of the American Society of Civil Engineers.

In Chapter 1 I discuss the significance of *American City* (1909–1940), *National Municipal Review* (1912–1941), and *The Survey* as sources for the new professionalism. Each was extremely useful, but *The Survey* and its forerunners (1901–1941) deserves special mention here for the range of interests and topics that it covered. In addition to a torrent of news and information on social work, social welfare, and social reform, it ran regular sections on developments in public health and urban planning and served generally as an index to the shifting concerns of liberal reform in the first half of this century. Its editor, Paul Kellogg, did a remarkable job of reaching out to professionals and nonprofessionals alike for over forty years.

Finally, I decided not to include in this bibliography all of the secondary sources—articles and books—on the new policy professionals. Instead I refer the reader to the chapter notes, which include those sources that played some specific role in my thinking.

Index

About the Author

DON S. KIRSCHNER, Professor of History at Simon Fraser University, British Columbia, is the author of *City and Country*. His articles have appeared in *American Quarterly, Mid-America, Historical Reflections,* and *American Studies.*